A Particular Duty

A Particular Duty

The Canadian Rebellions
1837 – 1839

Michael Mann

MICHAEL RUSSELL

© Michael Mann 1986

First published in Great Britain 1986
by Michael Russell (Publishing) Ltd
The Chantry, Wilton, Salisbury, Wiltshire

Typeset by The Spartan Press Ltd, Lymington
Printed in Great Britain
by Biddles Ltd, Guildford and King's Lynn

ISBN 0 855955 136 9

Contents

Acknowledgements

This book could not have been written without the willing and generous help of so many people. Above all I must express my gratitude to Major-General the Earl Cathcart and Mrs Colborne Mackrell for making available the Cathcart and Colborne papers and for helping me with pictures and encouraging me in so many ways. I must also thank Mrs Anita Burdett of the Public Archives of Canada in the Canadian High Commission in London, whose generous assistance opened up a whole series of avenues in Canada previously unknown to me; through her my thanks are due to Grace Hyam, Diane Bridges and Patricia Kennedy of the Public Archives of Canada in Ottawa. I must thank Michael Barthorp of Jersey for introducing me to René Chartrand of the National Historic Parks and Sites Branch in Ottawa, who has been enormously helpful, not only in sending me material but also in putting me in touch with the Macdonald-Stewart Museum in St Helen's Island, Montreal. I have to thank Mrs Elizabeth Hale of the David M. Stewart Museum, St Helen's Island, Montreal for permission to use the Archibald Hope watercolours, which were previously unknown to me. I also have to thank Mr Chartrand for putting me in touch with Mrs Elinor Kyte Senior of Montreal and Mrs Senior both for her interest and help in my work and for the invaluable insights which *Redcoats and Patriotes*, her excellent book on this period, provided.

My grateful thanks go to His Royal Highness the Duke of Edinburgh for putting me in touch with the Hon George Stanley of New Brunswick, whose unrivalled knowledge of Canadian military history has been a great help. Also my thanks go to Lieutenant-General Sir Robin Carnegie for introducing me to Christopher Fulton, himself an old 7th

Hussar, who has been to endless trouble to obtain material and pictures and whose own work I most gratefully reproduce. I must thank Mr Frank McLarnon of Signode in Montreal, who used so much spare time to cover the sites in Lower Canada on my behalf. I am very grateful to the Revd Andrew Wetmore of Montreal, who drove me around Lower Canada and without whose generous assistance I should never have been able to cover so much ground. In Britain my thanks go, as always, to the staff of the National Army Museum for their unfailing helpfulness and courtesy, not only in providing material but in giving permission to reproduce some of their pictures. I must express my gratitude to my fellow trustees of the Regimental Museum of 1st The Queen's Dragoon Guards for allowing me such unfettered use of their valuable material.

Finally, I cannot but express my gratitude and thanks to Mrs Henrietta Napier, who with great patience has typed all the manuscript and deciphered my writing, and to my wife for her forbearance in finding me so preoccupied for so long.

Introduction

There is very little written from British sources about the rebellion in Canada between 1837 and 1839. There are some excellent Canadian accounts, which very naturally concentrate on the events from a Canadian point of view and which deal with the political and military aspects of the time. British accounts are rare, and yet two cavalry regiments and no less than two regiments of Guards and twenty regiments of Foot were eventually involved from the British regular establishment, quite apart from the numerous Canadian militia and volunteer units. Furthermore there are some original sources which are extraordinarily rich in giving a picture of what it must have been like to serve as a British soldier in Canada at that period.

Wavell wrote in *Generals and Generalship*:

What I have tried to show you is that history is a flesh-and-blood affair, not a matter of diagrams and formulas, or of rules. When you study military history don't read outlines on strategy or the principles of war. Read biographical memoirs, get at the flesh and blood of it, not the skeleton. To learn that Napoleon won the campaign of 1796 by manoeuvre on interior lines or some such phrase is of little value. If you can discover how a young, unknown man inspired a ragged, mutinous, half-starved army and made it fight as it did, how he dominated, and controlled generals older and more experienced than himself, then you will have learned something. Napoleon did not gain the position he did so much by a study of rules and strategy as by a profound knowledge of human nature in war.

And that great master of the strategy of war, Clausewitz, wrote in his classical treatise *On War*: 'War belongs not to the province of arts and sciences, but to the province of social life.'

It has been my good fortune by a series of coincidences to have the privilege of going through two huge collections of original material covering the period. Some years ago Major-General the Earl Cathcart told me that he had been sorting out the papers of his great-uncle, who had commanded my old regiment, the 1st King's Dragoon Guards, in Canada from 1838 to 1844. I was asked whether I would be interested in going through these papers. They proved such a rich source of material that I made inquiries of the Canadian High Commission in London whether they could advise me about any other sources covering this period. Due to the great help which I received from Mrs Anita Burdett of the High Commission and from the Public Archives Department in Ottawa, I was made aware of the Colborne Papers. The Canadian Public Archives informed me that, whilst they carry photostat copies of these papers, the originals are still in the possession of the Colborne family. It was only then that I realised that this original material was still owned by a family who lived in a parish of which I had been the vicar, and whose owner had been my church warden. Thanks to the kindness of Mrs Colborne Mackrell I have been able to study these papers.

I have tried to cover the main events of these years in Canada, but more from the point of view of how it must have seemed to the British soldier serving in Canada than by 'outlines of strategy or principles of war'. I have been interested to see how they lived, what was of concern to them, of the way they overcame the rigours of a Canadian winter and adapted to the conditions then facing them in North America. It is always a temptation when reading the history of past events to apply to them the hindsight and wisdom of after years. But events such as these have to be seen and judged, so far as we are able, within the temper and standards of the time. If the account is unduly biased towards the activities of the King's Dragoon Guards, this is solely because it is from this regimental source that the richest supply of material has come. I have studied the regimental histories of all the British regular regiments involved and, with a few notable exceptions, it is remarkable how little is written about this period of their service. The National Army Museum does not even list these two rebellions as a campaign.

I hope that this account of those tumultuous years in Canada will fill a gap that certainly seems to exist on this side of the Atlantic, and that it will also throw some light on the way in which the early Victorian soldier fought and served, as well as providing an insight into his attitudes and mode of life.

I

The Background

The troubles that beset the provinces of Upper and Lower Canada over the years from 1837 to 1839 had their origin in the earlier history of Canada and in the birth pangs and growth of its more powerful neighbour, the United States of America.

In September 1759 Quebec fell to the British, and a year later the British army occupied Montreal, where the survivors of eight French battalions laid down their weapons in the Place d'Armes. French Canada (New France), with all its inhabitants, came under British rule. Then, following the surrender of the French garrison of Fort Niagara, the huge areas north of Lake Erie and Lake Ontario became open to English settlement. They were formally claimed for the Crown by Robert Rogers in 1760, although it was to be several decades before the fur-trappers and the traders dealing with the Indians were to be disturbed by widespread agricultural settlement in what was to become Upper Canada.

In 1775 the thirteen American colonies broke into armed conflict with the Crown and declared their independence from Britain a year later. For six years fighting and bloodshed pervaded the Americas, made all the more bitter because districts, towns and families were divided in their loyalties. Many individuals maintained their allegiance to the King, being castigated as Tories by the Continental Congress, or – as they preferred to think of themselves – as loyalists.

In 1775 Ethan Allan led an abortive American attack on Montreal, and this was followed the same year by a full-scale invasion of Canada under Richard Montgomery and Benedict Arnold, only thwarted the following year after a seige in which Quebec held out, and the defeat of the American ships on Lake Champlain by Sir Guy Carleton.[1]

I

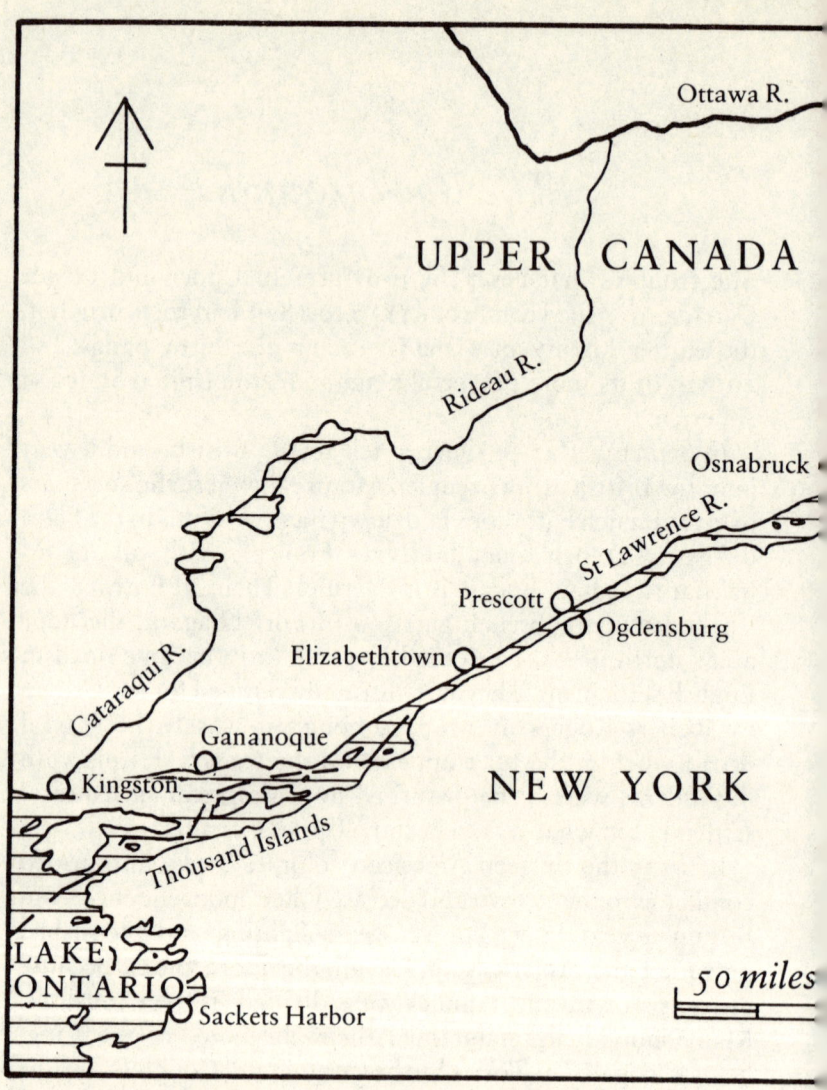

The St Lawrence Frontier

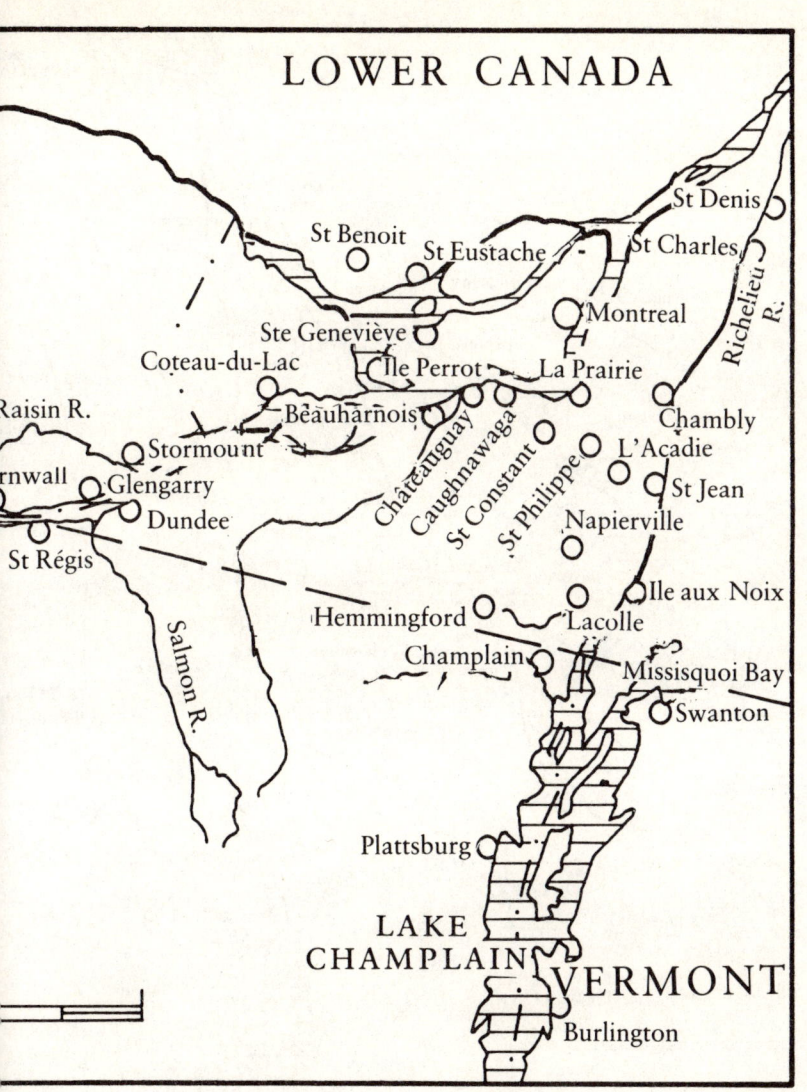

LOWER CANADA

St Denis

St Benoit
St Eustache
St Charles

Richelieu R.

Ste Geneviève
Montreal

Coteau-du-Lac
Ile Perrot
La Prairie

Raisin R.
Béauharnois
Chambly

Stormount
L'Acadie
Chateauguay
Caughnawaga
St Constant
St Philippe

rnwall
Glengarry
St Jean

Dundee
Napierville

St Régis

Ile aux Noix

Salmon R.
Hemmingford
Lacolle

Champlain
Missisquoi Bay

Swanton

Plattsburg

LAKE
CHAMPLAIN VERMONT

Burlington

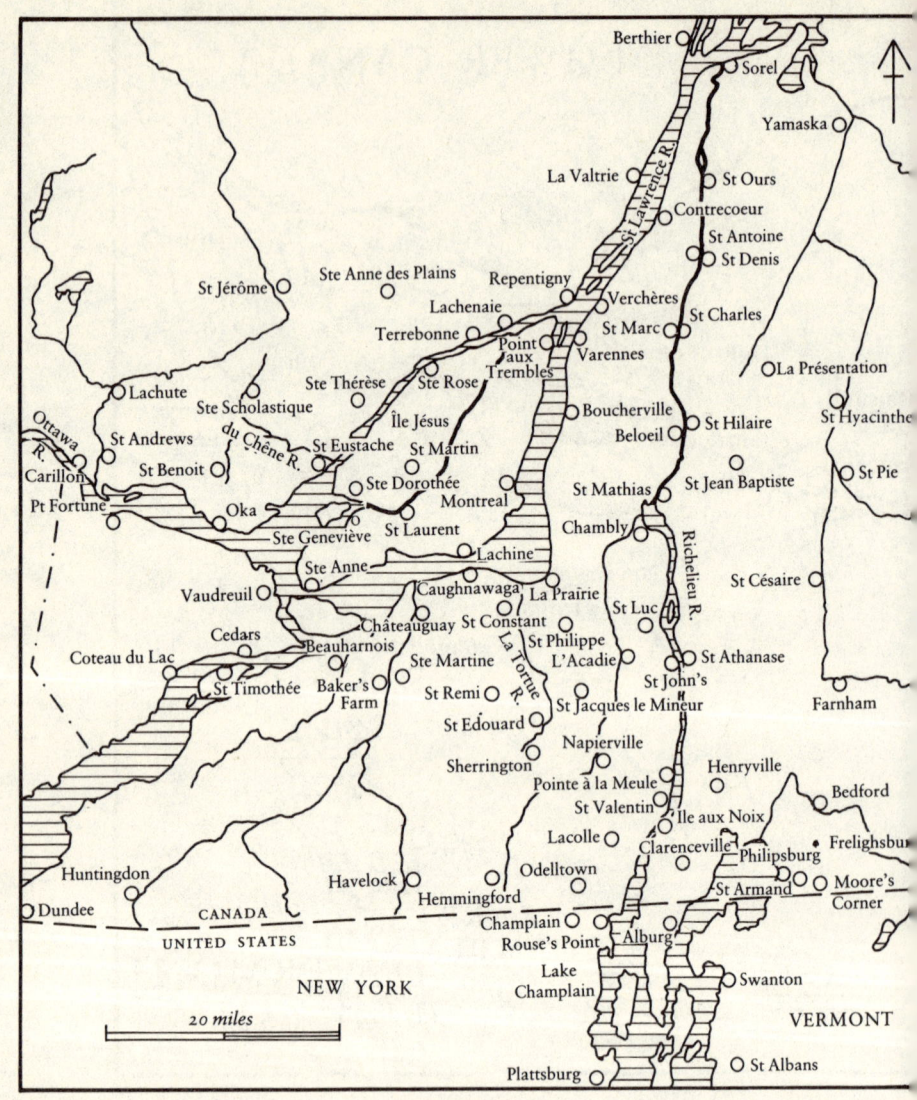

Lower Canada

As the war progressed and it became clear that the American colonists were gaining the upper hand, many of the loyalists decided that they could no longer live in a country whose allegiances were so opposed to their own. The first exodus took place when General Howe evacuated Boston in 1776, to

4

be followed by others up to and after the signing of the peace treaty in 1783, which granted independence to what had now become the United States of America. It has been estimated that perhaps as many as forty per cent of the population of the old thirteen American colonies were of loyalist conviction, to a greater or lesser extent, although not all of these were willing to leave their homes and kindred. Of the 50,000 loyalists who did leave, some 30,000 settled in Nova Scotia and attempted to build a new life there, whilst a further 7,000 went to Lower Canada, now the modern province of Quebec. After the surrender of Burgoyne at Saratoga and the fighting in New York State in 1779, many more loyalists settled in the Niagara area, and their number was swelled in 1783 after the evacuation of New York by the British. The steady trickle north of loyalists from that state and Pennsylvania included many of German or Huguenot extraction. It was only to be expected that having given up their homes and livelihood, and having endured great hardship and suffering, these new settlers along the frontier of Canada should not feel kindly disposed to their erstwhile countrymen, whom they looked upon as traitors. The feelings of bitterness against the United States of America went deep.

It was important to the British in Canada that the settlement along the frontier with America should be strengthened by those whose loyalty to the Crown was beyond question, and who could be counted upon to defend that frontier in times of emergency. Those who had borne arms for the King were made eligible for grants of land.[2]

A mere thirty years after the War of Independence, on 18 June 1812, the United States declared war on Great Britain, and Canada was put under the renewed threat of American invasion from the south. The causes of the war had little to do with Canadian-American relations, but it was clear to all that Canada offered the expanding American states a rich prize, which seemed to them to be available for the taking. The American Ex-President, Thomas Jefferson, wrote, 'The acquisition of Canada this year (1812) as far as the neighbourhood of Quebec will be a mere matter of marching', and

Congressman Henry Clay said: 'The conquest of Canada is in your power. I trust I shall not be deemed presumptuous when I state I verily believe that the militia of Kentucky are alone competent to place Montreal and Upper Canada at your feet.'[3]

The number of regular British troops in Canada was at a minimum, owing to the years of warfare with Napoleonic France. There was only one regular infantry battalion in Upper Canada, the 41st Regiment, and it made up two-thirds of the total garrison of 1,600 regulars in the province. In Lower Canada the situation was slightly better but the total of regular British troops and Canadian fencibles in the Canadas amounted to only some 5,600 men, with another 4,200 in Nova Scotia.[2,4]

In 1812 the Americans launched three attacks on Canada – on Detroit, on Niagara and from Lake Champlain, all of which were repulsed after heavy fighting. During the next two years hostilities along the frontier continued with mixed fortunes for both sides, but in 1813 reinforcements of Peninsular veterans arrived from Europe to strengthen Canadian resistance. The peace that was signed late in 1814 brought to an end a war which resulted in little advantage to either side, but which certainly deepened Canadian suspicions of American intentions and goodwill. It also became clear to the British that it was insufficient to depend upon local Canadian militia units for the defence of the frontier, partly because a militia drawn from a sparsely populated agricultural area could not be adequately trained and welded into an efficient fighting force, and partly because threats to individual homesteads, or the demands of harvest, inevitably rendered their attendance unreliable. The hard core of the defence had to be regular troops, but the effectiveness of any defence of Upper Canada also depended upon the ability of the British to command control of the lakes and waterways.

As both Americans and Canadians expanded westward, the occasions for friction and misunderstanding increased. The British still maintained garrisons in areas ceded to the Americans under the terms of the Treaty of Paris of 1783. When, in 1794, General Wayne's American forces defeated the Indians at the Battle of Fallen Timbers, near the newly built British Fort Miami commanded by Major Campbell, Wayne tried to force out Campbell by overawing him. Campbell refused to be overawed, but also declined to give assistance to the Indians. Along such an uncertain and developing frontier it was inevitable, too, that on the Canadian side of the border, especially in Upper Canada, there would always be a strong proportion of settlers who had crossed from the United States, and whose loyalty to the Crown and to the ideals of British government could never be relied upon. They looked upon themselves as Americans and not as Canadians. During the War of 1812 there were many instances of American-born settlers in Canada giving sympathy and help to the American invaders.

In Lower Canada the bulk of the population was French-speaking, and here the English-speaking Canadians were in the minority. In the early years of British rule great care had been taken not to offend the susceptibilities of the French-Canadian population, nor to place too great a strain on their feelings for the British Crown. This policy had been embodied in the Quebec Act of 1774, in order that it might be apparent that the rewards of loyalty would be greater than those of secession or rebellion. But following the War of Independence, the need to secure the frontier against American incursion became more urgent, and as the Americans outnumbered the Canadians by at least twelve to one, the British Home Government encouraged English settlement. This policy was opposed by the French Canadians, who comprised ninety-four per cent of the population and who, under the terms of the 1760 surrender, had been promised that their way of life would be respected. French Canadians pointed out that as their numbers had doubled since 1760 there was no need for English-speaking settlement, and they assured the Government that they would never throw in their lot with the Americans. However, the mood of the times was such that it was decided that Government policy must be directed towards demonstrating to the French Canadians the advantages and superiority of the British way of life obtainable under British rule.[2,4]

Given the self-confidence and national pride of the period, the British way of life was believed by those in authority to offer the best possible form of freedom, with the finest and most noble system of government under the Mother of Parliaments at Westminster. The Canadas were seen not only as a group of colonies, but as an extension of the British people overseas, where every Canadian should be able to enjoy the same privileges and duties as an Englishman. This growing missionary zeal to anglicise, and the methods used, were to provide one of the major causes for dissatisfaction, and eventually for rebellion, in both Lower and Upper Canada.

The rural French Canadians were poorly educated, conservative in their farming practice and subject to the feudal system of the seigneurs and the tithes of the Catholic Church. Conservatism and resistance to change made it difficult for them to meet the economic challenges posed by the development of wheat-growing in Upper Canada, while the shift in trade from fur to lumber and boat-building, though it offered seasonal labour to the 'habitants', was under the control of English-speaking merchants. As the development of Upper Canada progressed, the primitive farming methods of the French-Canadian peasantry could not compete and they were driven to subsistence farming.

The British authorities were concerned with the military security of the frontier and loyalty to the Crown. Immigration from England, Scotland and later from Ireland was encouraged, but the immigrants tended to be those who were unable or incapable of making a living in their own country. After the end of the Napoleonic Wars, the number of immigrants greatly increased, most of them disembarking at Quebec, with about a third of them settling in Lower Canada. Their numbers, adding to the natural fecundity of the French Canadians, exerted tremendous pressure upon the availability of land. To the French Canadians it seemed that the British were expanding rapidly, and taking from them their means of livelihood.[4]

From the British conquest of Canada in 1760 up to the end of the Napoleonic Wars, the attitude of most French Canadians had been one of loyalty to the British Crown. Their very conservatism made them abhor the ideas of the French Revolution; their loyalty was traditional, to a sovereign, to their feudal duties through the seigneurial system, and to the Catholic Church. But the combination of poor agricultural methods and subsistence farming, of the domination of the English-speaking mercantile interests, of natural over-population allied to an acute shortage of new land, made more acute by English-speaking immigration, and the gradual change in emphasis on the part of government from care not to offend French-Canadian susceptibilities to what seemed to be an outright policy of English domination, changed the mood of French Canada. Loyalty to the Crown turned into French-Canadian nationalism. This general discontent was given leadership by the growing alienation of the expanding French-Canadian merchant class, who comprised a mass of small businessmen, storekeepers, tradesmen, artisans and innkeepers. These shared many of the values and interests of their rural compatriots and viewed with alarm the growth of the English-speaking merchants who everywhere seemed to be stifling their initiatives and taking over their trade. Class-consciousness was added to race-consciousness, and both were seen as part of a deliberate policy on the part of the authorities to subjugate them, to destroy their traditions, and to exclude them from the benefits of the developments, economic and political, that were taking place.

The political expression of this discontent was voiced by the Canadian Party, which after 1826 came to be known as the 'Patriotes', under the leadership of the Speaker of the House of Assembly, Louis-Joseph Papineau. He was born in Montreal in 1786, the grandson of a cooper. His father improved the family's social position by becoming a notary in Montreal, and his son trained as a surveyor and notary. Louis-Joseph managed a number of seigneuries until he himself managed to purchase the seigneury of La Petite Nation on the Ottawa river. All the French-Canadian virtues and attitudes tended to combine in Papineau – peasant, bourgeois and aristocratic. He had the gift of matching his actions to the needs of a constantly changing situation, of responding to the desires of those whom he led. His followers saw him as upholding their values against hostile forces which were encroaching increasingly upon their way of life. Ambitious, he became Speaker of the House at the early age of twenty-nine. He was a man with a sense of mission who identified himself completely with the French-Canadian heritage and its interests, but as a *petit bourgeois* who had only recently acquired aristocratic status as a seigneur he saw those interests through the eyes of the French-Canadian élite; and this coloured his attitude to the peasants and labourers.[4,5]

In the elections of 1834 the Patriotes swept the board and Papineau, their acknowledged leader, attacked those symbols of British power and the English-speaking supremacy which he saw as constraining his people. Members of the House of Assembly were elected, and the House was under the political control of the Patriotes, but the Legislative and Executive Councils were appointed by the Governor and only had the power to advise. Papineau wanted the elective principle to be established throughout the political system, with the Governor bound by the advice he received. So the ethnic lines were drawn, for the English-speaking minority saw their financial and social interests challenged. Patronage lay in the hands of the Governor, as did many of the rights over the allocation of land. Trade and commerce were controlled by the English-speaking traders of Montreal, and whoever controlled Montreal, controlled the only access to and from Upper Canada.

There was one influential interest in French Canada that viewed the claims of the Patriotes with alarm – the Catholic Church. Under the French the Catholic Church had been supreme, and whilst it acknowledged the State in all things temporal, it had also exercised total power in all matters spiritual. It had believed in the divine right of the monarchy and the aristocracy, under whose protection it flourished, to whom it owed complete temporal obedience, and for whose stability it was bound to work. In return the State had allowed the Church freedom to control religious practice and the care of the poor and the sick, and granted it a monopoly over education. The clergy had received financial support from the French king, and were allowed by law to collect tithes and other fees in order to carry out their duties. Under the British most of the Catholic Church's privileges were continued. The French Revolution was therefore viewed with horror by the French-Canadian bishops and clergy, since it abolished the monarchy and the aristocracy, and did away with the privileges of the Church. Understandably, the French-Canadian hierarchy now hardened in its opposition to all the ideas that it saw as emerging from the French metropolitan Anti-Christ, especially those radical ideas associated with liberty, equality and the elective principle.

Monseigneur Lartigue, the Bishop of Montreal, who was a cousin of Papineau, saw the Church threatened from every side – by the Government, by the English-speaking minority and by the more liberal and republican ideas of the emerging French-Canadian middle class. He believed in the divine right of kings and in an established Church, which in Lower Canada could only be, in his view, the Catholic Church. The clergy were, to him, the élite of the nation, and the laity were servants of the Church. His strongly clerical and authoritarian views were intended to form a bulwark against the evils of liberalism, republicanism and Protestant encroachment. The bulk of the French-Canadian Catholic clergy, following their bishops' lead, were hostile to the ideas of the Patriotes; and they exercised great influence, especially within the rural areas.[4]

For the Patriotes an elected Legislative Council became the prime objective, first because it upheld the supremacy of suffrage over appointed officials, secondly because those appointed officials themselves represented the authority of the English-speaking minority in Lower Canada, and thirdly because that English-speaking minority held the power over so much patronage. As early as 1829 Papineau was writing about the Legislative Council that it was 'a body between which and the assemblies it is impossible that there be any rapprochement. Therein is the origin of all the abuses which impose strain on the provinces. The administrations insult the assemblies when they do not dominate them, instead of which, in principle, it is for the assemblies to influence the executive, to direct it.'[5]

These views were in direct contrast to those held by the succession of Governors, some of whom were more liberal than others. In their view government did not derive its authority from the wishes of the majority expressed through its duly elected representatives, but from the King and his appointed officers, and that only upon such principles could a sound foundation be laid for progress. A stable society should be based on religious faith and practice, and for that to succeed the Church must be established. As Canada was British, and as the King was head of the Church of England, it followed that the established Church in Canada had to be the Anglican Church, not as a matter of religious prejudice but of sound order. Other forms of belief would not be persecuted, and anyone could worship God in his own way, but the natural order in their view demanded that a British territory should have the English church. Loyalty to the Crown and the link with Britain was of paramount importance, and could best be upheld by a combination of loyalty, sound religion and strong economic ties with the homeland.[2,4]

In Lower Canada the English-speaking mercantile interests, the administration and the Anglican Church, from whom were drawn most of the members of Legislative Council, were in the happy position that their loyalties and self-interest coincided. The more immigration could be encouraged, the more economic progress could be achieved and the more the numerical balance between French and English Canadians could be redressed, the more the merchants would prosper, just as the Anglican Church would grow stronger and the Crown could depend upon strengthening the British connection.

The political objectives of the Patriotes were to concentate French-Canadian and English-speaking liberal attention on what they saw as misgovernment by an outdated aristocratic institution which stood for English-speaking supremacy and which perpetrated abuses of power and authority through a self-perpetuating oligarchy. Their aim was to secure the transfer of this political power from the English-speaking minority to the French-Canadian majority, and in the process to abolish both the old French feudal ties and the more subtle but nonetheless real British autocracy. Both sides started from opposing ideas, whilst they held in common strong beliefs in what form of government ought to prevail, and a passionate allegiance to their respective cultural and national origins.

These political objectives were polarised around the issues of revenue control, the elective principle, and economic prosperity. The Constitutional Act of 1791 had established the new province of Upper Canada and granted Houses of Assembly to both Upper and Lower Canada, mainly in response to liberal pressures. The Canadians saw these two Houses as being the counterparts of the Westminster House of Commons, but while their members gained many of the privileges of the Westminster model, there the resemblance stopped. All legislation passed by the Houses of Assembly was subject to the approval of the appointed Legislative and Executive Councils under the control of the Governor, who could himself be overruled by London. The control of revenue and expenditure in both Upper and Lower Canada became an immediate issue.[2,4,6]

In Lower Canada Papineau realised that he had to broaden his political appeal if the Patriotes were to attract the growing English-speaking vote, especially among the many Irish immigrants. Otherwise his support would be relegated to the rural French-Canadian areas, as the townships expanded with the influx of immigrant labour. He therefore sought to focus attention on what he saw as the abuses brought about by an outdated form of aristocratic government, which enabled a select few – and those English-speaking – to retain all power in their own hands. This also had the effect of drawing up the lines of ethnic consciousness, with the result that French-Canadian nationalism flourished under the banner of democratic principles and republican ideas. Following the overwhelming support gained in the elections of 1834, the Patriotes became more and more a French-Canadian national party. Even so, its nationalism was still very conservative, with many Patriotes upholding the French-Canadian seigneurial system and the ideals of the Ancien Régime. There was, however, a radical minority who were dedicated to social change, and these were among the most active and committed members. All were united in the primary aim of political independence.

Convinced by their own electoral success, Papineau and his party believed that revolution was inevitable, not only in the Canadas but also in Britain itself. In order to increase the political pressure, the Patriotes embarked upon an economic war. All French Canadians should feel obliged to support a boycott of British goods, especially textiles, woollens, beer and whisky, and build their own mills, breweries and distilleries. Patriotes must withdraw their money from the English-dominated banking system and deal only with fellow French Canadians. By these means Papineau sought to undermine the system, so that the authorities would be forced to give way or face economic collapse.[2,4,6]

The leaders of the economic boycott were young men, described by the Patriote Duvernay as 'vigorous youths, determined and well organised'. They looked upon wearing homespun clothing and drinking locally brewed beer and distilled whisky as a patriotic gesture and as evidence of their own commitment to the cause. Papineau, in answer to criticism of the economic boycott, declared:

Some will tell us: But you are destroying commerce! I reply first of all, that if commerce were inseparable from the triumph of our oppressors and from our degradation, then commerce must be destroyed! But this is not the case. Our efforts can give it a new and better direction. Multiply our flock, so as to have more wool, our cattle for food, for improving the land, for tanning more leather. Let us have more craftsmen to put out more abundant products; sow more hemp to have more linen, and, during our long winters, employ usefully at the loom our industrious and comely female fellow-citizens, and thereby help us liberate our country.[6]

As the political temperature increased, so did the split within the Patriote ranks. The radicals tended to be grouped around Montreal, the more conservative elements around Quebec; the former became known as the 'wolves', the latter as the 'lambs'. Matters came to a head in 1834, when the House of Assembly adopted the 'Ninety-Two Resolutions', consisting of a list of grievances embodied within a political programme of parliamentary reform and French-Canadian nationalism. The Quebec Patriotes, 'la petite famille', were unable to accept such a radical challenge to the established order, and this was to have profound effects upon the course of the coming rebellion. As the Quebec leaders increasingly distanced themselves from the Montreal leadership, and as they began slowly to exercise a more moderate influence, they were increasingly joined by other French-Canadian moderates who were aware and were concerned at the way in which Papineau seemed to be leading the Patriotes towards the use of force.[2,4]

In answer to the Ninety-Two Resolutions, London responded by replacing the Governor in Lower Canada and by sending out a new Governor who was to chair a Royal Commission to look into the grievances, and who, it was hoped, could exercise a steadying influence. The new Governor, Lord Gosford, tried to conciliate through compromise, with some success in Quebec, but he made little headway in Montreal. And when the Patriotes learned that the possibility of elections to the Legislative Council had been ruled out by London, they seized upon this as further evidence of British bad faith. At once they delivered an ultimatum to London, demanding the election of legislative councillors and calling a strike of assembly members until their demands were met.

As the situation rapidly deteriorated, Parliament was asked to intervene. The Commissioners reported in March 1837, and the same month Parliament replied by adopting Lord John Russell's Ten Resolutions, which rejected the Patriotes' demands, and authorised the Governor to pay civil service salaries, if necessary, without the consent of the House of Assembly. From this point on, the Patriotes began to prepare openly for armed conflict.[4]

In Upper Canada, while the background and personalities were very different from the Lower Province, many of the grievances were the same. There had long been friction between the House of Assembly and the Legislative Council, particularly over the control of money. As in Lower Canada, the Upper Canadian Assembly felt that it ought to enjoy the same rights as the British House of Commons, but a request to this effect was rejected by the Governor, who was in turn supported by London. Then there was the alien issue. Many Americans had settled in the new lands of Upper Canada as the drive westwards gained pace. Imbued with American ideas of democracy and individualism, they now demanded to participate fully as Canadian citizens. The Assembly supported their claims and asked that all American-born immigrants should be treated on the same basis as natural-born Canadians. This was a request which the British Government found very hard to accept in view of the province's recent history and their own British pride. Then the Assembly went a step further, demanding that existing policies should be changed so that immigration from the United States could be actively encouraged. London eventually ruled that all American immigrants must be treated as aliens on arrival, but that after a qualifying period of seven years' residence they could become British citizens provided they took an oath of allegiance and at the same time renounced their allegiance to any other country. These terms were bitterly resented by the independently-minded American immigrants.[2]

Executive authority in Upper Canada, and especially the control of patronage, lay in the hands of the Family Compact. This consisted of a closely-knit group comprising the senior members of the administration; they shared the same interests and ideals and in their hands rested the control of day-to-day affairs. They were a self-perpetuating oligarchy who, because they controlled patronage, saw to it that only like-minded persons were appointed to positions of power and influence in the province. At least half were drawn from second-generation loyalist families, being young men of education and proven loyalty to the Crown; the rest were men who had come to Canada more recently from Britain. Two of the leading members were John Strachan and John Robinson, both members of the Executive Council and later of the Legislative

Council. John Strachan was the Anglican rector of York, and later became Archdeacon and then the first Bishop of Toronto. Robinson became Attorney General in 1818 and Chief Justice in 1829. Their aim was to ensure that Canada remained an integral part of the British Empire, but the means they adopted to achieve that object were often ruthless, callous and self-seeking. They were frankly contemptuous of democracy, and sought stable government under an established Church; they conducted their affairs with arrogant energy. Inevitably they came into conflict with the more liberal American way of thinking and with the ideals of the radical elements of Upper Canadian society, especially among the Scottish and Irish immigrants.

The growing feeling against the Family Compact in Upper Canada found leadership in the person of William Lyon Mackenzie, a small red-headed Scot of cantankerous disposition, considerable idealism, and a vituperative pen. This misguided patriot saw himself as a crusading zealot and critic against the abuses perpetrated by members of the Family Compact. He worked untiringly, without thought or wish for personal gain, for a freely elected and open system of government and by his single-minded perversity gained a considerable following. Also, he had the tool to further his aims: he was proprietor and editor of a newspaper, *The Colonial Advocate*. Seemingly possessed by an urge to be scurrilous, he constantly printed sensational scandal, much of it invented, which exemplified his ability to indulge in the worst excesses of the gutter press.[2,7]

Opposition to the government in Upper Canada crystallised in the growth of the Reform Party, and centred around the alien question, the Anglican supremacy and patronage. Those in authority were deeply suspicious of the American-born settlers in Upper Canada, who they believed had as their aim the separation of the province from the Crown, and its incorporation into the United States. The Reformers, influenced by American ideals, wanted a freely elected form of what they described as 'responsible government'. There was little room for give and take.

On the question of Anglican supremacy, the Family Compact were in a less secure position. A permanent apportionment of land had been given to the Anglican Church 'for the support and maintenance of a Protestant clergy'. These clergy reserves amounted to a seventh in value of all land granted to every township, and totalled more than 800,000 acres. Furthermore, the Governor had the power to have at least one parsonage built in each township, with enough land attached so as to endow the living.

Only the Anglican Church, as by law established, benefited from these provisions. Opposition to the Government's land policy grew with the increase in immigration after the War of 1812. Strachan countered by offering the land of the clergy reserves for sale, and by the end of the 1820s the clergy lands were selling rapidly for good prices. Then the opposition shifted to political and religious issues.[2,7]

Many of the new settlers from Britain were of Scottish origin, and these Scots petitioned that the clergy reserves be also used for the support of the Church of Scotland. London took the view that 'the support of the Protestant clergy' included ministers of the Church of Scotland, but the Governor and Executive Council did not like this ruling and chose to ignore it. This became known to the Presbyterians and increased their sense of injustice.

But public opinion generally in Upper Canada had little sympathy with the favoured claims of either the Anglican or Presbyterian churches. In 1826 the Assembly claimed that all churches should be entitled to their share in the reserves, but that since there were so many denominations it would be better if the proceeds were applied to 'the purpose of education and the general improvement of the Province'. Certainly few of the settlers were Anglicans, with the Methodists and other Protestant Churches claiming the loyalty of the majority. John Strachan's determination to create a monopoly for the Anglicans gave cause for more ill-feeling. Thus the two issues of clergy lands and the alien question gave impetus to the rapidly-growing Reform movement in Upper Canada. Never far from the surface, too, lay the manner in which the

Family Compact exercised the power which patronage gave to them.[2]

Upper Canada had become 'Yankee' in outlook, with many of the frontier values of their American neighbour, a leaning towards sectarian religion, a deep suspicion of education and social standing, hostility to strangers, and belief in the values of initiative, hard work and democracy. These feelings were accentuated by the constant pressure of American influence and competition. Egerton Ryerson, a young travelling Methodist preacher, drew attention to the ills under which his congregations suffered, but it was William Lyon Mackenzie who gave these views publicity in *The Colonial Advocate*. Within the Assembly it was Dr John Rolph who led the opposition. Rolph, a doctor and a lawyer, was a complex character, but a skilled orator and debater and he was supported within the Reform Party by Marshall Spring Bidwell, Peter Perry, and Dr Baldwin and his son Robert.[2,7] Bidwell, American-born, had taken the oath of allegiance and in spite of attempts to declare him an alien was re-elected to the Assembly.

Mackenzie was incapable of taking a moderate stand; he saw himself as an agitator and a disturber of the status quo. He stood for plain speech and no deference to those in authority. *The Colonial Advocate* soon became widely read throughout Upper Canada. It did not stop at criticism but descended to scandal and libel of the most vicious and personal kind, with the result that a party of young men, whose families had been subjected to abuse, broke into the newspaper office and destroyed the printing press. Mackenzie instituted and won a civil action for damages which not only enabled him to set up a new and better press, but made him a hero in the cause of freedom.[2,7]

In 1836 Sir Francis Head arrived as Governor of Upper Canada, with instructions to conciliate provincial opinion. However, he quickly formed an adverse opinion of the Reformers as 'republicans' who would never be satisfied by concessions. He found himself confronted by growing opposition from the Assembly, who voted to stop supplies. He responded by refusing his assent to bills already passed. He then dissolved the Assembly, and in the ensuing election the Reform Party suffered defeat. Sir Francis Head had the political sagacity to make the election issue a simple one of loyalty to the Crown versus republicanism, and so secured the votes of the recent immigrants and the Roman Catholics, as well as the Methodists. But Sir Francis could not rest content until he had destroyed all traces of republicanism, and when he started to dismiss from office men whom he suspected of having sympathy with the Reformers, he alienated that moderate opinion which had previously supported him.[2]

The situation in Upper Canada was now exacerbated by influences beyond its border, partly by the severe economic depression which was affecting both Britain and America, and partly by the growing tensions in Lower Canada. Mackenzie, who was in contact with Papineau, and the Patriotes, was now determined upon armed rebellion. Most of the Reformers refused to support him, although the attitude of Dr Rolph remained ambiguous. When British policy towards Lower Canada changed in early 1837, with Lord John Russell's Ten Resolutions, Mackenzie in Upper Canada toured the province organising and addressing public meetings, appealing to their hearers to become 'more Canadian' and intimating that they would only secure their just rights by the use of force. 'Foreign' governments were condemned; Canadians could best secure their freedom against a cruel and oppressive regime by being joined to the United States as a semi-independent state within a Union covering the whole of North America.

If Mackenzie's leadership of the Reform Party had driven out most of its moderate members, he himself was past caring. He seemed to be driven by a dynamic energy and restless spirit to pursue his extreme objectives regardless of any other considerations. So, by the autumn of 1837, matters in both Lower and Upper Canada were drawing to their climax.

2

Rebellion in Lower Canada

By the beginning of 1837 there was a hardening of attitude among the Patriotes of Lower Canada, assisted by the growing economic crisis. Poor harvests had affected Britain and America, as well as Canada, and this added to the social hardship suffered by the French-Canadian habitants. On 13 April the paper *La Minerve* commented on Lord John Russell's Ten Resolutions: 'The anxiously awaited news of the Commons relating to this country has arrived at last. The story we have to tell is one of new acts of oppression.'

The Patriote leaders decided to broaden their base of support by stirring up popular opinion, though not to the point where the moderates might become alienated. The radicals were now determined upon revolution, but first they wanted to increase their support and to bring back into their fold the waverers of Quebec, and to win over those who still looked for a peaceful solution. The Patriote leader, Wolfred Nelson, wrote: 'I am vexed by Mr Papineau's and Mackenzie's admission that we had decided to rebel. It gives justification to our adversaries and denies us the right to complain of having been attacked.'[4]

From early days the Patriotes had set up an efficient network of parish and county committees under a Permanent Central Committee based in Montreal, on which were represented deputies from each of the parish and county committees. Communication to and from the rural areas to the centre worked rapidly and well.[6]

The Patriotes, through their Permanent Central Committee, decided to step up their economic boycott of all British goods, and at the same time to organise parish meetings and public gatherings. This action was intended to lead to a popular convention of representatives from each of the counties of

Lower Canada, who would then present the British Government with their demands. If these demands were not heeded, they would resort to armed rebellion, which would be accompanied by a declaration of independence and the setting up of a provisional government. Even though the Patriotes' ultimate intention was revolution, it was to be given a semblance of political propriety in order to gain the support of moderates, and those who still looked for a peaceful solution.[4]

The first rally took place at St Ours in the Richelieu County on 7 May 1837 and drew a crowd of 1,200, who were addressed by two of the radical wing of the party, Wolfred Nelson of St Denis and Dr Cyrille Coté of Napierville.[6]

On 14 May two more rallies were held at Montreal and at St Marc-sur-Richelieu, and at the latter it was declared, 'Better a bloody but just and honourable fight than cowardly submission to a corrupt power.'[7] The Montreal rally, which was poorly attended, was addressed by Papineau, who appealed for support for the economic boycott of British goods. These rallies were accompanied throughout Lower Canada by numerous parish meetings.

In June the number of rallies increased dramatically, particularly around Montreal. On 1 June three were held, at Chambly, St Hyacinthe and Ste Scholastique, and at the latter French and Canadian flags were flown accompanied by Patriote songs. French-Canadian nationalism was increasing and English-speaking Canadians who had lived in peace for years among the French-Canadian majority in Lower Canada now found themselves ostracised. Papineau endeavoured to woo the Irish settlers and was often accompanied by O'Callaghan, a Patriote of Irish immigrant origin and editor of *The Vindicator*, an English language paper which supported the Patriotes. The habitants had by now taken the radical message to heart and the burning of barns and threats to the property of the English-speaking Canadians – and of the Catholic clergy where they disapproved of Patriote sentiments – increased rapidly.

The main support for the Patriotes came from the valley of the Richelieu south of Montreal, and along the River du Chêne to the north west of the city. Between Montreal and the American border, rallies were held at Yamaska, St Grégoire, Longueuil and again at St Hyacinthe, where a crowd of between one and two thousand attended. North west of Montreal 1,000 people met at Ste Rose, and 4,000 came to hear Papineau from the counties of Lachenaie and L'Assomption, and a smaller number in Berthier.

In July, on American Independence Day, there were calls for American support of the Patriote cause at a rally at Missisquoi, and Papineau drew a crowd of 4,000 at Napierville. On 6 August a rally was held west of Montreal at Vaudreuil, with a gathering of all the Patriote leadership. South of Montreal St Constant was the scene of a final rally with many Patriote leaders personally present, including Amury Girod, Cardinal, Lacroix, Chénier and Brown.[4]

Rallies were also held around Quebec, but here enthusiasm for the Patriote cause was less ardent than in Montreal. Because of this Papineau made a special effort to support Augustin-Norbert Morin, the most energetic of the Patriote party in the area. At St Thomas there was a crowd of over 1,800 people, and rallies at Lislet and Bellechasse were well attended. But at Kamouraska the powerful seigneur, Amable Dionne, exerted sufficient influence to deter even Papineau. At Charlevoix and Deschambault, Morin on his own managed to stir the crowds, but he failed to establish a following of any substance in the major towns. Étienne Parent, the editor of the right-wing French-Canadian paper *Le Canadien*, warned his readers that Morin was working towards rebellion, and he consistently attacked those who advocated violence and independence, accusing them of encouraging anarchy and of going out of their way to provoke the authorities to take action against them.

On the other hand the Patriote press, and particularly *La Minerve*, under Ludger Duvernay, and *The Vindicator*, under its Irish editor, Daniel Tracey (who was later succeeded by E. B. O'Callaghan, Papineau's constant companion), declared their intention of instructing Canadians 'to resist every usurpation of their rights'. As early as in 1832 *La Minerve* had attacked Papineau for using peaceful means, and in July 1837 wrote of the Bishop of Montreal, 'M. the curé of Quebec preaches passive obedience, which is to say servitude.'[2,6]

The opposition to the Patriotes in Quebec came to a head in August when the awaited convention of representatives from the counties gathered in the city. It turned out to be a confrontation between the Quebec moderates and the Montreal extremists, and resulted in the Quebec leadership withdrawing their support. From then on, the focus of attention centred on the Montreal area, but even in the areas of the Patriotes' greatest support there were many French Canadians, who, while wanting reform, were not prepared to resort to armed force and rebellion. These moderates were dubbed Tory Canadians or Chouaguens.[5]

Following a rally in the city on 29 June, the Patriotes established a revolutionary caucus and groups of Patriotes were organised in order to prepare for action. In September Dr Robert Nelson, at the inaugural meeting of a new association called the Fils de la Liberté, encouraged his audience 'to try to overthrow the government if we consider ourselves strong enough'.[4] From now on preparations became overtly military. The Fils de la Liberté were organised into sections, each responsible for training its members in drill, weapon training and in exercises.

It was the French-Canadian students and young professional men who formed the leadership of the Fils de la Liberté, and they were joined by the artisans, unemployed, and apprentices. It was essentially a youth organisation whose aim was 'to emancipate our country from all human authority save that of the bold democracy residing in its bosom'. Its members sang 'Moi, je préfère ma patrie: avant tout, je suis Canadien'. They were led by Thomas Storrow Brown and André Ouimet, who headed the military and civil wings. The civil wing consisted of six sections corresponding to the six militia districts of Montreal, and the military wing was formed so that these six civil sections could furnish six battalions when called upon.[6]

On 23 October the Patriotes organised a rally at St Charles which was expected to lead to the calling of the general convention at which they would declare a state of independence and set up a provisional government. Papineau was invited to speak. The night before, he and O'Callaghan drafted resolutions to be presented to the Great Confederation which, it was hoped, the rally would promote.

Wolfred Nelson presided next day, with a crowd of four to five thousand people present, with representatives from all the six counties, and armed men on guard, and with a plentiful supply of banners around a liberty pole. Papineau still favoured the economic boycott. Nelson, Rodier and Brown supported Dr Coté, who said that it was useless to send petitions to England, 'America is ready to help, Upper Canada is in rebellion and we must follow their example.' And Nelson openly defied Papineau, saying, 'I am of a different opinion to Mr Papineau. I claim the time has come to melt down our pewter plates and spoons into bullets.' M. Viger, President of the Banque du Peuple, recalled 'the applause of the crowd from which there came not a single disapproving voice showed clearly that a revolution had already taken place in their hearts, and all that was left was to proclaim it by some overt act of opposition to the government. During this meeting many donations were made for buying arms and munitions of war for defence in case of attack.' Dr Kimber from Chambly said, 'I was at St Charles and never in any country has there been seen such an assemblage determined to be rid of the English government.'[4,6]

The commander of the British military forces in Lower Canada was Sir John Colborne, an energetic and experienced soldier who had been Governor of Upper Canada until replaced by Sir Francis Head. He was a Peninsular veteran, and the man who commanded the 52nd Foot at Waterloo, on whose initiative that regiment was wheeled onto the flank of the Imperial Guard and whose volleys against those picked troops helped to raise the cry, 'La Garde recule!' On 6 October Sir John felt it necessary to warn the civil authorities, 'The game which Mr Papineau is playing cannot be mistaken and we must be prepared to expect that if four or five hundred persons be allowed to parade the streets of Montreal at night singing revolutionary songs, the excited parties will come in collision.'[8]

After the St Charles rally the clergy and the seigneurs became alarmed, but as early as July Bishop Lartigue of Montreal had told his clergy to refuse absolution to any who encouraged resistance to 'the government under which we have the happiness to live'. In October, on the day after the St Charles rally, the Bishop issued a *mandement* condemning the 'pernicious doctrines of democracy', and the evils of thinking in terms of independence. For those who refused to heed his warning, the Bishop made it clear that rebellion would result in the denial of absolution and the refusal of a Christian burial conducted by the Church.

The Patriotes increased their preparations for rebellion. On 6 November Sir John Colborne's fears were vindicated. The Fils de la Liberté clashed in the streets of Montreal with members of the Doric Club, a group of aggressive loyalist young men. The Fils de la Liberté marched through the city in silence, each man carrying a club, but soon brawls developed with the young loyalists and then spread into a series of running street fights in the course of which the Patriote leader, Storrow Brown, was hurt in the eye. During the night military pickets were posted at key points throughout the city, and the volunteer Montreal Royal Artillery paraded through the streets in a show of force. This was followed a week later with a proclamation which forbade all unauthorised military activity, and which sought to raise volunteer units of infantry, artillery and cavalry to help maintain law and order.[2,6,8]

Around Montreal, and particularly in the area along the Richelieu valley between the city and the American border, Patriote harassment of government officials increased. On 10 November a farmer, Dupins, and an innkeeper, Gervais from St John, gathered the Patriotes to attack the garrison. At St Edouard a merchant aroused the people, and at Longueuil another merchant, François Charron, sold powder and shot in order to kill 'the red pigs'. At St Césaire, Chambly and in many of the rural areas around Montreal, the French-

Canadian middle-class radicals were stirring the revolutionary pot and bringing it to the boil.[4]

On 1 November Sir John Colborne received a letter from one of his informants which said:

It was rumoured yesterday that 6 French officers have arrived at Rasco's Hotel. I strongly suspect it is true. They even march thro our streets with revolutionary flags by night; and go out by day publicly and on Sabbath-days even to practise. It may further be expected that not a few turbulent Americans will gladly foment and promote this revolt, but the greater evil and danger would result from the aid of French adventurers familiar with revolution and blood, and fitted to train the Canadians to fight and commit all manners of excesses on life and property. The country people are becoming like brigands, attacking isolated houses where British families reside.[C1]

At this time there were throughout Canada eleven regular British battalions of infantry, none of which was up to their full strength; the 2nd Battalion the 1st Foot, the Royal Scots, the 15th Foot (the East Yorkshires), the 24th Foot (the South Wales Borderers), the 32nd Foot (The Duke of Cornwall's Light Infantry), the 34th Foot (Border Regiment), the 43rd Foot (Oxfordshire and Buckinghamshire Light Infantry), the 65th Foot (York and Lancaster Regiment), 66th Foot (The Royal Berkshires), the 83rd Foot (Royal Ulster Rifles), the 85th Foot (King's Own Shropshire Light Infantry) and the 93rd Foot (Argyll and Sutherland Highlanders). These were stationed: 1st, 24th and 32nd Foot – at Montreal and in the area around; 15th, 66th and 83rd Foot – at Quebec and in the area around; 34th, 43rd, 65th and 85th Foot – in New Brunswick; 93rd Foot – arrived at Halifax early in 1838.

The 15th and 24th Foot had been stationed in Upper Canada until May and October 1837 respectively, but in view of the threatening situation in Lower Canada, the Governor of the Upper Province, Sir Francis Head, not believing that there would be trouble in his area, allowed Sir John Colborne to move them as reinforcements to Quebec and Montreal. Also the 83rd Foot, who had been stationed in Nova Scotia, were moved into Quebec in June.[C2]

The Patriotes decided to hold their Great Convention at St Charles on 4 December. To prepare for this, Papineau, O'Callaghan and Nelson moved to St Marc on 14 November, leaving Montreal the day before. Papineau had been warned that the authorities were considering his arrest, and this news greatly distressed him.[4]

Sir John Colborne believed that the time had come to act decisively, and on 16 November warrants of arrest were issued for Papineau and several other Patriote leaders. Lieutenant Ermatinger, with Constable Malo and fifteen troopers of the Royal Montreal Volunteer Cavalry, went to St John's and to St Anthanase to execute the warrants. They succeeded in arresting Dr Davignon and Dr Lionnais, together with a lawyer called Desmaray. On the way back to Montreal 150 Patriotes from Longueuil, commanded by two farmers, Bonaventure Viger and Joseph Vincent, set upon the party and freed the prisoners after a sharp fight in which several men on each side were wounded, the Volunteer Cavalry having two officers and one trooper wounded, and three horses killed. However, as the troopers were only armed with pistols and were outnumbered by ten to one, they soon had to beat a retreat as best they could.[4,8,9]

This action greatly heartened the Patriotes, and news of their success travelled fast. The Patriote leaders realised that time was running out before the Government acted, and they hastily started to establish camps at St Charles and St Denis. Dr Cyrille Coté and Lucien Gagnon assembled a band of 150 men at Pointe-à-la-Meule, and Rodier and Dr Lacroix warned the militia captains to assemble. Wolfred Nelson had some 800 men at St Denis, of whom about half were armed, and was joined there by Papineau and O'Callaghan. At the St Charles camp the Patriote leadership was under Storrow Brown, who had arrived from Montreal where he had been wounded in the street fighting of 6 November. He was visited by Papineau and O'Callaghan, who promoted him to 'General'. The number of men at St Charles varied from hour to hour between 400 and 1,000. Wolfred Nelson also visited St Charles from his camp at St Denis and offered 'General' Brown reinforcements of two

28

guns and 300 men, but Brown, too full of confidence and a sense of his own importance, declined the offer, as he did another from Mailhot and Dr Coté at St Mathias of 1,000 men.

The naive and amateur idealism of the Patriote leadership is illustrated by the way in which Amury Girod, a Swiss soldier of fortune, who had previously served in the Mexican cavalry, wrote in his diary, in an entry dated 15 November:

The people of St Charles detained Debartch, prisoner, for some days; because they supposed that this traitor wished to go to Quebec to advise rigorous measures against those who had signed the declarations and Resolutions of the Assembly at St Charles the 23rd or 24th October. By the interposition of Joseph Cartier, joined to his own explanations, Debartch was permitted to depart. Debartch gave a paper, written with his own hand, by which he promised to do nothing against the above mentioned patriots, and particularly against Dr Wolfred Nelson of St Denis, Dr Duvert and Duvert the Notary of St Charles, and Father Drolat of St Mark, and Boucher Belleville of St Charles.

Boucher Belleville suddenly entered the room, very elegantly dressed, but with a very disconcerted countenance, exhibiting altogether the most ridiculous figure in the world. He entreated me to follow him out of the house with so much earnestness that, in truth, I thought he was mad. However, seeing that several people were waiting for me in the entrance, I concluded that something extraordinary had happened. I found there first, O'Callaghan, trembling with cold, and I think with uneasiness also. He wore a very elegant surtout, his head was concealed by an immense red shawl, which formed a singular contrast with the paleness of his face. Second, Papineau, in a Capote, but presenting a marked difference in his appearance from the former, because he was tranquil, composed and although allowing nothing to escape his attention, he manifested not the slightest symptom of apprehension.

After the ordinary compliments they informed me that the Governor had fulminated Warrants against me, and others, as accused of High Treason, and they required that I should go with them to seek a shelter from the impending danger. With a great deal of trouble I persuaded them to go to Duchernois' house that we might see what was to be done. They proposed to me to flee to the River Chambly, they desired to know my opinion, on the measures the public ought to adopt against the injustice of the government. I do not remember who, but I think it was Boucher, who first proposed that a Convention should be called, and that a Provisional Government should be established. We agreed to his proposals, but, he added, that this step, being equivalent to an Act of Open Rebellion, it would be well to devise the means of organising the people, and of procuring arms and ammunition. We all assented to this proposal, and then began to talk about our departure.

As for me I will not, I said, take the same road with you. Go you to St Denis; see Nelson, be ready to procure arms. I will go to the North, and see what can be done there from Grand Brulé. You shall hear from me. Just at that moment, Duchernois arrived. He had been very ill, Boucher was very hungry, O'Callaghan oppressed with fatigue. Papineau alone did not articulate a single syllable.

Our departure became again the subject of deliberation. They had come in a canoe with two men from Pointe aux Trembles. These men began to form conjectures concerning ourselves and the object of our journey. This induced me to change my intention of descending the river with them. O'Callaghan asked them how much they thought themselves entitled to for their trouble. They mentioned the sum of four shillings. But he, seeing the suspicious looks of these men, gave them five shillings. I could not help observing to him that if he went on at that rate, the route which he intended to take would be known to the Government before twelve o'clock that day.[C4]

Sir John Colborne, decided to nip the incipient rebellion in the bud. The rioting in Montreal, followed by the battle with the Royal Montreal Volunteer Cavalry, indicated that civil disturbance was rapidly degenerating into open rebellion. He therefore decided to disperse the various rebel encampments along the Richelieu river, and to take their leaders into custody. He planned a two-pronged attack: one column of troops would move down the Richelieu from Chambly to attack the camp at St Charles; at the same time a second column would proceed up the Richelieu from Sorel to St Denis; then, having dealt with the rebel camp at St Denis, this column would continue along the Richelieu and link up with the St Charles column to form a united force.

Early on 18 November, four companies of the 1st Foot (Royal Scots) and two 6-pounder guns set out from Montreal under the command of Lieutenant-Colonel Wetherall. This force crossed the St Lawrence River and set out for Chambly. En route they came into contact with some rebels, who took to the woods, which were then combed by a company of the Royal Scots under Captain Bell, who managed to capture some prisoners. On the 19th, Captain Bell was sent to Montreal with despatches, and on the way was challenged by a party of rebels who ordered him to halt. Bell refused, and rode for his life. He was saved by the speed of his horse and the cover of the gathering dusk.[9]

Colonel Charles Gore, the Deputy Quarter Master General, set out from Sorel on 22 November with the other column for St Denis. The troops under his command consisted of elements of the 24th Foot, the 32nd Foot and the 66th Foot, with one 12-pounder gun. The distance to be covered was eighteen miles, but Gore made a detour to avoid St Ours, thus adding another eight miles to the journey. The rain poured down and when that stopped it was followed by snow and a sharp frost. The men had been issued with moccasins and blanket clothing, but they were soon soaked to the skin, and then the wet clothes froze on their backs. The column lost cohesion, men became separated, horses sank into the mud, harness snapped. Gore pressed on, however, and after a march lasting twelve hours over appalling roads the advance guard, consisting of the Light Company of the 32nd Foot under Captain F. Markham, reached the outskirts of St Denis at 9 am.

The Patriotes numbered about 800 men under the determined and resourceful leadership of Wolfred Nelson, but only half at most had firearms. At 5 am on 23 November a scout brought news of the approach of the British column. Nelson threatened his men with dire consequences if they deserted and said he would cut their throats. Even such warnings did not have universal effect; the local blacksmith, Modeste Roy, admitted later: 'I hid in the cellar, where I stayed until it was all over.' Papineau and O'Callaghan remained in Nelson's headquarters, but they had quietly left St Denis by nine o'clock, when the British arrived. They were seen later near St Charles, and from there they fled to the United States. Papineau was heard to say at St Charles that he was afraid that the British

31

would take St Denis. Papineau's failure, at the hour of crisis, to assume the active leadership of the rebellion which his political activities had made inevitable damaged his standing and caused a split within the Patriote ranks.

Nelson had those of his men who possessed firearms posted and ready, barricaded in the stone house of the Saint Germains and in nearby buildings. The remainder, armed with scythes and pitchforks, were gathered behind the church. As soon as the Light Company of the 32nd appeared, the Patriotes opened fire. Gore decided to press the attack with his exhausted and frozen troops. He sent out flanking bodies, one to the west along the river, another to the east towards a wood, and a third central column down the road into the village.

The British charged three times and three times they were beaten back, taking shelter among piles of wood and behind fences. The Patriotes were reinforced by a party from St Ours numbering about a hundred men. The British were, by 3 pm, running short of ammunition and saw no hope of being reinforced, so Gore started to withdraw. The 12-pounder – too light to make any impression on the stone houses – was abandoned in the mud, along with the wounded, who numbered about twenty men, half of whom were from the 24th Foot, whilst the 32nd Foot lost two men killed, five wounded and four missing. Captain Markham, commanding the Light Company of the 32nd, was hit by two bullets through the neck; then, as the British started to retire and he was being carried to the rear by Sergeant Allcock and a private soldier, a third bullet went through the calf of his leg and a fourth grazed his knee. Gore now withdrew his men in some disorder and retreated back to Sorel.[4,6,8,9,10,11]

An officer of the 32nd Foot, Lieutenant Weir, had been sent from Montreal on the morning of 22 November with despatches for Colonel Gore ordering the Colonel to take the Sorel detachment of troops with him to St Denis. Weir arrived at Sorel at 10 pm, after Gore's force had left. He set out at once in order to catch up with Gore, but took the direct route to St Denis via St Ours, whereas Gore's force had gone by the back road in order to avoid the rebels in St Ours. Weir was captured by the St Ours rebels, who took him to St Denis.[9,11]

On 22 November, at seven in the evening, Colonel Wetherall's column marched from Chambly with four companies of the 1st Foot and one of the 66th Foot, made up of sixty men commanded by Lieutenant Johnston, and twenty of the Royal Montreal Cavalry under Captain Davies together with the two guns. His intention was to attack St Charles on the following morning. First of all the force had to be ferried across the river in scows, an operation which took four hours to complete. It was a foul night, very dark with the rain coming down and the roads deep in mud. Next morning (23 November), by eleven o'clock, they reached the house of Colonel de Hertel, Seigneur of Rouville at St Hilaire, but the soldiers were caked in mud, exhausted and wet through.

Major Gugy, a Swiss Huguenot magistrate who accompanied the force, wrote:

Not one of the force knew anything of the roads or people, nor do I believe that more than one spoke French. The storm raged so fearfully, the rain poured in such torrents, and the frost set in afterwards so intensely that men and horses were equally fatigued – all so exhausted as to be unable to cope on broken or woody ground successfully with any resolute enemy.[12]

The Colonel gave over his house to the officers and allowed the men to use his barns. He supplied the officers with wine, and the men were given a generous helping of spirits. The soldiers dried out, cleaned up and rested at St Hilaire for the remainder of the 23rd. A message arrived from Colonel Gore, telling of the failure at St Denis. Wetherall decided to wait for reinforcements and for fresh orders. The force remained at St Hilaire for the whole of 24 November, when the grenadier company of the 1st Foot, who had set out later, joined them.[8,9]

At 8 pm on the 24th, Colonel Wetherall marched his force out of St Hilaire, in order to deceive the Patriotes into thinking that the attack was about to begin. Having marched for two hours, the force returned to St Hilaire and to a good night's rest. The rebels, however, who were soon warned that the British were on the move, manned their positions throughout that night.

On the morning of 25 November, Colonel Wetherall moved off with 280 men, two 6-pounders and some of the Montreal Volunteer Cavalry. They soon came under fire from the Patriotes stationed in houses alongside the road. The fire was immediately returned, the houses were cleared, and were then burnt as an example. The advance into St Charles was pressed forward, while some of the rebels kept up a straggling fire from the other side of the river.

By 2 pm the force had arrived at the outskirts of St Charles to be confronted by an earth breastwork and houses manned by the Patriotes. Wetherall halted the companies in column on the right of the road, out of range of the Patriotes fire, and summoned the rebels to surrender. In reply the Patriotes gave a cheer and fired a volley. The two 6-pounder guns then opened up on the breastwork and houses, with round shot and shrapnel, but without much effect as the barns and houses had been loopholed and the rebels kept well under cover.[9]

The infantry of the 1st Foot and 66th Foot then deployed into line, and advanced, with the Light Company of the 1st Foot extended on each flank in skirmishing order. The Patriotes at once opened fire, and at the same time moved some 300 men from St Charles into a wood on the right flank of the British advance. At once the Grenadier Company of the 1st Foot stormed the wood and drove out the rebels, who retired back into the town. The centre companies of the 1st Foot and the single company of the 66th Foot were now ordered to take the town. They made a detour to avoid the breastwork and then wheeled to the left and charged, cheering and catching the rebels in the flank. The Patriotes meanwhile maintained a heavy fire against the advancing troops. Colonel Wetherall's horse was killed under him, as was the Adjutant's of the 1st Foot, Captain McNichol. In this charge, which took place over newly ploughed land made solid by hard frosts, one sergeant and four privates of the 1st Foot and one private, William Atkins, of the 66th Foot were killed. Sixteen men of the 1st

Foot and four of the 66th were wounded, two of whom died later.[9,12]

At one point in the fighting about fifty Patriotes appeared on bended knees with weapons reversed. The Royal Scots, thinking that they were surrendering, advanced; whereupon the rebels fired, killing the sergeant and wounding others. The Royal Scots massacred all these rebels, allowing no quarter.[13]

Once into the town the fighting was severe, with no quarter asked or given. As Private Charley Plumb of the 1st Foot remarked calmly afterwards, 'Well, them fellers fought well. I worked amongst them till my bayonet was bent on a tough back-bone, yet I only killed three on 'em!' And Private Bulger of the same regiment said, 'What a head that fellow had, who was just going to shoot the Captain there, till I sent him to the other world' – which he achieved by plunging his bayonet into the man's ear and through his head. He then stood on the body in order to pull out his weapon. Lieutenant Johnston of the 66th Foot was mentioned in General Orders for his bravery on this day. The Patriotes fought bravely and refused to surrender, and many were burnt alive as the soldiers set fire to the wooden houses and barns. In all only twenty-eight Patriotes were taken prisoner. After the fighting the parish priest's house was converted into a hospital for the wounded, and the church was used to accommodate the soldiers. Every house from which a shot had been fired was burnt in punishment (most were built of wood). A large amount of arms and ammunition was destroyed, and two guns which were captured were spiked and thrown into the river.[9]

'General' T. Storrow Brown, the Patriote leader, claimed later that the defenders of St Charles had only 'some half dozen kegs of gunpower and a little lead'. Certainly the variety of weapons of every calibre held by the Patriotes must have made the adequate supply of ammunition very difficult.[8] But Brown had reason to make excuses, for a deserting Patriote labourer from St Hilaire, François Dache, saw him 'on horseback escaping towards Maska'. The Patriotes were badly let down by their leaders: another, called Tétro, who styled himself a captain of the Republic of Canada, fled once the fighting started, having previously exhorted his men 'Mes enfants, be brave, pay close attention, don't miss those scoundrels, aim well and truly, aim at their hearts, stomachs, heads, no mercy, no quarter.'[4]

Throughout that night gunpowder exploded from time to time, as fire within the burning houses reached the various stores of rebel ammunition. A herd of pigs broke loose and started to feed on the corpses of the slain, many of which had been roasted in the fire. So the soldiers shot the pigs. A diary was found in the house of the parish priest, Curé Blanchet, giving exact details of the movement and timings of the column.[9]

The next day, the 26th, was a Sunday, and gradually a trickle of relatives and inhabitants came into the town to look for the bodies of the dead and to see to their property. Two young women approached Captain Bell to seek his assistance in finding their father.

I went along with them, and, alas, he was indeed found with his head shattered to pieces, and a most dreadful corpse, frozen like a log, with his limbs extended in the manner in which he fell, and the blood and brains congealed and forming part of the horrid mess. These poor girls, with some assistance, had him placed upon a sleigh and covered up. One of them never shed a tear, the other was in agony.[9]

That Sunday was spent looking after the wounded, burying the dead, and getting the soldiers and their weapons into a fit state for future action. The eight British dead were buried on the spot; the Patriote dead, who numbered about fifty, were buried in a mass grave in the churchyard by the Curé Blanchet. The parish priest from St Denis, some six miles away, had also been summoned, shown the damage done to the town, and been made to inspect the corpses of the rebels. This made him sick. He was then sent back to St Denis and told to spread the news amongst his people of what would happen, to any Patriotes who did not surrender.

On 30 November, Colonel Gore, having heard of Wetherall's success at St Charles, set out once more from Sorel for St Denis. This time his detachment had been reinforced and consisted of four companies of the 32nd Foot, two companies of the 66th Foot, and the Light Companies from the 24th and 83rd Foot, with one 12-pounder howitzer. The troops embarked on a steamboat and tried to force a passage through the ice on the Richelieu river. It proved too much for them, so they were disembarked and marched to St Ours and then on to St Denis. The Patriotes had become discouraged by Wetherall's success at St Charles, although their casualties in the first battle with Gore's troops had been only twelve killed and four wounded. On the night of 30 November they abandoned St Denis, so when Gore arrived there on 1 December he was able to enter and occupy the town without opposition. Gore left three companies of the 32nd Foot and a gun, under command of Major Reed of the 32nd, to act as a garrison, while he pushed on with the remainder of his force to join up with Wetherall at St Charles. He later moved on to St Hyacinthe, searching the area for rebels and reasserting British authority.[9,10,11]

At St Denis the abandoned 12-pounder was recovered, along with the British wounded who had been left behind by the retreating Patriotes. The soldiers then discovered Lieutenant Weir's body in the Richelieu river, partly hidden under large stones and lying in two feet of water. As soon as they pulled the corpse from the river, they could see its mutilated condition. This so infuriated them that in carrying out Gore's orders to burn rebel property they set fire to the whole town; only two houses survived being rased to the ground.[6,8,9,11]

Patriote accounts of Weir's death claim that he tried to escape on the approach of the British troops, but that, unknown to him, he was secured by a strap to the cart in which he was sitting. As he jumped from the cart the strap brought him to the ground, whereupon his captors lost their heads and started to hack at him, until eventually one of them shot him. The mutilated corpse was then thrown into the river, and covered with stones to hide it from view.

The main body of Patriote resistance along the Richelieu had now been broken. The Patriote leaders, Papineau, O'Callaghan, Duvernay and Nelson had fled to the security of the

United States. The Longueuil Patriotes, and those at Pointe à la Meule, Ste Mathias and St Hyacinthe, dispersed after the Patriote defeat at St Charles and the recapture of St Denis by Gore. Colonel Wetherall, who was to be awarded the CB for his action at St Charles, and who was later presented with a gift of plate by the grateful seigneurs and gentry, now led his troops back to Montreal. At Pointe Olivier a group of Patriotes attacked his column, but were easily repulsed and dispersed. On arrival in Montreal the soldiers received a rapturous welcome; the citizens had been on tenterhooks whilst the troops were away, because of a sizeable Patriote force to the west who were threatening to put Montreal to the torch.[4,6,8,9]

Those Patriote leaders who had sought refuge in the United States assembled at Swanton, just south of the Canadian border, and having collected together two guns and arms and ammunition from American supporters, they managed to assemble a force of about 200 men. On 6 December, led by Dr Coté, Gagnon, Bouchette, Duvernay, Kimber and Rodier, they invaded Lower Canada, carrying with them extra arms and ammunition with which to equip those Patriotes who they believed would come to join their ranks. Just across the border from Vermont, at Moore's Corner, they were met by 400 English-speaking Canadian volunteers from the Missisquoi and St Armand Loyal Volunteers. There was an exchange of shots, and the Patriotes fled back to the United States, abandoning their two guns, their extra arms and ammunition and a plentiful supply of banners.

Sir John Colborne now collected his available troops at Montreal in order to deal with Patriote resistance to the north and west of the city. The first ten days of December were spent in resting the soldiers and getting ready for forthcoming operations. At Vaudreuil and at Rigaud there were some 125 Patriotes in each place. Patriote camps had been set up north of Montreal, at St Eustache and St Benoit, in early November. At St Jérôme and Ste Scholastique the Patriotes began to organise themselves; on 20 November a party of St Jérôme Patriotes occupied New Paisley and ordered the Scottish settlers there to hand over their arms or have their village burnt to the ground. Another foray of 400 Patriotes to Lac des Deux Montagnes resulted in the seizure of stores and arms from the Hudson's Bay Company's post and from the local Indians, including a supply of muskets and ammunition.[4,6,8,9]

Amury Girod, who had set out from Varennes on 15 November, arrived in St Eustache a few days later, but the local Patriote leadership, under Joseph Girouard and Dr Chénier was generally uncoordinated and incapable of instilling discipline in the ranks. Morale rose when two Montreal lawyers Peltier and Hubert, arrived with exaggerated news of Gore's defeat at St Denis: W. Nelson had gained the victory and 197 soldiers had been killed, with six taken prisoner. Also 3,600 cartridges, six barrels of gunpowder and three field pieces had been taken.[C4]

Girod continues in his diary:

I received information that the troops were on their march from St Andrews, to take Grand Brulé. I sent expresses in every direction. Girouard was recalled (from a visit he was making to Ste Scholastique), but sent back word that he could not return before tomorrow. More than six hundred persons mostly men [gathered] in less than an hour, and assured me that others were coming. Dr R Nelson sent me word that the City [Montreal] was in a state of terror, that there were very few or no troops there, and that his brother and friends calculated on a diversion on this side of the river. So I determined upon going, the following day, to Montreal to storm it. Archambault was despatched with a letter.[C4]

The entry for the following day, 25 November, reads:

The alarm bell was rung in Ste Scholastique. Girouard returned. He, Barsolone, Chénier, the priest, Doumechelle and myself assembled in Council. I laid my plan before them. Barsolone spoke at first against it. Chénier only thought of revenging himself on his enemies, in River Du Chene, and declared he would do nothing else. Girouard appeared to temporise, and the priest sided with him. So they resolved to keep on the defensive. I repented for the first time that I had placed my confidence in such hesitant men.[C4]

On 5 December Lord Gosford, the Governor, proclaimed martial law in and around Montreal. On 13 December Sir John

Colborne marched on St Eustache with two brigades commanded by Colonel Maitland and Lieutenant-Colonel Wetherall, numbering some 2,000 men. The 1st Foot, 32nd Foot and 83rd Foot, together with five guns and some rockets, formed the regular contingent, together with the Royal Montreal Volunteer Cavalry, the Montreal Volunteer Rifles, Globenski's St Eustache Loyal Volunteers and Leclerc's Volunteers. Two companies of the 24th Foot, stationed at Carillon and commanded by Major Townshend, joined Colborne near Grand Brulé on 14 December. Maitland's brigade was made up of 32nd and 83rd Foot, while the 1st Foot and the Loyal Volunteers were brigaded under Wetherall. The first night was spent at Ste Martine, and on the morning of the 14th the force set out for St Eustache. Colborne made a detour to avoid the ferry on the main road, opposite which stood St Eustache church which was known to be fortified and used as a strong point. Instead a crossing was made over the ice some three miles below the town. The ice supported the infantry but finally gave way, with the loss of one ammunition tumbril.[8,9,11,14,15]

Morale in the Patriote camp had sunk to a low level. A Montreal innkeeper had brought news of the defeat at St Charles, which the Patriote leaders tried to hide from their men. Girod exclaimed that 'all those who brought news like that were impostors'. However, there were defections and resignations in the Patriote ranks. Girouard was the most respected Patriote in the area, but he was reluctant to take command. There were no such hesitations about Girod who assumed the rank of general with Chénier as his colonel, and four Montreal lawyers, Hubert, Peltier and the de Lorimier brothers, taking on posts of leadership. Girouard and Dumouchelle went to St Benoit and assumed command of the 300 men there.[4,6]

At St Eustache the parish priest, Paquin, and the priest at Ste Rose, Turnotte, blew hot and cold. Girod wrote:

Paquin wanted to enter into political conversation, but the knowledge I had of his previous conduct and his recent treason enabled me to silence him in a short time. Turnotte proved himself to be quite a false fellow. When alone with me and his brothers, he acted the part of a Patriote, and said in our presence to one of his habitants 'The time is now come, when it is impossible to continue neutral, and it is necessary to take a determined stand.'[C4]

Nevertheless, once the soldiers were known to be on their way to St Eustache, Paquin persuaded some 500 of the 1,000 Patriotes with Chénier and Girod to disband and return to their homes. However, Abbé Chartier of St Benoit spoke to the Patriotes, 'encouraging them to revolt' and helping them to fortify St Eustache. By the time the British arrived at St Eustache the total number of Patriotes did not amount to more than 600 men.

Globenski, who was the seigneur of St Eustache, led his loyal Volunteers by a shorter route than the main body, going across Isle Jésus to a point on the opposite side of the river to St Eustache. Once in position the Volunteers opened fire, and this was the first warning that the Patriotes received that the troops were upon them. Chénier gathered 150 Patriotes and had started across the ice to attack the Volunteers when they heard the sound of a cannon fired from the river bank they had just left. They turned and saw the full might of Colborne's array, stretching down the road that skirts the river, their bayonets glinting in the winter sunshine. The sight was too much for the Patriotes' discipline. They broke and fled back to St Eustache. Chénier at once rallied them and started to post them in the church, convent and presbytery, all of which had been barricaded.

George Bell of the 1st Foot recalled: 'I mounted a paling, and first saw, glittering in the sun, the double spires of the church which was doomed to ruin, and to entomb many of its then unfortunate and fated inmates.' Colborne had sufficient force to be methodical; he deployed his artillery and started a bombardment, concentrating upon the stone houses and the solidly built church. At the same time he deployed his infantry in a circle around the town, but out of range of the Patriotes' muskets. Before the cordon closed many of the Patriotes fled towards St Benoit, among them 'General' Girod, who got away on a sleigh, which he had had prepared in advance for such an eventuality. The Abbé Chartier also returned to his flock at St Benoit, going to the house of Girouard, where he saw Girod.[4,6,8,9]

Colborne continued the bombardment for an hour, while the infantry were getting into position around the town. He then moved his guns up the main street, opposite the church, and opened fire at short range. The 1st Foot were ordered forward at about 2 pm, and with fixed bayonets advanced to be met with fire from the presbytery. This they stormed, driving out the Patriotes, and then set fire to the building. Some of the Patriotes were able to escape under cover of the smoke, and they crossed the ice-bound river, only to be shot down or bayoneted by Globenski's Volunteers, who were waiting for them concealed in a wood.

The fire spread to two more houses in which the Patriotes were barricaded. As they were driven out by the flames they were shot down, and as the smoke thickened the British under its cover ran up the street to the church, got around behind the building and forced an entry from the rear. By this time the flames from the burning houses had spread to the church, and the Patriotes had no choice but to stand and fight, to be burnt alive, or to make a run for it. George Bell of the 1st Foot relates: 'There was no escape, and they died as they fought, regardless of life.'

As a body of Patriotes made a rush out of the burning church, a Volunteer captain recognised one of them, and shouted to him, 'What are you doing here, Forget?' He received the reply, 'Fighting for my country.' But within minutes Forget and his two sons were lying dead in the churchyard. Chénier, the only Patriote leader to remain with his men, and whose leadership had inspired them, had remained in the church, and eventually leapt out of a window into the churchyard. George Bell tells how he also

was killed in the churchyard, a ball having passed through his body, entering his left side under the ribs. This shot saved the Government £500, being the reward offered for his apprehension. He was a genteel-looking young man, about twenty-four years old, and had a wife and family. I took the stock from his neck, which was made of the common cloth of the country, it being a system amongst those unfortunates not to wear anything of British manufacture.

By four o'clock most of St Eustache was in flames. George Bell describes the scene:

The wounded were most severely riddled. Many of them bled to death for want of surgical aid. I found one poor fellow with his arm shattered above the elbow with a grapeshot. Some soldiers were just going to despatch him when I came up. He was crying for mercy, and the blood was pouring from the wound most rapidly. I took off one of my moccasin strings, and bound his arm tight, which stopped the effusion of blood. It was amputated the same night, and I believe he recovered. I had some difficulty in saving a few other prisoners from the soldiers, who were much excited. I walked about the most part of the night, not being in a sufficiently composed state to lie down. The town was in flames. The cries of the wounded were piercing, many of them being roasted alive. The heat of the fire melted the snow, and the street was in a puddle. The soldiers were cutting down houses, to prevent the fire reaching the hospital, and altogether the scene was too terrible to permit me, fagged as I was, to retire to my humble billet.

The fire reached the church clock just at twenty minutes past two, and the roof fell in at about six, burying in its ruins many an unfortunate misguided wretch. I saw their ruins next morning, some only partially burned, others almost entirely consumed.[9]

Patriote casualties were difficult to determine accurately; probably about 70 died, and about 120 were captured. Colborne lost one man killed, and nine wounded. The 32nd Foot had one man wounded, and most of the British casualties were suffered by the 1st Foot, who bore the brunt of the fighting in St Eustache itself. Chénier's corpse was taken to the inn, where it lay for some days before being buried.[4,6,8,9,11]

The next day, 15 December, Colborne set out for St Benoit, having issued a warning that if he met resistance he would burn the place to the ground. On arrival the town was deserted, for the Patriotes and their leaders had dispersed into the country around. In spite of the lack of any opposition St Benoit was burnt. George Bell wrote: 'This being one of the chief seats of their disloyalty for years back, we burned the whole town, church and all, and then retraced our steps to Montreal, bringing home 108 prisoners, many of them wealthy men, and leaders of the blind.' Later the blame for the sack of St Benoit was shifted onto the Volunteers. 'The irregular troops were not to be controlled, and were in every case, I believe, the instruments of affliction,' wrote a regular officer.

Girouard, who was captured later, wrote from prison:

It would be impossible for me to describe to you the desolation which [Colborne's] march and the barbarous scenes accompanying it spread through our homes. A considerable number of the inhabitants were assembled in my courtyard which, as you know, is very large; they were lined up and two cannon placed in the gateway were aimed at them, while they were told they would be exterminated in a few minutes. There are no insults and outrages which were not heaped upon them, no threats which were not made, to intimidate them into declaring the hiding places of those who were called their leaders. Not one would give the least indication. Some officers having learned that Paul Barazeau had guided me to Eboulis, they tortured him to tell my place of retreat. They put a pistol to his throat and several times placed him on a block; threatening to behead him, but the generous Patriote held his ground, and the barbarians' violence was wasted.

Then began scenes of devastation and destruction more atrocious than any seen in a town taken by storm and given over to pillage after a long, hard siege. After completely pillaging the village, the enemy set fire to it and reduced it from one end to the other to a heap of ashes.[6]

Ste Scholastique and Ste Thérèse, which also surrendered and gave up their arms and ammunition, were spared and were occupied by the 32nd Foot. The main body of troops returned to Montreal, reaching there on 17 December. The two companies of the 24th Foot, who had joined the force from Carillon under Major Townshend, were used to clear the countryside of rebels before being sent to Chippewa near Niagara in Upper Canada on 21 December. Amury Girod, who had escaped, evaded capture for some days, but as his pursuers caught up with him he blew out his brains as he was being taken prisoner. George Bell remembered how he 'saw him brought into Montreal on a train immediately after his death. He was considered a reckless ruffian, and proved himself a coward.'[8,9,10,11]

With the end of the operations in the area of the Two Mountains, the rebellion of 1837 in Lower Canada was at an end. Its failure was mainly owing to the inadequacies of its leadership. Mailhot wrote to Duvernay in 1839: 'Those people are good at pushing others to the front, and keeping back themselves, always ready to blame those they have pushed ahead if they do not succeed, and if they do, always ready to take the benefit and glory themselves. Thus are our leaders.'[4] But equally the rebellion failed because of the strong and determined military leadership of Sir John Colborne. In April 1838 Ludger Duvernay wrote to Dr Robitaille from the United States: 'The people in general were not ready for the fighting, which came earlier than expected. The government acted with trickery in causing them when they were not expected. It knew our weakness then in our want of organisation.'

Sir John Colborne acted promptly and carried out preventitive action swiftly and efficiently, catching the Patriotes unawares. It says a great deal about the naïveté of the Patriote leadership that, when preparing armed rebellion, they thought it their right to be left alone until they were ready.

3

Trouble in Upper Canada

The defeat of the Reform Party and the triumph of the Family Compact in the elections of 1836 in Upper Canada gave the Governor, Sir Francis Head, an exaggerated sense of confidence in his ability to control the situation. This confidence was increased by the growing tide of immigration, which Head believed would strengthen loyalty to the Crown. Many of the new settlers in Upper Canada were Protestant Irish. Whereas in Ireland Orangemen were constantly on the alert for what they saw as the subversive machinations of Catholics, in Upper Canada their natural 'Britishness' took the form of extreme loyalty to the Empire. There were few French Canadians in Upper Canada, and although it would be necessary to watch Catholic activities in the Lower Province, it was clear to the new Orange settlers that the immediate menace lay with the Reformers who proclaimed republican sympathies and plotted independence from the British Empire.

When the first Orange lodges were formed in the early 1820s in Upper Canada, the authorities treated them with considerable reserve and suspicion. In the atmosphere of 1837, however, those who proclaimed themselves to be more British than the British, and whose aggressive loyalty to the Crown was beyond doubt, were seen as a welcome counterbalance to the discontent being fostered by William Lyon Mackenzie and the Reformers.[2]

In addition to the Protestant Irish influx, there had been a much smaller but equally significant arrival of men of education and means from Britain. These were officers, professional men, and substantial farmers who found the post-war years in Britain particularly hard. They came to seek new opportunities and to establish their fortunes in a young country where the constraints of an overcrowded and economically depressed post-war Britain would no longer stifle their sense of initiative. Catharine Traill, wife of a British officer on half pay, wrote that these new settlers were 'the pioneers of civilisation in the wilderness, and their families, often of delicate nurture and honourable descent, are at once plunged into the hardship attendant on the rough life of a bush settler'.[2,16] Many of these newcomers failed to realise their dreams, and returned to Britain after a few years; others left the backwoods for the townships; but enough remained to provide leadership, which, although not necessarily sympathetic to the Family Compact, was utterly loyal to the Crown.

The unconcealed triumphalism with which the Governor treated the Reformers did little to assist the policy of reconciliation being urged from London. Sir Francis Head took an active dislike to Bidwell and Mackenzie, and Robinson, the Chief Justice, a mainspring of the Family Compact, became the Governor's chief adviser.

Meanwhile the farmers of Upper Canada were struggling against the severe economic depression, and because they lived on the brink of insolvency, it was they who felt the hard times most keenly. Hardship and the discontent arising from it were rife in the rural areas. The extremists among the Reformers, having been defeated when they followed constitutional means, now turned their thoughts to more drastic measures. Mackenzie, who had handed over his paper *The Colonial Advocate* following the destruction of his press, started another even more radical newspaper which he called *The Constitution*, founded as it was on 4 July 1836, the sixtieth anniversary of the Declaration of Independence. 'Tories! Pensioners! Placemen! Profligates! Orangemen! Churchmen! Brokers! Gamblers! Parasites! Allow me to congratulate you. Your feet are at last on the people's necks.' He invited people to join in 'this bold, dangerous but delightful course of preparing the public mind for nobler actions than our tyrants dream of'.[2,7,8]

Mackenzie, closely in touch with the ferment in Lower Canada, decided in the summer of 1837 upon armed rebellion. In late July, at a meeting of radicals in John Doel's brewery in

Toronto, a list of grievances was adopted, admiration for the Patriotes of Lower Canada was expressed, and every community in Upper Canada was to be urged to hold public meetings of protest. Finally a Congress of Delegates from both Upper and Lower Canada was proposed, which would be convened at Toronto in order 'to seek an effectual remedy for the grievances of the colonists'. Mackenzie was elected to be the agent and secretary of this self-constituted Committee of Vigilance.[7]

Armed with this authority, Mackenzie organised Committees of Vigilance throughout the province. He published the Toronto declaration in the *Constitution* on 2 August, and then travelled to the north. He was at Newmarket on 3 August, then at Lloydtown, Boltontown, and on the 12th he was at Esquesing. Like the Patriotes of Lower Canada, Mackenzie urged a boycott of the banks, and sought to embarrass the Compact by encouraging his followers to 'exchange your bank notes for gold and silver'. 'Farmers of Upper Canada, you will be richer and happier if these vile Banking Associations' are destroyed. Among farmers on the verge of bankruptcy and dependent upon the banks, these words found ready ears.[2,7]

A group of Orangemen attacked twenty-six mounted farmers as they rode to attend a meeting and were crossing the Humber river. They managed to drag the two rearmost from their horses, but the remaining twenty-four Reformers jumped from their horses into the water, and set upon their opponents, freeing their two companions. At Esquesing, on 12 August, the magistrates were ready to read the Riot Act and a group of Orangemen were also in the offing, so the Reformers withdrew to a private house for their meeting. Throughout the summer and autumn of 1837 the meetings continued, and the Reformers began to drill and engage in shooting practice. Some of the more prudent disguised their activities under the cloak of turkey shoots. Tom Sheppard, who later fought in the rebellion, remembered how

Mike and I then lived at the mill back of Lansing, up Yonge Street. We would take our muskets and join other Reformers who were

48

drilled by an old soldier who worked I think in Mackenzie's printing office. We drilled at Uncle Jake Fisher's Farm in Vaughan. Mackenzie used to ride from the city (with his brace of pocket pistols under his belt) to watch the old soldier put the farmers through their facings.

A less optimistic onlooker described another meeting:

Three or four hundred men and boys marshalled or rather scattered in picturesque fashion hither and thither. A few mounted lancers, well appointed but with a great variety of uniform, others having only a carving knife at the end of a fishing pole. The captain of lancers was proprietor of the village store, and might be seen shortly after the military display, plumed helmet in hand, vaulting over the counter to serve one customer a penn'orth of tobacco and another a yard of check cloth.[7]

Through the late summer and autumn of 1837 the economic climate deteriorated. An Upper Canadian farmer, who was to die of his wounds in the forthcoming rebellion, wrote:

The author has been in Canada since he was a little boy, and he has not had the advantage of a classical education at the King's College, or the less advantages derived from a District School. The greater part of his life has been spent watching over and providing for an increasing and tender family. He had in most instances to make his own roads and bridges, clear his own farm, educate himself and his children, be his own mechanic, and except now and then, he had no society but his own family. He had his bones broken by the fall of trees, his feet lacerated by the axe, and suffered almost everything except death. He waited year after year in hope of better days, expecting that the government would care less for themselves and more for the people. But every year he has been disappointed.[2,17]

Mackenzie now sought to develop this discontent and to persuade his followers that independence was within their power. He encouraged them to think of themselves as 'patriots' rather than 'loyalists', as more Canadian and less British. 'Foreign' and 'Colonial' ties were denounced, whilst the advantage of becoming an independent state of the United States was extolled. Canadians had the same right to redress, by force if necessary, the grievances which the old Thirteen

Colonies had abolished by rebellion, and to join with them in a new and vibrant North American national identity expressed through a political Union.

The Governor, Sir Francis Head, then played straight into Mackenzie's hands. His confidence had been bolstered by the results of the election; he was dismissive of the reports of growing discontent and saw the activity of the Reformers as the antics of a lunatic fringe. He was determined to rely upon the loyalty of the vast majority of the ordinary people of the province. Mackenzie would eventually overreach himself, so let him 'stamp and foam' until he went so far that he could be arrested on a charge of treason. In this mood, and conscious of the very real dangers building up among the French Canadians in Lower Canada, he agreed in October that Sir John Colborne might remove the 24th Foot from Fort Henry in Kingston and from Fort York in Toronto in order to reinforce the troops in the Lower Province.[2,7,10]

The 24th Foot had moved from Montreal to Kingston in 1835. In the summer of 1837 the headquarters of the regiment moved to Toronto, leaving three companies at Kingston. As with many of the regular British infantry regiments stationed in Canada at that time, desertion was a problem for the 24th Foot. During 1836 sixty-three men deserted and in 1837 another forty-seven, reducing the strength of the regiment to 374 NCOs and men. A welcome draft from Britain arrived on 28 July 1837 of 111 men, bringing the regiment's strength up to nearly 500. The 15th Foot, who were stationed in Upper Canada during 1836 until 11 May 1837, when they were moved to Quebec, also suffered a high rate of desertion; in the six months between January and June 1836 there were seventy desertions, of whom only four rejoined the colours, and in the following six months another three sergeants and seventy-one privates deserted, of whom twelve rejoined and twenty-nine were caught and court-martialled. The Inspecting Officer commented:

The Service companies of this Corps are in excellent order, but the desertions from them have far exceeded those from the other Corps in these Provinces. I can, however, only attribute the great loss by desertion which the 15th Regiment has sustained to the long period which most of the companies were stationed at Toronto, and the inducements which were held out to them to pass into the United States during the time they were in the Upper Provinces.[10,18]

Upper Canada was now left with no regular troops except for two remaining companies of the 24th Foot stationed at Carillon on the American border. The stand of arms in the City Hall at Toronto was left unguarded; Fort York in Toronto and Fort Henry at Kingston were 'open and empty'. As Mackenzie told his followers, 'A steamer had only to sail down to the wharf and take possession.'[2,7,8,10]

The loyalists in Toronto were not slow to see the possible dangers of their situation, and pressed the Governor to take precautionary measures. The Reformers were not able to keep their plans secret, and Sir Francis Head was kept fully informed, even to the projected date of the uprising. Nothing, however, was able to shatter his confidence, and the most that he would agree to do was to appoint Colonel James Fitzgibbon to be Adjutant General with the authority to raise two battalions of militia. He also agreed to import an additional stand of arms from Montreal, which were then placed in the unguarded City Hall of Toronto. Colonel Fitzgibbon had begged him to hold the last detachment of the 24th Foot in Toronto, as they marched through the city from their station at Penetang en route for Montreal, and received the reply 'I do not apprehend rebellion in Upper Canada.'

On Monday 9 October Jesse Lloyd, Mackenzie's liaison with Papineau in Lower Canada, arrived in Toronto to tell Mackenzie that the Patriotes were about to make 'a brave stroke for liberty', and that they looked for the same from the Reformers in Upper Canada. Mackenzie sent a scout to make sure that Fort York really was empty, and another to track the movements of the Governor; he then called a meeting the same evening at John Doel's brewery. Mackenzie pressed for instant action, using those Reformers in and around Toronto to seize the Governor, who was at Government House guarded by a solitary sentry, take him to the City Hall, where they could take possession of the arms and ammunition stored there and then to proclaim a provisional government. The steamer in the bay would be seized and sent to Fort Henry at Kingston to secure it for the Reformers. The Governor would be given a choice of setting up an elected Executive Committee, responsible to an Assembly, which would itself be subject to new and 'fair' elections, or if Sir Francis Head refused to do that, the Reformers would declare a state of independence.

Mackenzie was going too far and too fast for his more cautious colleagues. They wanted more time to think and deliberate, and they were apprehensive about seizing the arms. Mackenzie argued that if 'those who persuaded Head to place four thousand stand of arms in the midst of an unarmed people', surely 'they seemed evidently not opposed to their being used'. The Reformers were prepared to agree with Mackenzie that they wanted reform if it could be achieved, and that they were prepared for rebellion if it could not, but they were not ready to act on the spur of the moment. They wanted more time to think and to get ready. Mackenzie failed to shift them.

Dr Rolph had not attended the meeting, and so Mackenzie sought him out the following evening and got him to agree that a rebellion without bloodshed was possible. Mackenzie then turned his attention to Dr Morrison, and eventually both Rolph and Morrison agreed to join the rebellion provided Mackenzie would make a final tour of the Committees of Vigilance within the Province, get their agreement, and then report back to Rolph and Morrison so that a final date for the uprising could be set. Dr Rolph would then agree to lead a provisional government. Mackenzie knew that he could not succeed without their support, and reluctantly agreed to the delay.

In early November Mackenzie set out on his tour of the north of the province. Rolph and Morrison, in his absence, took steps to cover their tracks, but Mackenzie was determined to stiffen their resolve by forcing their hand. News from Lower Canada of the Patriotes' rebellion convinced Mackenzie that the moment for action had come. While touring the north, he met with the more radical Reformers, Jesse Lloyd and Samuel Lount, and set a date of 7 December for the rebellion without consulting Rolph and Morrison. Lount and Captain Anthony Anderson were to be in command of 5,000 men, who were to gather at Montgomery's Tavern north of Toronto at the Eglinton crossroads. Rolph and Morrison were given no choice but to comply, for Mackenzie had allowed the date to become widely known in order to bring additional pressure upon them.

Rolph was concerned at the lack of professional military experience among the Reformers, and Mackenzie sent a plea by messenger to Colonel Anthony Van Egmond, a Dutchman who had served under Napoleon and who was living in the far west of the province in the Huron tract. He was invited to become the supreme commander and to make haste to join the proposed assembly at Montgomery's Tavern.[2,7,8]

At the end of November Mackenzie made a final trip to the north, carrying with him handbills to be distributed which urged:

Brave Canadians. Do you love freedom? Do you hate oppression? Then buckle on your armour and put down the villains who oppress and enslave our country . . . We cannot be reconciled to Britain – we have humbled ourselves to the Pharoah of England, to the Ministers and great people, and they will neither rule justly or let us go. Up then, brave Canadians! Get ready your rifles, and make short work of it. Woe be to those that oppose us, for 'in God is our trust'.

News had come in of the Patriotes' success at St Denis against Colonel Gore, and Mackenzie wanted to make final arrangements with his followers.

Whilst Mackenzie was away, it became clear to Rolph that Mackenzie's lack of caution had alerted the authorities, and he insisted that the date for the rebellion be advanced. Mackenzie only heard late on 3 December of the change of plan, and that the new date for the rebellion was to be the following day. He hurried back to Montgomery's Tavern. Then came news of the Patriote defeats in Lower Canada, and Rolph in Toronto tried to persuade his colleagues there of the hopelessness of their

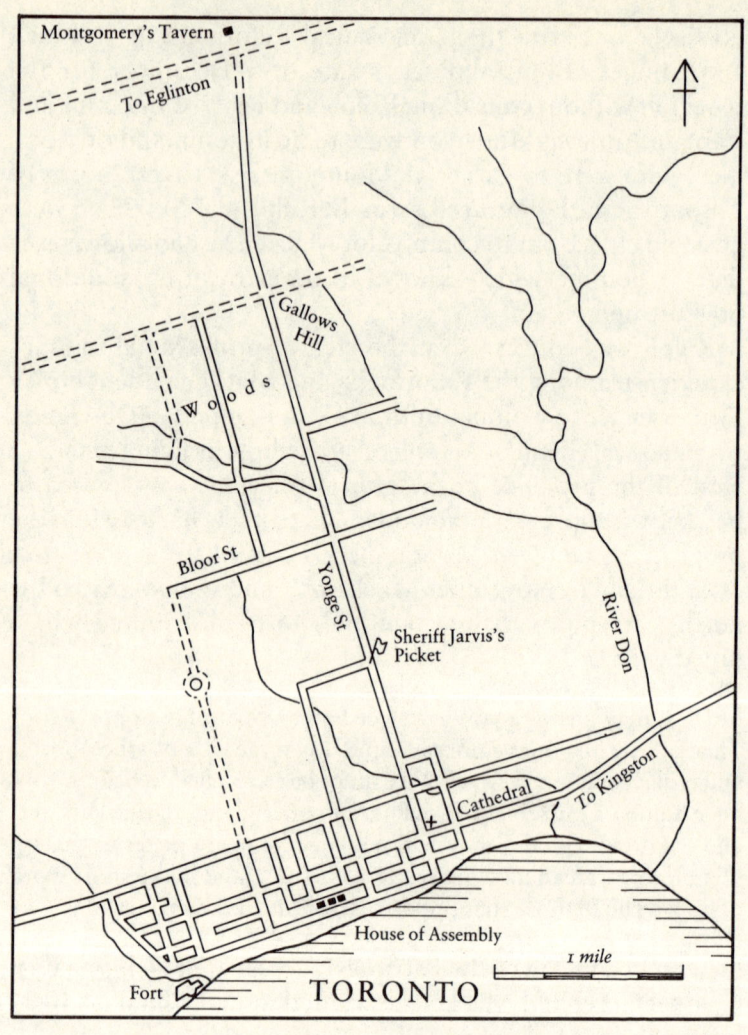

Montgomery's Tavern

To Eglinton

Gallows Hill

W o o d s

Bloor St

Yonge St

Sheriff Jarvis's Picket

River Don

Cathedral

To Kingston

House of Assembly

1 mile

Fort

TORONTO

situation. But it was too late, for the men were already marching to gather at Montgomery's Tavern.

In Toronto Fitzgibbon had begun to take precautions, in spite of Sir Francis Head's confidence. He posted a militia guard on the City Hall, and two sentries on Government House. When he tried to arrange that trustworthy loyalists should be warned by the ringing of the bell of Upper Canada

College, he was told by the mayor that he was interfering, and the Chief Justice, John Robinson, said, 'I am sorry to see you alarming the people in this way.' At a meeting held at Government House on 2 December, the Governor and his immediate advisers believed that 'not fifty people in the Province could be got to take up arms against the Government'. When Fitzgibbon joined the meeting, his warnings were treated as added evidence of his alarmist tendency to exaggerate. However, it was agreed that a warrant would be issued for Mackenzie's arrest.

During the late evening of 4 December, and all through that night, men began to gather at Montgomery's Tavern until by the morning of 5 December between seven and eight hundred had collected under the leadership of Lount and Anderson. By the time enough men had gathered it was too late for any action to be taken, for they had marched too far and were too exhausted. However, rebel pickets were posted down Yonge Street towards Toronto to prevent movement in and out of the town. The Tavern had recently changed hands, and the new landlord refused to feed anyone without cash payment. There was no news from Rolph within the town, and of those who had assembled 'many had no arms, others had rifles, old fowling pieces, Indian guns, pikes'. Many started off home again when they found that there were no muskets or weapons available for them.

Mackenzie, unable to contain his restlessness, persuaded Anderson and five others to accompany him on a mounted patrol towards Toronto, to contact Rolph and Morrison and bring them to join the main body of rebels. Soon after they had left, three horsemen came galloping down the slope from Eglinton towards Montgomery's Tavern on their way to Toronto. The rebel guards ordered the riders to halt, but they carried on towards Toronto. The guards opened fire, and one rider fell backwards off his horse, another was captured, but the third galloped on to the town. The fallen man turned out to be Colonel Robert Moodie, a well-known loyalist from Richmond Hill, and he was mortally wounded.

Colonel Fitzgibbon in Toronto was growing increasingly

anxious, and by 10 pm he decided to rouse the Governor. Sir Francis Head heard what he had to say and then returned to bed. Fitzgibbon decided to make a personal reconnaissance, but meeting Alderman Powell, who had decided to explore as far as Montgomery's Tavern, Fitzgibbon returned to Toronto. As Powell and his companion climbed Gallows Hill they came face to face with Mackenzie's mounted patrol. Mackenzie rode up, pistol drawn, and took the two men prisoner, but did not search them. Mackenzie sent the two prisoners back to Montgomery's Tavern under escort of Anderson and some of the patrol, while he rode on with the others.[2,7,8]

As Anderson took the prisoners up the road, they were met by the remaining horseman of Colonel Moodie's party, who shouted out, 'The rebels have shot poor Colonel Moodie and are advancing on the city.' Powell shouted for help, but the rider raced past them. Anderson made Powell and his companion ride ahead of him. As they came near to Montgomery's Tavern, Powell drew a pistol, which he had hidden, and shot Anderson dead, the bullet hitting him in the neck. Powell and his companion turned their horses and rode down Gallows Hill as fast as they could, coming up with Mackenzie. Powell fired point blank at Mackenzie's face, but the priming flashed in the pan and the pistol misfired. As soon as Powell reached the town he roused the Governor and gave a warning that brooked no dismissal, and which also destroyed the rebels' last chance of achieving any surprise.

Sir Francis Head ordered the alarm to be sounded, and gathered together a group of loyalists under Fitzgibbon, including the Chief Justice, Attorney General, civil servants and members of the leading families, who armed themselves and prepared to defend the town. They numbered about 200 men. Messengers were sent off to summon the militia from neighbouring districts to march to Toronto as quickly as possible.

Back at Montgomery's Tavern, rebel morale was low. Their only competent military leader, Anderson, was dead and because of his inexperience Lount was unwilling to take over command. The combination of bad whisky, little food, and

56

rough sleeping conditions, together with the loss of any chance of surprise upon which their best hopes lay, had all had their effect. Mackenzie behaved as though 'he was going to have a fit'. One of those present said later:

Little Mac conducted himself like a crazy man all the time we were at Montgomery's. He went about storming and screaming like a lunatic, and many of us felt certain he was not in his right senses. He abused and insulted several of the men without any shadow of cause, and Lount had to go round and pacify them by telling them not to pay any attention to him as he was hardly responsible for his actions.[7]

The arguments about what to do, and who should lead went on until at last it was reluctantly agreed that Mackenzie should lead them. At eleven o'clock in the morning the men were told to form up outside the tavern. Mackenzie came out, dressed in several overcoats buttoned up to the chin, mounted a white pony and harangued the 800 men who were by now assembled, telling them that opposition would be slight and that the Governor could only muster about 150 Tories to oppose them, and some of those would be schoolboys. By about midday they left Montgomery's Tavern, and headed towards Gallows Hill and Toronto. When they reached the brow of Gallows Hill they halted and re-formed into two columns half a mile apart.

Just before two o'clock Robert Baldwin and Dr John Rolph, who had ridden out from Toronto, were sighted by the rebels' advance picket on Yonge Street. To the rebels' astonishment, those very men whom the rebels had been led to believe were their future heads of state came under a flag of truce to offer a full amnesty if only the rebels would disperse and go home. Mackenzie refused to accept Baldwin's and Rolph's word, and they were sent back to Toronto to get these terms in writing; he did, however, agree for the time being, not to march beyond the Red Lion Inn at Bloor Street. As Baldwin and Rolph rode away, Mackenzie and Lount moved their men up to Bloor Street.

While these discussions were taking place, Colonel Fitzgibbon in Toronto had paraded 200 Volunteers in the market place. The core of this force was Fitzgibbon's own company of Volunteers, which he had formed in 1834 and had drilled twice weekly. Their numbers were augumented by those members of the administration and loyalist families whom the Governor had gathered together. Sir Francis Head took the additional personal precaution of placing his wife and family on board a steamer in the harbour. The loyalist Volunteers spent the morning waiting calmly in the midst of a town torn by rumour. In order to gain time the offer of an amnesty for the rebels had been decided upon, to be carried by ambassadors whom it was hoped the rebels would believe. Bidwell was invited to go but refused, and so Rolph and Baldwin who were intent upon 'hedging their bets' had agreed to set out.

While Baldwin and Rolph were away, militia Volunteers from the outlying districts started to arrive in Toronto. They came from as far as Niagara and Coburg, with the news that more were on the way. By the time Baldwin and Rolph returned to Toronto, Fitzgibbon's force had risen to almost 1,000 men and the offer of a truce and an amnesty was now withdrawn. Baldwin and Rolph were sent back to the rebels a second time to give them this news, and Rolph took the opportunity to tell Mackenzie that in his view the town was still open to them if they attacked at once, and moreover there were some 600 sympathisers within the town who would then join them.

It was now early evening, and the rebels at length agreed to advance under Mackenzie's leadership. Some riflemen were sent on ahead, followed by a motley collection of men armed with pikes and pitchforks. As the riflemen advanced down Yonge Street they were watched in the gathering dusk by a picket of some twenty to thirty loyalist Volunteers under Sheriff Jarvis, stationed on Yonge Street on the outskirts of the town. The rebels got to within a hundred yards of the picket when Jarvis gave his men the order to fire, and the rebels were greeted by a ragged volley. As soon as the Volunteers at the picket had fired, they dropped their muskets and fled back to Toronto. Lount, who was in command of the rebel riflemen, ordered them to return the fire, which they did, falling to the ground as they fired in order to give their rear ranks a clear field of fire. But those behind, seeing their entire front rank disappear, thought they had all been killed, and this was too much for them. As they turned tail, their panic communicated itself to the rest of the rebel host, and all but Lount and his front rank turned and fled. Lount maintained his ground for a time, but then, as they were on their own, he withdrew with his riflemen. One rebel had been killed, a cooper from Sharon and a former British soldier, and two others mortally wounded. The rebel force now retreated back up Yonge Street to Montgomery's Tavern.

During that evening of 6 December, militia reinforcements under Colonel Allan MacNab arrived by boat from Hamilton and other militia bodies began to arrive from Oakville, Port Credit and Perth. Sir Francis Head decided to appoint Colonel MacNab as Commander-in-Chief, but neglected to tell Colonel Fitzgibbon, who only heard that he had been superseded later that night, having spent his time trying to organise the Volunteer militiamen as they dribbled into the town. Dr Rolph now decided that discretion was the better part of valour, sent a message to Mackenzie telling him that the cause was lost and that the men should be sent home, and then left Toronto to seek refuge in the United States.

Mackenzie ignored Rolph's warning, and instead set out with a mounted party and proceeded to hold up and rob the mail coach, taking its passengers prisoner to Montgomery's Tavern. Late that evening Colonel Van Egmond arrived at the tavern from Huron, to find that the rebel force had dwindled to 500 men. Mackenzie wanted to attack again the next day, but Van Egmond and Lount maintained that the best they could hope for would be to defend their present position and trust that reinforcement from the rural areas would arrive. It was agreed that sixty riflemen should be sent down to the east of Toronto by the River Don to act as a diversion.[2,6,8,19]

On the next day, 7 December, Colonel Fitzgibbon, who had again taken over command on MacNab's personal insistence, organised the newly arrived militia Volunteers into companies, and set officers in command of them. He then split his force of 1,200 men into three columns; and at noon Fitzgibbon, with MacNab, led the centre column up Yonge Street to the accompaniment of two bands, with the flanking columns advancing half a mile to either side. Two cannon, under command of Major Carfrae of the militia artillery, followed. At one o'clock the centre column was sighted by the rebel sentries in front of Montgomery's Tavern, and they raised the alarm.

Van Egmond and Mackenzie turned out their men, who now numbered only some 400 (the sixty riflemen having left to take up positions east of Toronto). Of these 400, probably less than half carried firearms. About 150 were posted in a small wood beside Yonge Street, some way below Montgomery's Tavern; another fifty took up position to the east of the road behind fences and what cover they could find; the remainder, unarmed except for pikes and pitchforks, waited around the tavern.

As the militia drew within range, the rebel riflemen opened fire, whereupon the militia deployed to either side of the road, and Major Carfrae brought up his two cannon. As the guns opened fire, the sound of round shot crashing through the trees further undermined the rebels' morale. Then the two flanking columns appeared, and the rebel riflemen started to withdraw towards the tavern. Major Carfrae advanced his cannon, and one shot going through the window of the tavern so scared the inmates that they took to their heels. The panic spread and in a matter of minutes the rebel force had evaporated.

Mackenzie fled, pursued by Colonel Fitzgibbon and some officers for some way, but he managed to elude the pursuit and eventually made his way to the sanctuary of the United States. Sir Francis Head ordered that Montgomery's Tavern be burnt to the ground. Colonel Van Egmond was taken prisoner together with Samuel Lount and another rebel leader, Matthews. Ninety-two other rebels were taken to Toronto. Marshall Spring Bidwell, who had not been involved in the rebellion, was given the choice by Sir Francis Head of returning to the United States or standing trial; he chose the former course.[2,7,8,19]

There was one more flicker of rebellion in the west of the province when Dr Charles Duncombe gathered a small band of rebels in the area of London, but his party was dispersed as bodies of militia were quickly dispatched from Toronto and approached him from several sides. As the collapse of the rebellion became obvious, some rebel sympathisers marching to join their comrades decided to change sides and joined the militia instead. Although the rebellion had been crushed, Upper Canada's troubles were not yet over. A new threat was to come by armed intervention from across the United States border.

4
Holding the Fort ·

The two rebellions of 1837 in the Lower and Upper Provinces had alarmed the British authorities. The Lower Canadian uprising had been the more serious, and had commanded much support among the French Canadian population, but in Upper Canada there were fears of continuing American involvement, which soon proved to be only too well founded.

The fiasco around Montgomery's Tavern took place on 7 December. Mackenzie, having escaped, made his way to Buffalo in the United States, arriving there on the 11th and, in spite of the price on his head of £1,000 and in spite of being recognised on a number of occasions, he was not arrested. Mackenzie had been able to inspire some hundreds of farmers and country people to take up arms, but he had not succeeded in establishing a substantial following, as was shown by the way in which the militia drawn from the local population all over the province hurried to support the Government.

Mackenzie was greeted with enthusiasm on his arrival in Buffalo, and a public meeting was called for that very night. To the Americans Mackenzie appeared to be a patriot who was endeavouring to throw off the tyranny and despotism of British rule, which still prevented Canadians from realising their freedom. Here, to them, was another potential War of Independence, a popular movement of democratic Canadians about to be cruelly suppressed by the autocratic use of British regular troops. The natural generosity and sympathy of the Americans was aroused, and the crowd dispersed only after it had been promised that Mackenzie himself would address them the following day. A guard of young Volunteers set a watch over the house where the exhausted Reform leader slept.

Next day Mackenzie spoke to a large and enthusiastic crowd, telling them of the oppression being suffered by Canadians, and of their fight for reform and the establishment of democratic institutions. Canadians would never be free so long as they were held down by the military might of an autocratic British Governor, owing allegiance not to Canadian but to an English monarch. As soon as he had finished speaking, an American, Thomas Sutherland, appealed for volunteers to join him and to cross the border to assist their Canadian brothers. Another American appealed for gifts of arms and ammunition to be left at the Eagle Tavern.[2,7]

On 15 December Mackenzie and a party of Canadian and American volunteers broke into the United States Army arsenal and equipped themselves with arms and ammunition. They then took over an American paddle steamer, the *Caroline*, and occupied Navy Island, some three miles from Niagara and part of Canadian territory. Mackenzie proclaimed the setting up of a Provisional Canadian Republic, with himself as chairman, and hoisted the Patriote tricolour flag with its two stars symbolising the two Canadas. Rewards of Canadian land and money were promised for each new recruit that joined them.

American volunteers soon started to arrive in numbers. A visitor to Rochester in New York State wrote, 'There is excitement here, forty soldiers marching the streets today under drum and fife; two pieces of cannon went off this morning, and three fourths of the people here are encouraging the cause of the Patriots.' By the end of December the *Caroline* had ferried to Navy Island supplies, ordnance and enough volunteers to bring the force up to 200 men. In addition Rensselaer Van Rensselaer arrived to take command. He was the son of an American general who had fought in the War of 1812, and probably saw himself in the same role as that of Sam Houston, who had just established the new State of Texas. Later Mackenzie was joined by his wife, who helped to make flannel cartridge cases for the cannon. The rebel artillery on Navy Island started to bombard the Canadian village of Chippewa.[7,20]

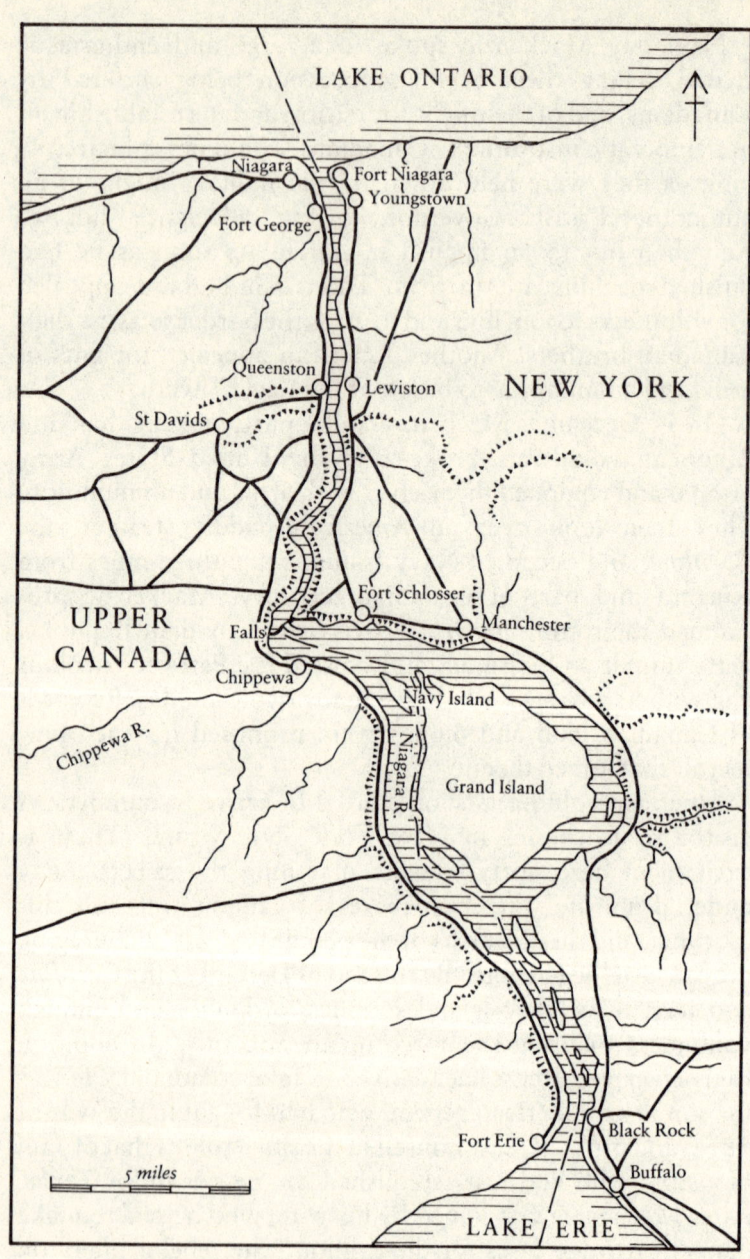

LAKE ONTARIO

Niagara

Fort Niagara
Youngstown

Fort George

NEW YORK

Queenston

Lewiston

St Davids

UPPER
CANADA

Fort Schlosser

Falls

Manchester

Chippewa

Navy Island

Chippewa R.

Niagara R.

Grand Island

Fort Erie

Black Rock

Buffalo

5 miles

LAKE ERIE

The Niagara Frontier

On the Canadian side of the River Niagara, Colonel MacNab had moved down from Toronto and was in command of the militia and Volunteers. Having seen the *Caroline* ferrying arms and reinforcements from the American mainland to Navy Island, he ordered Commander Andrew Drew RN to board the ship, cut her out and destroy her. On 28 December Drew's party found the ship moored on the American shore; she was boarded after a fight in which one American was killed and several were wounded on both sides. The ship was then cut loose and fired, and was watched from Navy Island as it drifted, burning, down the river.[7]

At Chippewa, on the Canadian side, Colonel MacNab was reinforced by two companies of the 24th Foot on 21 December, followed by the rest of the battalion under Colonel Hughes a few days later. Together with militia and Volunteers the force opposing Mackenzie's 200 Volunteers now numbered 2,500 men. There were hesitations about launching an attack on the island itself because of possible American reactions, but as British batteries were established a bombardment of Navy Island was begun.[10]

The burning of the *Caroline* when moored on United States territory raised a storm of protest from the Americans, and the President threatened the 'pirates' with the utmost rigour of the law. Tension along the border increased, and Americans demanded revenge and retaliation.[2,20]

A report sent to Lord Palmerston in London, dated 21 February 1838, read:

It appears that on 13th December last a numerous armed body composed chiefly of American citizens had openly invaded and later taken possession of Navy Island, a part of the British possessions. This body was under the command of an American named Van Rausseleas [sic], who affected to establish in Navy Island, in conjunction with the Canadian rebels, a provisional government for the purpose of revolutionising Canada.

From 13th to 29th inclusive Van Rausseleas [sic] and his followers kept possession of Navy Island, and were guilty of repeated acts of warlike aggression on the Canadian shore, and also on British boats passing the island. During all this time there was constant communication between the American shore and Navy Island, and a constant reinforcement of warlike men and warlike stores was supplied from the State of New York, and principally from Fort Schlosser.

On 29th two discharges of heavy ordnance were made on a British boat from the American shore near the fort. On the same day the 'Caroline' came down the river from Buffalo, and after landing at Navy Island several men and packages, which it is impossible not to see contained stores of war, it made two trips between Fort Schlosser and Navy Island, and transported from the former to the latter place a six-pounder and other warlike stores. Fort Schlosser itself appears to have been largely provided with shot of various descriptions and other ammunition. The Lieutenant Governor had on 13th apprised the Governor of the State of New York of the proceedings which had occurred, but no answer had been sent to that communication. Under these circumstances we are of the opinion that the place where the 'Caroline' was moored was not firstly entitled to the privileges of a neutral territory, and that the British forces with a view of self-preservation were fully justified in attacking the 'Caroline' and treating her as a belligerent vessel.[C5]

MacNab kept up a steady bombardment of Navy Island, which undermined the morale of the Patriotes. Mackenzie, as cantankerous as ever, continually quarrelled and argued with Van Rensselaer. With the loss of the *Caroline* there was no effective means of supplying the island with heavy stores, and after two weeks it was decided that they would have to abandon their position. By this time the American President, Van Buren, under diplomatic and commercial pressure, was forced to intervene. As the Patriotes returned to the United States shore their weapons were taken from them by regular troops of the United States Army, since many of them had been seized from American Government arsenals. Van Rensselaer was arrested on charges of breaking the American laws of neutrality. Mackenzie refused to have anything further to do with Van Rensselaer and retreated with his wife to Rochester in New York State. So the shortlived Provisional Canadian Republic died.[6,7]

The British Government in London was now sufficiently alarmed to set in motion urgent measures to remedy the situation. It became known in Quebec in early January 1838 that the resignation of the Governor, Lord Gosford, had been accepted, and on 20 February he handed over to Sir John Colborne, who was to act as Administrator. In London in January Lord John Russell had announced to the House of Commons that the Constitution of Lower Canada was suspended, and that Lord Durham was to be sent out as a Special Commissioner, with authority to pass ordinances, in consultation with five members of the Executive Council. He was, in addition, to make recommendations on the future government of the two provinces, and for this purpose he was to form a Special Council made up of three members of each Legislative Council and ten members of each House of Assembly. The news of the suspension of the Lower Province's Constitution reached Quebec in February and was proclaimed on 20 March, and on 5 April Sir John Colborne announced the names of the Special Council.[21]

At the same time large reinforcements of troops were ordered to prepare for service in Canada. Within Canada itself, such preliminary steps as were possible were set in motion. The Governor of New Brunswick, Sir Colin Campbell, had written to Sir John Colborne offering such regular troops as were under his command, and in a further letter dated 27 December he wrote that, 'The 43rd and 85th have ere now reached their destination, and I hope that their presence will enable you to put the disaffected and rebels at defiance until you receive sufficient reinforcements.'[C6]

The 43rd Regiment had one wing stationed at Fredericton and the other at St John's. The orders to march from New Brunswick to Quebec arrived in mid-December at a time when the Canadian winter was at its most severe. Captain Mundy of the 43rd described the journey:

On 11th December the headquarters, after much trouble in fitting the men and baggage into the sleds (fourteen in number) left Fredericton. The cold was great, and the ground too bare of snow for good sleighing. At the River Tobique we encountered our first serious difficulty, being upwards of four hours crossing our eighty men over the stream, which was running blocks of ice. Left the Grand Falls, and driving thirty three miles on the frozen river reached the French settlement of Madowaska. Some horses knocked up – dreadfully cold – piercing wind with sleet. Here we found the commissary from Quebec with provisions, but he had failed in getting carrioles, and our New Brunswick drivers with great difficulty were bribed to continue the march. On the 17th, we fairly plunged into the eternal forests, from whence we did not emerge until 22nd evening, on the banks of the St Lawrence. I brought up the rear always, and after all this excessive cold and fatigue a wretched log camp (there were six of them on the route built for us), open at the top, smoking so dreadfully that we could not open our eyes; a bed of pine branches, a supper of salt pork, biscuit, and unmilked tea in a tin pot, the heat of the fire singeing our moccasins, whilst our fur night caps were frozen hard to the walls of the hut, the snow on the roof, dripping through on our luxurious couch. The surgeon's thermometer went down two evenings to 24 and 30 degrees below zero, or 62 of frost.

At one of the camps, when we rose in the morning, the sleds and baggage were found entirely buried in snow, and one's strength could not fold the frozen blankets covering the poor horses. The drivers behaved with the greatest bravery and loyalty, and were relieved by the carrioles and French drivers of Canada. I can give no idea of the dreariness of our forest marches. During our four days strange march along the St Lawrence, we were daily fed and lodged by loyal Canadians and priests. Several persons came from Quebec to meet us and offer assistance en route, and our passage of the river and arrival at the city were extremely striking and exciting. Two companies were thrown across the river in canoes at once – the paddlers singing merrily – the quays and wharfs crowded with spectators. All gave us a most terrific cheer. And thus, on 28th December, the ragged, unshaven, smoke-dried, toil worn, frostbitten 43rd entered triumphantly their barracks – an ancient Jesuit convent.

The regiment had travelled 370 miles in 18 days across appalling country in the height of a Canadian winter.[22]

The 85th Regiment, and later the 34th, followed the 43rd, having concentrated at Fredericton; the 85th left there on 16 December, arriving in Quebec on 2 January, and then moving on to Sorel. The men had been issued with two pairs of moccasins each, two blankets, warm mitts and ear covers.[24]

The 32nd and 83rd Regiments were ordered to move from

the Lower Province to Upper Canada. Early in January 1838, the headquarters of the 32nd embarked for a passage up river from Montreal to Kingston and became frozen in among the Thousand Isles. After some days they left their boats, crossed the ice on foot and marched to Kingston, sending detachments to Toronto and New London. The 83rd Regiment sent two companies to Amherstburg in Upper Canada, while the headquarters remained in Montreal.[11,14]

In London, Lord FitzRoy Somerset at the Horse Guards was issuing the orders for substantial reinforcements to embark for Canada. In a letter dated 27 February 1838 he wrote:

The period is now approaching when the troops under orders for embarkation will be put on board the ships appointed for their conveyance to British North America. At the date of this letter, the whole of this force is distributed as follows:

1st Dragoon Guards	6 troops	All four regiments
7th Hussars	4 troops	in Ireland in
23rd Foot		readiness to be
71st Foot		embarked
11th Foot		On passage from Gibraltar to Bermuda
73rd Foot		At Gibraltar
Grenadier Guards	2nd Battalion ⎱	Both in London
Coldstream Guards	2nd Battalion ⎰	
65th Foot		At New Brunswick and Halifax
93rd Foot		At Halifax
1st Foot	2nd Battalion ⎫	
15th Foot		
24th Foot		
32nd Foot		All
34th Foot	⎬	in
43rd Foot		Canada
66th Foot		
83rd Foot		
85th Foot	⎭	

Thus showing a force of   6   Troops 1st Dragoon Guards

	4	Troops 7th Hussars
TOTAL	10	Troops in Ireland
	9	Battalions in Canada
	1	Battalion between Halifax and New Brunswick
	1	Battalion at Halifax
	4	Battalions to be sent from home, Gibraltar and Bermuda
	2	Battalions of Guards
TOTAL	17	Battalions

The permanent barrack accommodation in British North America may be stated as follows:

Chambly	1,362	Coteau du Lac	460
Quebec	1,909	St John's	104
Montreal	493	Three Rivers	340
St Helens	61	Sorel	440
La Prairie	1,378	Blair Findie	82
Ile aux Noix	419	Rideau Canal	60
La Chine	250	Others	284

TOTAL Lower Canada   7,642

Kingston	624	Amherstburg	124
Toronto	354	Fort Wellington	96
Fort George	376	Others	48

TOTAL Upper Canada   1,622

Halifax	2,017	Sydney, Cap Breton	84
Windsor	24	Prince Edward Island	200

TOTAL Nova Scotia   2,325

Fredericton	240	St Andrew	30
St John	270		

TOTAL New Brunswick   540

In this state of things, and considering that in the summer months reinforcements can always be sent from Halifax to Quebec, I would suggest as follows: that of the troops now about to proceed to British North America the 11th Foot should be conveyed from Bermuda to New Brunswick; the 73rd from Gibraltar to Halifax; the 23rd from

Ireland to Halifax. The 71st and 2 Battalions of Guards to Quebec.[C7]

The strength of British regular troops in Canada was to be increased to a total strength of 500 cavalry and 10,600 infantry.

1st Dragoon Guards	300 men
7th Hussars	200 men
	————
TOTAL	500 cavalry

15 battalions of Foot at 600 men	=	9,000
2 battalions of Guards at 800	=	1,600
		————
TOTAL		10,600 infantry

With a force of this size being assembled in Canada steps were also taken to strengthen the command and staff structure. Lord FitzRoy Somerset wrote to Sir John Colborne from the Horse Guards on 6 January 1838:

Since I wrote to you on 30th Sir William MacBean has informed Lord Hill that his health will not admit of his proceeding to Canada, and Major General Clitheroe, formerly of the Guards, has been selected in his stead. The Major General will proceed in the course of a week. I send you the list of officers who have been selected for employment in Canada, and have been instructed to embark with the least delay possible. I hope you will find them useful.

Lord Hill has been authorised to add to the staff in Canada one Assistant Adjutant General, one Assistant Quartermaster General, two Deputy Assistant Adjutant Generals, and two Deputy Assistant Quartermaster Generals. His Lordship will leave it to you to make these appointments subject to the restriction adverted to in my letter of the 30th regarding field officers serving with their regiments. Many of those who are going out will prove valuable staff officers, but you will soon discover their several merits.

Your last despatch I acknowledge officially. Lieutenant Colonel Frederick Campbell also goes by this packet to take command of the artillery. He is Sir Colin's brother, as you will at once see when he appears before you. You will find him a very zealous officer.[C8]

This letter was followed by one from Lord Hill dated 9 January 1838:

Her Majesty's Government having directed that the military force in British North America should at the earliest possible period be increased to 10,000 men, including a force of from four to five hundred cavalry, but not including artillery and that this force – should be held in readiness to embark for Quebec as soon as the season will permit.

Her Majesty's Government moreover directs that 25 military officers should, with the least possible delay, be commissioned for special service, and despatched to Lower Canada to place themselves under your orders. I have, with Her Majesty's approbation, selected the following, and they have received my instructions to proceed via New York to your Headquarters with the utmost expedition:

Lt Col Robert Mickle	Lt Col Joseph Patterson
Lt George Cathcart	Lt Col Ernest Gascoygne
Lt Col Robert Loring	Lt Col Clerke
Lt Col Benjamin Browne	Lt Col William Marshal
Lt Col Charles Turner	Lt Col Cox
Lt Col Charles Taylor	Lt Col William Williams
Major Frederick Fraser	Major John Campbell
Major Sir G T Temple	Major Plomer Young
Major Lewis Carmichael	Major Robert Anstruther
Major George Hall	Major Charles Stead
Major L D Pritchard	Major Sir James Hamilton
Capt Rottenburgh	Capt G C Swan
Capt I Bynge Creagh	

I have to add that the commanding officer of each of the regiments of cavalry has been ordered immediately to select a competent officer to proceed to New York for the purpose of purchasing horses for the regiments as soon as they shall receive orders to that effect from you. They will be accompanied by a few rough riders of good character in plain clothes, and by the veterinary surgeon of the 7th Light Dragoons, and they will be furnished with detailed instructions. The officers and men, when selected, will be ordered to proceed to Liverpool for embarkation to New York, to call upon Mr Buchanan, Her Majesty's Consul, and request from him advice and information as to the rank which they should pursue in proceeding when required by you to Canada.

Major General Clitheroe, one of the Major Generals appointed to your staff, is the bearer of this despatch.[C9]

Apart from these official postings other young officers were eager to gain employment. Lord Hill wrote to Sir John Colborne on 15 January 1838:

Mr Goring who was a Lieutenant in the King's Dragoon Guards, and sold out some little time ago, being wholly unemployed, has determined to proceed to Canada. I could not hold out to him any hope of military employment, having determined not to sanction the employment of volunteers, but being acquainted with his brother, I am unwilling to withold from him a letter of introduction to you as a favour.[C10]

And Lord Lynedoch wrote in similar vein in April:

I wish now to recommend to your notice Paymaster MacCurrin, of the 1st Dragoon Guards, just going to embark at Cork with his regiment. I have taken a great interest in him, he was present at the Battle of Waterloo, and was warmly recommended for promotion.[C11]

Sir John Colborne was bombarded with similar letters bringing young officers to his attention and seeking employment for others. As an immediate measure the twenty-five officers selected by Lord Hill for 'a particular duty' and for 'a special service' were to be posted in the troubled areas and along the frontier with the United States. It would be their duty to inspect and assist the militia and Volunteers, and generally to act as a calming influence in the localities in which they would be stationed. Lieutenant-Colonel George Cathcart was placed in command at Montreal with the task of collecting and consolidating weekly reports from these officers and submitting this intelligence to Sir John Colborne. He was also put in charge of all the Volunteer and militia cavalry in the Province, as well as the Volunteers in the Island of Montreal. The second-in-command of this group of staff officers, Lieutenant-Colonel Mickle, was established at Quebec.

In a letter written from Montreal to his father in England, dated 25 March 1838, George Cathcart describes the general situation in the Lower Province.

Martial Law is proclaimed here but Lord Gosford, before he went, hampered it with so many cautions that Sir John (Colborne) who is all firmness and promptitude and an officer of the right sort, cannot act upon it except to keep the rebels under arrest in jail. They say that Sir Francis Head has acted with less scruple in the Upper Province and that Sutherland has been tried by Court Martial of Militia Field officers and shot. Sir Francis Head is, I believe, due here today on his way home. The Upper Province is now all safe internally and the United States are exerting themselves to prevent mischief on their side.

Here in Lower Canada it is very much a division of party politics between the French Canadians and the Anglo-Irish population. The French male population between the ages of 18 and 60, who are fit to bear arms are about 70,000. The Loyalists are 14,000 exclusive of regular troops. The Militia being chiefly disloyal are neither armed nor called out. The Volunteers who are loyal are both armed and well organised and already blooded.

The St Lawrence which intersects the whole country longitudinally gives that facility for the movement of troops so that our force can be more than doubled for purposes of concentration, in a matter of a few hours by means of sledges in winter and steamboats in the summer. The civilian population capable of bearing arms which is as I have mentioned, 70,000, are unarmed, unorganised, and scattered over an area from Gaspé to Montreal, a distance of nearly 400 miles. Thus I think we are at all times able to muster these provinces unless by some mistaken policy we quarrel with our present loyal supporters and disgust them with our ingratitude.

All parties will, I think, agree with the Union of the two provinces which would equalise the representation and be a benefit to both provinces. The old French law must be abolished but yet this is not at all incompatible with the rights and interests of the French but on the contrary would be for their benefit. It is well known that the Upper Province flourishes whilst the Lower Province does not, because with the old French feudal tenancies nobody can purchase property in Lower Canada without the risk of a disputed title.

The Upper Province would also benefit by a Union because at present they have no sea-port and with water communications direct to the sea through the Lower Province, they are by customs duties and difficulties obliged to develop the less advantageous trade with the United States. This is not only less advantageous to them, but also to the Mother Country.[CAI]

In Upper Canada American incursions continued. On 8

January the American volunteer who had supported Mackenzie at Buffalo, Thomas Sutherland, having seized arms from the Michigan State arsenal and commandeered several vessels, set out for Amherstburg. He landed on Bois Blanc Island, where he read out a proclamation, and on the 9th the commander of one of the commandeered vessels, Edward Mueller, sailed his ship, the *Anne*, up to Amherstburg and started to bombard the town. But he went too close to the shore, so that the Canadian militia were able to shoot the helmsman, and board the *Anne*, capturing not only the ship but 200 muskets and most of Sutherland's stores which were on board. Sutherland then retreated back to the United States where he was arrested.

On 22 February Van Rensselaer, freed from US custody, headed a band of some 400 volunteers who had been recruited and armed by him in New York State, and led them to French Creek on the American side of the St Lawrence River, some twenty-five miles below Kingston. From there they took possession of Hickory Island in the Upper Province and some miles nearer to Kingston. The militia from the Midland and Jamestown Districts were mustered and marched for Hickory Island, but Van Rensselaer and his men fled as soon as they received intelligence of the approach of the militia.[C19]

A party of American Volunteers from Michigan occupied Fighting Island, and were dispersed by a company of the 24th Foot under Lieutenant Kelsall who were stationed at Amherstburg. A small cannon, some new muskets bearing the mark of the US Army and ammunition which had been abandoned, were captured. A more serious attempt was made under the leadership of a wealthy Ohio man, Bradley, from Sandusky when 'a body of American brigands, armed to the teeth with rifles, pistols, bayonets and large carvers as sharp as razors, called bowie knives', landed on 28 February on an island at the head of Lake Erie. Point Pelée was some twenty miles from the Canadian mainland. The Americans seized the inhabitants and looted their houses. They then began to prepare for an attack on Amherstburg. A detachment of the 32nd and 83rd

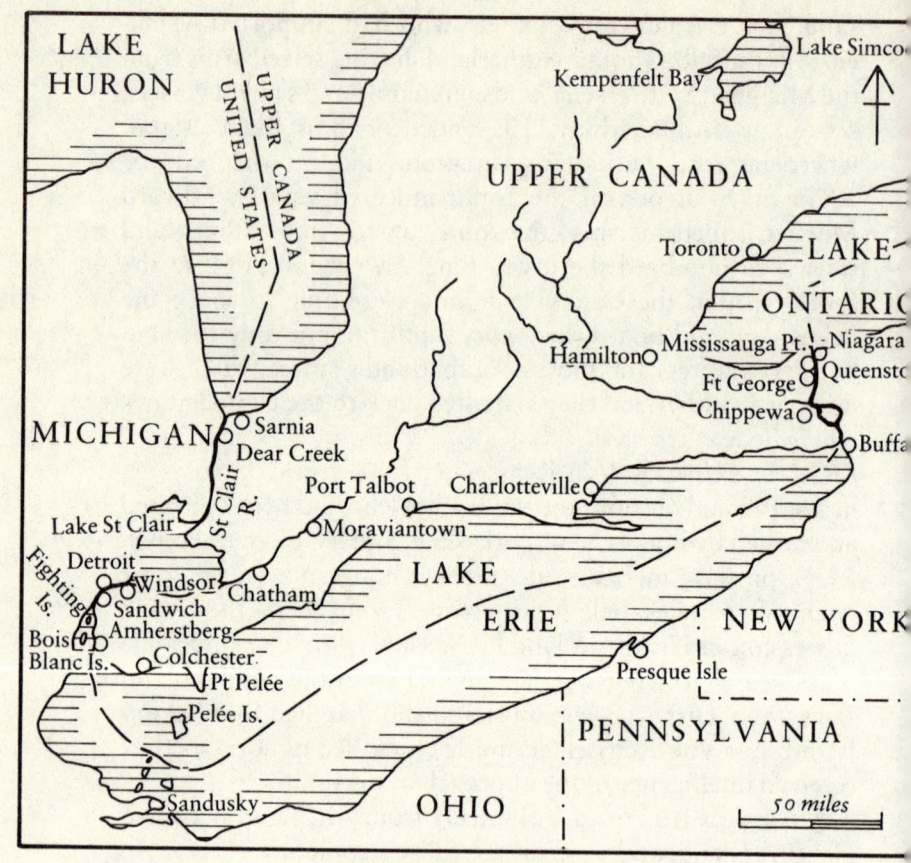

Western Upper Canada

Foot, together with a party of Volunteer cavalry, set out from
Amherstburg under Colonel Maitland of the 32nd, travelling
in sleighs over the ice of the lake, covering the eighteen miles to
Colchester by the evening of 2 March, and arriving at Point
Pelée by daybreak, a total distance of some forty miles. Two
companies of the 32nd with the Volunteer cavalry under
Captain Browne were detached and sent round to the south of
the island in order to cut off the Americans' retreat. Colonel

76

Maitland with the rest of his force advanced through deep snow from the north, with two cannon in support, and forced the Americans to retire to the south. Finding themselves surrounded, the Americans attacked Captain Browne's detachment as it only numbered 100 men, and also because that direction provided a line of retreat back across the ice to Sandusky. The Americans advanced on Captain Browne in formation, preceded by a line of skirmishers who took cover behind large blocks of ice and opened fire. Captain Browne found himself outflanked, so he formed his small force into an extended line and charged with the bayonet. The sight of cold steel was too much for the Americans who, although they outnumbered Browne's force by four to one, broke and fled to the woods, and from there to their sleighs. They made off in these back to the American shore, but not before leaving over seventy of their number killed and wounded. The 32nd suffered more than thirty casualties, all of whom were wounded, but two of these later died, Captain Browne received a brevet majority for his gallantry. Sutherland and Theller, released by the American authorities, after the affair at Bois Blanc Island, were on their way to join Bradley at Point Pelée when they were intercepted and arrested by Colonel Prince.[11,14,C19]

Representations were constantly made by the British to the American authorities to prevent these incursions. It was not so much that the American authorities did not wish to take action, it was more that they did not have the resources to police a long frontier and an unruly population. A report from Toronto to Sir John Colborne of 19 February stated that 'General Brady [of the US Army] has been able to recover 3 or 400 stand of arms, which the Brigands had carried off, that had just been removed from the Arsenal at Dearborn to Detroit for the use of the Militia Companies which were being embodied to preserve the peace, besides 30 or 40 additional muskets'.[C12]

Concern was also expressed at the preparations being made from within the United States for a fresh invasion. The

American State Department in Washington tried to reassure the British; John Forsyth wrote on 7 February that advice had been received:

from Lieut General Sir John Colborne, that preparations are making for a hostile invasion of the Province of Lower Canada by a body of armed men assembled at Plattsburg and Champlain in the State of New York, and that the assemblage, composed partly of French Canadian outlaws, and partly of inhabitants of the United States, is understood to be fast increasing in numbers, and to be furnished by the neighbouring American population with arms and ammunition, for the furtherance of an unlawful and piratical assault upon a part of H. M. Dominions, and communicating this information in order that this Government may adopt prompt and effectual measures, for restraining this threatened attempt, from within its jurisdiction, against the security of H. M. Dominions, and against the lives and property of H. M. subjects.

I hasten to make known to you that no official intelligence has reached this Department of the circumstances stated in your Note. The President has however directed me to inform you that General Scott's attention has been called to the rumours of movements near Plattsburg which had reached the War Department, and that orders will now be extended to that officer to repair to that part of the frontier in person. As General Wool has been in Vermont, in the neighbourhood of Plattsburg and Champlain, the President does not doubt that he has interfered to prevent any violations of the law, if any were intended, by citizens of the United States, or other persons within our jurisdiction.[C13]

In February, however, those Patriotes who had fled to the United States were preparing to move. Robert Nelson had been gathering arms and supporters at Alburg, Vermont and he intended to invade Lower Canada in conjunction with the raids being planned by Mackenzie into the Upper Province. Nelson was warned by the American authorities that, whilst General Wool would not stop them from entering Canada, any attempt to return with their weapons would be considered as an invasion of US territory and would be dealt with accordingly.[23]

On 28 February, Nelson, along with Dr Coté and de Lorimier, crossed the frontier at night with 600 men, equipped with 1,500 muskets and 8,000 cartridges, together with three cannon mounted on sleighs. The cannon had been the gift of American sympathisers, most of the muskets had been seized from the Vermont State arsenal at Elizabethtown, and the cartridges had been manufactured by the Patriotes themselves.

By morning the Patriote force had dwindled to about 150 men, most of the American volunteers having had second thoughts, but this did not deter Nelson from proclaiming a 'Republic of Lower Canada' and handing out a manifesto which abolished the seigneurial system, and expropriated all Crown land and clergy reserves, as well as breaking the ties with Britain.[4,8,23]

As the Patriotes started their advance into the Lower Province, they were met by Major Warde of the Royal Scots in command of the Missisquoi Volunteers, who soon despatched the 'Republican Army' back to the United States, where Nelson and Coté were arrested by General Wool and their followers disarmed by regular United States troops. As Sir John Colborne wrote to Lord FitzRoy Somerset, 'The officers of the United States Army have acted, I think, honestly and with great vigour and prudence under very trying circumstances.'[C15]

On 1 March the 43rd and 85th Foot stationed at St John's were ordered to march on Henryville as a precautionary measure, because it was believed that a considerable concentration of Patriotes had gathered around Henryville to join Nelson's foray across the frontier should it succeed. The column set out with two guns but on approaching Henryville it was learnt that Nelson's attempt had been countered, that any Patriotes gathering around Henryville had dispersed, and that the American General Wool had disarmed Nelson's men as they fled back across the frontier. On 3 March the 43rd and 85th returned to St John's.[22,24]

In Canada the British Government wanted a policy of firmness combined with conciliation. Lord Glenelg wrote from London to Sir John Colborne on 30 January:

I have laid your despatches before The Queen, and it has afforded

Her Majesty sincere gratification to find that the promptness and decision of your measures has been entirely successful in effectually checking the progress of the revolt. The Queen has observed with regret the statement in your despatch that acts of violence had been committed by some of those whose feelings had been exasperated by the outrages previously perpetrated by the insurgents. Accounts of such proceedings have appeared also in the public journals, though I trust with exaggeration. I am aware how difficult it must be under the circumstances in which the Province is placed to prevent acts of retaliation, but I am confident that you will have anticipated the desire of Her Majesty's ministers to confine the miseries necessarily attendant on this civil context within the narrowest possible limits, and that in your own person, and by means of the officers, you will have used every endeavour to repress all wanton destruction of property, and to prevent any unnecessary individual suffering.[C14]

The 43rd Foot, who had made the winter journey from New Brunswick to Quebec, were ordered early in January to provide headquarters and two companies to escort a large convoy of arms and ammunition for the volunteer units around Montreal. The cavalcade consisted of 114 carrioles stretching over a distance of more than half a mile. The remaining four companies of the regiment followed behind, and the whole convoy was able to sleigh along the ice of the St Lawrence River. Three companies were then posted to St John's, where on 1 February they were joined by the rest of the regiment.[22] The officers on 'particular duty' were proving of varied value. Some did not speak French and so were of limited use. George Cathcart, who spoke French fluently wrote to his father in April:

I am going out tomorrow to be stationed at St Hyacinthe on the river Yamaska which was the centre and focus of the rebellion. I am there to get acquainted with all my neighbours and to report to Headquarters. Now that things have subsided into comparative tranquillity and that the disaffected see they have been deserted by their leaders and that their cause is hopeless, they desire to return to good order. There are so many alarmist and false reports and the party spirit runs so high between the French and English parties that the Magistrates are afraid to act for fear of misrepresentation in some cases and in others they might still be influenced by party prejudice to act improperly. Therefore resident impartial and observing officers, reporting direct to Headquarters, are to be sent and it is hoped that it will encourage the former and hold the latter in check. These additional officers are now to be stationed at St Denis, St Charles, St Césaire and Nicolet between the Richelieu and Yamaska rivers and to report to me. I shall in turn report to Headquarters and keep them in concert. The roads are in a bad state at this season and it is only today that the river has been passable for horses.

We have some very efficient though irregular Corps of Cavalry along the frontier and here at Montreal we have three troops. However in this country there is no room for more than one squadron to act in line since, where reclaimed, the land is enclosed and surrounded with lanes and large wooden fences, which intersect it in all directions.

We are not now alarmed here about an American intervention any more but there may still be a border affray with lawless refugees and it is essential to keep up a good defence.[c15]

However, in Upper Canada the possibility of American incursions taking place were still uppermost in people's minds. Colonel Foster wrote to Sir John Colborne on 19 February 1838 from Toronto:

There is every hope and expectation that the Brigands at Detroit will soon be dispersed. I am concerned to say that the alarm increases at Kingston. The militia in the post are not fully to be relied on. The two companies of the 83rd ordered from the London District have been detained under the peculiar circumstances of the Western Frontier by Colonel Maitland. Perhaps Your Excellency could spare a company from Montreal which would restore confidence to the inhabitants of Toronto, I must say the most large town in the Province.[c12]

Van Rensselaer, released after the Navy Island affair, tried to assemble a force of American volunteers at French Creek with the intention of seizing Fort Henry at Kingston. They landed on an island near Gananoque, but took no further action, and the Americans soon dispersed when they learnt of the Canadian preparations being made for their reception.

From the American side of the border opposite Lower Canada those Patriotes who had sought refuge were actively planning further moves. Robert Nelson started to establish a new underground movement within the Lower Province. Les Frères Chasseurs, or Hunters' Lodges, were a secret society which could be mobilised for military action at the appropriate time with lodges widely scattered over the area between Montreal and the American frontier. New members were bound by secret oaths and initiation ceremonies. The French-Canadian habitants were still suffering from the effects of the economic depression, and to this was added the evidence of the 1837 rebellion, with its trail of burnt houses and plundered farms. Coté and Gagnon, de Lorimier and Mailhot and their followers walked the roads of the Province and quietly set up their clandestine organisation in the fertile recruiting ground of French Canadian bitterness and poverty.

A peasant would be invited to a farmhouse late at night where the scene would on the surface be one of a peaceful family evening, until he was led to an inner room, forced to his knees, and blindfolded. After a period of waiting in the dark, he would be asked to take the oath, which bound him to secrecy on pain of death and the destruction of his property. The oath would require him to be bound by the rules of the lodge, to assist his fellow members in every way and to place himself and his family at the service of the Hunters. Once he had sworn, he was asked what he wanted, to which the required answer was 'Light'. The blindfold was then removed and he saw himself surrounded by his fellow Frères Chasseurs with their guns and knives pointed at his heart, and a flaming torch in front of him, showing him what would happen to him and his property should he ever betray their secrets.

The organisation of the Frères Chasseurs was divided into five ranks. Each Chasseur answered to a raquette or snow-shoe, whose command consisted of some nine Chasseurs. The raquettes were organised into groups of six who answered in turn to a castor, and beaver, who commanded the equivalent of a company. Over the castor there was an eagle, whose command was roughly equivalent to a battalion of 500 men, and in command of the eagles were the grand eagles whose responsibility covered a district.

Mailhot was the grand eagle of the Montreal Lodge, and de Lorimier of the Two Mountains area to the north west of Montreal. But de Lorimier found a distinct lack of enthusiasm in an area that had received the full attention of the military during the previous winter, so he moved to the Beauharnois district where Eustache Masson was active. It was in the previously untouched Châteauguay area where the Frères Chasseurs enjoyed the greatest success under Dumouchelle, its eagle.[23,25]

Robert Nelson wrote from Plattsburg in the United States to J. B. Ryan, one of his castors, in July:

I know not when you may receive this, but as I have very little time hereafter, I avail myself this spare moment to convey to you our request, and send a few of the proclamations of the provisional government of Lower Canada which I am desirous you should distribute in your part of Canada to the best advantage.

According to agreement McKenzie, with a large force, and well provided for war, took up his march on Thursday evening last towards Upper Canada. On Friday morning his army was safely encamped near Gananoque about 18 miles below Kingston, and last evening a ship from Montreal came to hand saying he had taken Kingston. This news was confirmed by a despatch from Sir John Colborne to George Wool (US General) at Champlain this morning. On the first report of McKay's movements at Watertown all the spare troops possible were sent on towards Upper Canada, and this morning we learned that Sir John is on his way thither, having taken the largest number of regulars he could with him. We have arranged that Wool and Colborne and company are under the firm persuasion that we have secretly sent on our men and means to the assistance of McKay and this is confirmed by the apparent absence of our men and ammunition.

We are informed on this evening Wool will move west to guard the St Lawrence frontier, disregarding us, and that will much facilitate our entry into Lower Canada on Monday night and Tuesday morning. Our force is abundant for our purpose, so if you can possibly co-operate, our success will be of earlier attainment. I would advise you to make your way with all possible speed to Three Rivers, if you have men enough, when we shall by rapid movements join you after having recovered Montreal. If your force is insufficient for this first route, then make your way to St Hyacinthe, and thence to Sorel, where you may take up quarters until you receive instructions; if again your force is still less, move on with what you can muster to Missisquoi Bay, St John's and La Prairie. Collect all you can of firearms.

Papineau has abandoned us, and this through selfish and family motives regarding the seigniories, and inveterate love of other French bad laws. We can do well without him, and better than if we had him, a man only fit for words, but not for action.

We have the most positive assurance of a lively and cordial reception on our arrival. We have named you a Captain, but I do not send you the commission now, it is unnecessary.[C16]

Nothing came of these plans, and Nelson's intelligence was at fault, although the Patriote leadership continually deluded itself into believing what it wanted to believe.

In the meantime the authorities in both Upper and Lower Canada were concerned with the number of prisoners held in the gaols from the 1837 rebellions. In Upper Canada the trials for treason went on throughout the spring and summer of 1838, presided over by Chief Justice Robinson. Colonel Van Egmond never came to court, because he died in the Toronto gaol from an illness contracted as a result of the appalling prison conditions. Samuel Lount and Peter Matthews were tried and condemned to death. Mrs Lount managed to submit a petition to the Governor for clemency on behalf of her husband which had 5,000 signatures. By 1 March Sir Francis Head was replaced as Governor by Sir George Arthur, who had previously been Governor of British Honduras and for twelve years before that in charge of the convict settlement in Van Diemen's Land. The continuing incursions from the United States throughout the spring of 1838 had served to maintain the political temperature. While the Governor could see that tempers would never be cooled by too harsh a policy towards the rebels, there was the need to set an example and deal firmly with the ringleaders. Lount and Matthews were kept in prison in irons for four months and were then executed by hanging. Two others, Anderson and Montgomery, the tavern keeper, were also condemned to death but their sentences were commuted to transportation. Ninety-two prisoners in all were sentenced to transportation to Van Diemen's Land. 'We were all kept in jail on Toronto Street until June 8th,' wrote one prisoner, 'when they packed us off to Kingston on the steamboat. The mothers and wives of the rebels crowded around to see the last of us as they thought. I tell you it was hard parting from the old folks, who stood there on the wharf looking after the steamer until we were out of sight.' Some of the prisoners managed to escape while being held at Fort Henry in Kingston, and got away to safety in the United States.[2,6,7]

In Lower Canada the situation was more difficult. The pressure from the loyalists and from the Family Compact, as well as the military, was for harsh and exemplary measures. The local courts in Lower Canada, however, were reluctant to sentence. So the prisoners were not brought to trial, and as many were accused of crimes committed before martial law had been proclaimed, their lawyers applied for a writ of habeas corpus and demanded their release. The Commandant of the Montreal gaol, Lieutenant-Colonel Wetherall, was threatened with proceedings for contempt for refusing to release such prisoners on request. Lord Gosford had asked to be relieved in November 1837, and Sir John Colborne took over from him as temporary Governor of the Lower Province on 27 February 1838. A total of 515 prisoners were being held, of which 501 were in Montreal, and 5 in Quebec. By May, Sir John Colborne was writing to London to say: 'I find from the Attorney General that 326 prisoners accused of high treason have been liberated by my authority from the jail in Montreal; that there are 161 now confined, and that not less than 72 of these are supposed to have been among the principle promoters of the late revolt, although some of these were more actively engaged than others.'[C17] Sir John Colborne had the Habeas Corpus Act suspended for three months, and the fate of the remaining 161 prisoners was left to await the arrival of the new High Commissioner.[4,6,7,23]

The work of the officers on particular duty was now beginning to take effect. George Cathcart at St Hyacinthe wrote to his wife on 5 May 1838:

St Hyacinthe is a pretty village situated on a wide and rapid river. It is a very populous parish having in it nearly 10,000 souls of which there are not more than three or four who can speak English fluently, and most of them not a word. I was well received as soon as they found out who I was, and that I was not come to look after old offenders, but only to see into their present state of loyalty.

Monsieur Papineau is the uncle and guardian of Mr Desolles who is the seigneur and who lives here and has great influence. Almost all the people were more or less implicated.

I have made acquaintance with the curé, the magistrates and the Director of the College and also about half a dozen gentlemen of the place who live on their means and nothing else. I have a constant levée and get on fluently with them all, setting one party to tell tales of the other, and thus I am pretty well informed myself of all the secret history of my neighbours.

I have Lt Col Gascoigne at St Denis, Baron de Rottenburg at St Charles and Major Mackenzie Fraser at St Césaire and they all report to me, so that without a single soldier, we hold this district in pretty good check and the confidence shewn by sending us without troops does much more towards a permanent awe than any military restraint.

I have put on my uniform of an afternoon to ride out, but in the morning I walk about in my red boots for the village is very muddy. I chat with all the farmers of whom there is a great influx on both the two weekly market days. I have not called on either Mme Desolles nor Madame Papineau because they are, of course, in a very uncomfortable circumstance since Papineau is outlawed with £1,000 offered for his apprehension. They say he has gone to France.[CA3]

A few days later Cathcart wrote again:

I interceded for two state prisoners belonging to my seigneurie and my request was instantly granted and they were released. The men have been to call on me to thank me and I had the pleasure of witnessing the joy of the whole village at their unexpected return. Of course this has increased my influence which was my object and now no opportunity is lost of shewing their respect. This is satisfactory as having drawn my line at once and declared that I was not come to punish past offences but only to survey the present and do all the good in my power, they come to me with the utmost confidence. Since the Magistrates cannot act without me, I have constant opportunities of doing good for the poor people who deserve it, and of keeping the bad ones in order . . .[CA4]

I do not expect [he wrote to his father on 27 June] to leave here until the day after tomorrow, since on that day the usual militia registration is to go on. Many of the inhabitants object to parading under their Colonel who was an arch-rebel, and who used his authority last winter to induce them to go to St Charles and St Denis as rebels. A deputation came to me last Sunday to say they would rather pay the fine than serve under that Colonel. However I told them to appear at the muster and to consider it as an order from the Queen. I am to have an address presented to me by the County, but I shall not be sorry to wind up my affairs here and to take on a more military occupation.[CA5]

Before George Cathcart left St Hyacinthe, sixty-two of its leading citizens, including the colonel of the militia, the postmaster and the schoolmaster, handed him an address, which was read by the curé and dated 30 June.

We, the representatives of the people of St Hyacinthe, wish to say that during your stay with us, you have acted as a just man. During the political troubles, which unhappily disturbed us, you were desirous of being a peacemaker. You listened to all with impartiality and you were zealous in rendering Justice. All this deserves our lively appreciation. Nor do we forget the interest you exercised in favour of political prisoners who, thanks to you, were restored to the bosom of their families. We shall cherish the recollection of your benevolent actions and we hereto subscribe to it with gratitude.[CA6]

In Upper Canada the American incursions continued. On 29 May a party of Americans under the leadership of one Bill Johnston, disguised themselves as Indians and, shouting 'Remember the *Caroline*', boarded a Canadian civilian river steamer called the *Sir Robert Peel* at Walls Island near Ogdensburg. They robbed the passengers and seized their baggage and then set fire to the vessel, which was completely burnt out.[8,C19]

There were further troubles in June. On the 30th the Governor, Sir George Arthur, wrote:

We had just concluded a very successful campaign against the rebels and patriots on the Niagara frontier, when fresh work has opened out in the west. Today I have received report after report from Colonel Maitland informing me that these vagabonds are landing in considerable numbers, and what is worse, a number of rebels have also appeared in the London District most suddenly and well armed. Colonel Maitland, having applied for another regiment immediately, I have ordered the 34th to proceed to the London district tomorrow morning at daylight.[C18,C24]

The 24th Foot had one company at Lake Erie, but this new gathering of rebels near Niagara caused three more companies to march from Toronto to Niagara where they dispersed two encroachments from across the border. The first of about 150 men from across the Niagara River into the Short Hills under the leadership of a man called Moreau attacked a detachment of Volunteer cavalry – the Provincial Dragoons – in Pelham. The yeomanry resisted until the building in which they were sheltering caught fire, after which twenty-seven of them were captured. The second invasion was across the Detroit River. These three companies shortly to be reinforced by a squadron of cavalry from the newly arrived King's Dragoon Guards remained at Niagara. The 43rd Foot, together with a battery of artillery and a party of sappers and miners were moved from Montreal to Upper Canada on 30 June, reaching Kingston on 3 July. From there they advanced on Niagara to support the 24th Foot with the militia and Volunteers arriving there on 6 July.[2,10,22,C19]

Yet another incursion occurred in July when about fifty men crossed into the Upper Province from Palmer in the United States and attacked the remote settlements of Sarnia and Dear Creek on the St Clair river. They robbed and locked up several settlers and then retreated back to the United States. Also in July an officer of the militia, Carey, was murdered in the night by a band of men who came over from the United States and returned there.[C19]

The American Volunteers Sutherland and Theller, who had subsequently been captured after the affair at Point Pelée, were brought to Quebec in June together with eight other prisoners. When they were landed at the wharf they were escorted to the citadel by an officer and thirty men of the 2nd Battalion Grenadier Guards. On the way they were followed by jeering crowds, and needed their escort.[26]

The situation in both Upper and Lower Canada changed as more and more reinforcements started to arrive from Britain and from overseas. But the continued threat from across the American frontier was stirring up strong feelings. The Select Committee appointed to report on the state of the province said:

The civilised nations of Europe will learn, with astonishment, that it ceases to be a question, whether the 'Great Republic' of the United States of America boasting of the superiority of its Institutions over those of every other country, has the power of controlling its citizens within the limits essential to the maintenance of peace, and the honourable performance of treaties, solemnly entered into by it, with foreign powers. The occupation and conquest of Texas, in the south, and the assembling of an armed force on its Eastern frontier, openly recruited in its principal Cities and Towns, commanded by its citizens, and by them also supplied with arms, ammunition, clothing, money and provisions, and transported in the presence of, and unrestrained (if not encouraged) by its Magistrates and Public Officers, in steamboats and other vessels into the Province, and landed in it for the avowed purpose of overthrowing the Government and wresting the Colony from the Crown of Great Britain, sufficiently prove – that, if countries bordering on the United States desire to protect themselves from the inroads of freebooters, pirates, fugitive traitors and outlaws, they must look for security to their own fleets and armies, and not to the honourable forbearance of the American people, or the efficiency or moral influence of the Government.[C19]

These were strong words, but American action and official failure to restrain action had stirred up strong feelings.

5
Reinforcement

In Britain urgent steps were being taken to see that the promised reinforcements arrived as speedily as was practicable. The 2nd Battalion of the Grenadier Guards at Windsor and the 2nd Battalion of the Coldstream Guards in London were warned on 23 January 1838 to hold themselves in readiness for embarkation for Quebec, each battalion to be made up to 800 rank and file. On 16 February the Grenadiers were moved to London, and both battalions were brought up to strength by transfers from their 1st and 3rd battalions, the senior guardsmen with less than eighteen years' service being selected. On 22 March both battalions were inspected by Lord Hill, the Commander-in-Chief, who gave his 'best wishes for their welfare while employed abroad in the service of the country', and was sure that they 'would do honour to the high reputation of the Brigade of Guards'. The Grenadiers embarked at Portsmouth in the *Apollo* and *Inconstant* and sailed on 9 and 10 April. The Coldstream embarked on the *Edinburgh* and *Atholl* and sailed from Portsmouth on 17 April. All four ships arrived in the St Lawrence on 9 May, anchoring off Quebec that evening. On the 10th both battalions disembarked, the Grenadiers going to the Jesuit Barracks and the Coldstream to the Citadel.[26,27]

In the meantime the British Government had appointed the Earl of Durham as Governor General and High Commissioner for the whole of Canada. By an Act which reached Quebec in February and was proclaimed on 20 March, the Constitution of Lower Canada was suspended. Lord Durham arrived in Quebec on 29 May, and the Artillery and Brigade of Guards lined the streets, parading with their regimental colours. He was given far-reaching powers, with a brief to carry out an inquiry into all the problems facing both Upper and Lower

Canada, and to make recommendations for their solution.[2,4,23,26,27]

In Britain four regiments serving in Ireland had been ordered to Canada, two regiments of cavalry, the 1st King's Dragoon Guards and the 7th (Queen's Own) Hussars, and two battalions of infantry, the 23rd and 71st Foot. The King's Dragoon Guards needed a new commanding officer, as Sir George Teesdale was to retire, having commanded the regiment since 1815. Lord Cathcart, the father of Lieutenant-Colonel Cathcart, who was on a 'particular duty' at St Hyacinthe in Lower Canada, received a letter dated 4 May from his daughter-in-law, Georgiana, in London, saying:

I received a letter from Lord Fitzroy Somerset requesting to see me at the Horse Guards on a matter of importance to the interests of Colonel Cathcart. I therefore went yesterday and was received with great politeness and kindness. He told me that Lord Hill contemplated giving the command of the King's Dragoon Guards to George, and that he had thought it the best plan to enquire from me if George would like it, and if he is able to pay the difference between Cavalry and Infantry, £1,635. I answered that I was quite sure George would like it very much, that as to the money I did not know of any relation who was able or willing to purchase for him, and that he had not the money or any part of it ready, but I hoped we might raise it by mortgaging our house at Brighton for which we have paid £4,000. He then said the regiment is now at Cork, embarking for Canada, that it would be as well it should be known who is to command it, therefore it should be settled immediately. If Sir George Teesdale is impatient for his money, Lord Somerset would get Cox to advance it, and I am to let him know when my arrangements are completed.[CA7]

On 24 May George Cathcart wrote to his father: 'I saw a rumour about my having the King's Dragoon Guards. I do not wish it, but if it should happen, I must make the best of it.'[CA8] In a further letter of 7 June he wrote: 'Sir John [Colborne] asked if I had heard anything from the newspaper reports of the King's Dragoon Guards. I told him I had not. He said he hoped it might be true as he wished to see me in command of the cavalry out here.'[CA9]

In London, Georgiana Cathcart had received a gift of £635 from one relative and an interest-free loan of £1,000 from George Cathcart's brother. As a result, a commission dated 11 June 1838, signed Victoria Regina, 'appoints you [Lieutenant-Colonel Cathcart] to be Lieutenant-Colonel of her First Regiment of Dragoon Guards from 11th May 1838'.[CA10] On 27 June George Cathcart wrote to his father: 'As you may suppose, I am very much pleased at my appointment and very thankful to the kind friends who accomplished it, and I am quite sure it is one that will give you the greatest pleasure.'[CA11]

Meanwhile the King's Dragoon Guards left Cork on 30 March for Dublin, arriving there on the 31st and embarking six troops, on four transports, *Stentor*, *Maria*, *The Marquis of Huntley* and *Calcutta*, which sailed for Canada on 3, 4 and 5 May. Some dismounted men embarked in a steamboat, and returned to Cork where they transferred to a transport, the *Prince Regent*, which sailed on 12 May. Prior to embarkation the regiment was equipped with new carbines with percussion locks. One squadron of two troops of the King's Dragoon Guards remained in Britain and, together with one squadron of two troops of the 7th Hussars, proceeded to York, where the two squadrons formed a depot for both regiments.[28]

The 7th Hussars embarked four troops, totalling 336 men, on four transports, *Elizabeth*, *Vanilla*, *Arab*, and the dismounted men with the King's Dragoon Guards on *Prince Regent*. The 7th Hussars arrived at Montreal between 8 and 24 June, and the *Naval and Military Gazette* of 14 June read:

The arrival of a detachment of the 7th Hussars at Montreal occasioned considerable excitement in the city, and immense crowds were on the island wharf all day, witnessing the landing of the horses – a novel importation from England to Canada. Considering the length of the voyage, the horses looked well, and excited very general admiration. The men all wear moustaches, which makes them look formidable.[29,30]

The King's Dragoon Guards arrived at Quebec by 22 June and were ordered to proceed to Trois Rivières. Two troops of the 7th Hussars were sent to Chambly.[29] The men, and twenty horses per troop of the KDG which had come from Britain, went by steamboat from Quebec to Trois Rivières, but as the service establishment was fifty-four men and seven staff sergeants per troop with forty-five horses, arrangements had to be made to purchase the necessary horses to complete the establishment.[28] In March Lord FitzRoy Somerset had sent on ahead an officer and some rough-riders from the King's Dragoon Guards and 7th Hussars, together with the veterinary surgeon of the 7th Hussars, in order to purchase horses. They had gone in plain clothes from Liverpool via New York, and had been busy since their arrival.[C9] Cathcart went to look at his new command, and wrote to his father on 27 June:

I came over here yesterday to see the horses they have bought, and have seen for us as nice a lot of 70 horses as I ever saw. They have been well and carefully selected, and many hundreds rejected. The state has been sent to me in due form from the KDG's, by which I see we have 35 Officers' horses and 14 troop horses died on the voyage. We still want about 120 to complete.[CA11]

On 3 July the KDG were issued with swords of the new pattern and with new bearskins for their helmets, and on 7 June George Cathcart formally took over command of the regiment.[28]

The 23rd Foot received orders in March 1838 to prepare for foreign service. On 22 May six service companies under the command of Lieutenant-Colonel Ross embarked at Cork for Nova Scotia, where they landed on 13 June. Four depot companies were left in Ireland.[31] The 71st Foot embarked at Cork on 20 April in HMS *Malabar* and in spite of bad weather arrived at Quebec on 15 May, from where they marched to St John's and Kingston.[32]

The 11th Foot, who had been stationed in the Ionian Islands in the Mediterranean, were on passage from Gibraltar to Bermuda, and the 73rd Foot were at Gibraltar. Lord Hill wrote to Sir John Colborne on 9 January 1838 that

the 11th have been ordered to proceed to Bermuda, there to await the opportunity of being conveyed to Canada, and the detachment to complete those companies to 600 rank and file will shortly proceed from Cork to Bermuda in the 'Sovereign' transport. The service companies of the 73rd will be joined at Gibraltar by the detachments necessary to complete them to 600 rank and file in the 'Boadicea' transport, and will proceed to Canada as soon as the navigation of the St Lawrence is open.[C20]

The 93rd Foot from Ireland had reached Quebec in January 1838 and had been sent to Halifax as garrison, having had a very crowded passage on two freight ships.[33]

In addition to the troops sent to Upper and Lower Canada, those whom Sir Colin Campbell had so promptly despatched to the help of Sir John Colborne from New Brunswick and Nova Scotia had to be replaced. The 65th Foot were in the West Indies, and were embarked at Barbados on HMS *Cornwallis* for Canada on 7 December 1837, landing at Halifax on 2 January 1838. On 8 January four companies were sent on to St John's and Fredericton, where the whole regiment was concentrated in June.[34] In due course the 11th Foot also arrived in New Brunswick from their long journey via Bermuda. In December 1838 Lord Glenelg informed Sir John Colborne:

In order to replace the regiments withdrawn from Sir Colin Campbell's command, the 36th Regiment was, in August last, ordered to proceed to Halifax, where it will probably have already arrived. Orders have since been issued for the conveyance to the same place of two additional regiments, the 37th and the 69th, from the West Indies; the former from Jamaica, the latter from the Windward and Leeward Islands. And if, as is probable, the officer in command of Her Majesty's troops in Jamaica should be able to spare yet another regiment, beside the 37th, from that station, the Admiral commanding in the West Indies has been instructed to provide the means for conveying this additional regiment to Halifax. All these regiments will be made up to 100 men in each company for which purpose additional men from the depots of the 37th and 69th Regiments to the amount of about 280 rank and file will proceed immediately from Cork to Halifax in Her Majesty's Ship 'Inconstant'. There will thus be three, and probably four, additional regiments in Nova Scotia at an early date, a force which will, I trust, be sufficient to answer any demands which you may be compelled to make on Sir Colin Campbell, and at the same time to provide for the security of that and the neighbouring provinces.[C21]

The provision of all these additional troops and the bringing up to strength of the battalions already in Canada had put a severe strain on British military resources, for an extra 8,000 men had had to be found. Parliament was told that this had been accomplished without interfering with reliefs, but this was not true. The 15th Foot had been due to return to Britain in 1837, and had to be held in Canada. In addition the 71st Foot had only left Canada in 1834, and were now ordered back again. Some of the additional men required to bring battalions up to strength so taxed the resources of the depots that 100 men from at least one other regiment had to be drafted to make up the deficiences.[20]

On 5 July George Cathcart was writing to his father:

I received orders to take command of my regiment, and came into Montreal. I found that from some alarm in the Upper Province, Sir John Colborne had decided to send a Squadron [of the King's Dragoon Guards] to Niagara. The first cavalry ever up there. I went down in a steamboat, and in two hours' time I had my Squadron on board. I returned with them to Montreal where we arrived at 7 am. By 9 am the mounted men (for we had only 40 horses) were on their march to Lachine, about 9 miles, where they embarked, and so on by the St Lawrence. The dismounted men and the heavy baggage are gone by the Rideau Canal. I have the Riding Master [Lt Hammersley] and the Veterinary Surgeon already in Upper Canada to buy horses for the remaining 48 dismounted men.

The squadron was made up of A and E Troops, commanded by Captain Martin. As Cathcart commented, 'It will be something new on the landscape of Niagara to see a heavy dragoon in the foreground.'[28,CA12,CA13]

On 8 July he was writing:

It is with equal pride and pleasure that I find myself most unexpectedly appointed to the command of this splendid regiment. We have 70 very good horses here, bought chiefly in the States, and many of them will soon be fit for duty as they have been ridden and are naturally of a very tractable sort. As soon as I have another

Squadron ready should Sir John call for it in the Upper Province, I hope to go also. At present I have a good deal to do to put matters of interior economy in the proper equilibrium again, out of which they have been a little shook by the circumstances of their departure [from Ireland] and frequent changes of command. But I never had more willing or better disposed people to deal with in all ranks from the officer to the private. We are getting horses fast enough and very good and those brought out from England are splendid.[CA13]

On 15 August he wrote to his aunt, 'I have a remarkably nice corps of officers, among them Mr Turner, brother to Lord Winchelsea's son-in-law, a very gentlemanlike, as well as ornamental officer.'[CA20]

These matters of interior economy covered every aspect of regimental life, for George Cathcart was an extremely energetic and efficient officer and he was taking over a regiment whose previous commanding officer had held his office for twenty-three years. In a cavalry regiment his first concern was with the horses and standard of horsemanship. He told his father in a letter of 25 July:

I am getting on well with my new horses. I put them all into the ranks as soon as possible, taking care to put the best riders on the worst broke nags, and every morning from 5 am to 7 am they have been at Adjutant's drill. My own horse is a good one, clever, correct and good-tempered. I am always there myself, and in three weeks of this steady work we have brought them to do everything essential for service, or to be found in the book, even to cantering in line. Threes-about was difficult at first, but this may always be dispensed with by wheeling about instead. They stand still well, which is no easy part of the lesson at first, and they now stand the sword exercises like old ones. Yesterday I had my first field day with the officers. I practice much of what is now called advancing 'by single files from the right of threes', and which used to be called from 'the right of threes to the front-file'. This is most essential in this country, when going through stumps of trees.[CA14]

A fortnight later he was writing:

We are in cantonments here, with 2 Squadrons now complete in horses, and I may say well-mounted. They are not equal to English horses in power and vigour, but their appearance, their tempers, and their action is certainly superior to the average rate of English troop horse. I must say I think we are better mounted than any foreign cavalry I ever saw, except those who had Hungarian or the better sort of Polish horses, and we have seen much worse mounted cavalry do great things with Murat at their head. I work here on an excellent piece of ground. Three Squadrons rank entire. The men ride well, and by keeping them to an hour's drill every morning, and by putting every horse into the ranks at once without asking questions, and requiring everything to be done as usual. My invaluable Adjutant, Captain R Hollis, and I, together, have got them in one month as steady and fit for service as you would wish to see. For instance, we march past according to all the book, including cantering past in column of troops. We advance in line and gallop (not charge) and do all the things at any pace. Besides that we do anything we will among old dead stumps of trees, broken ground by 'single files from the right of threes'. In this formation we can manoeuvre by Squadrons thrown forward or back a flank. I have now come to only 3 field days and 3 watering orders a week to let the nags get fat.[CA15]

On 28 August Major-General Clitheroe, the general officer sent out by London ahead of the reinforcements, inspected the King's Dragoon Guards. The regimental entry reads, 'The four troops at Headquarters [Trois Rivières] were inspected by Major-General Clitheroe who expressed himself satisfied with the appearance and conduct of the Regiment, and the admirable description of horses, which had been procured, and already rendered fit for service.'[28]

Canada had not previously been a station for British regular cavalry, and a number of problems arose. The Military Secretary at Quebec wrote on 9 July inquiring 'what sum per horse, daily, will in your opinion be sufficient remuneration for shoeing, and for a supply of Veterinary stores, in addition to the halfpenny per diem for each horse authorised to be charged in the public accounts'. Lieutenant-Colonel Whyte of the 7th Hussars made out a careful comparison between British and Canadian costs, and Cathcart replied that

a farrier must be much overpaid in England at a penny a day, or else the same duty cannot be properly done for the same money in this country (where coal and good iron are nearly double the price) without loss. And although I do not wish farriers to make money, for that leads to ruin by drunkenness, I should be sorry to see them thrown into debt and difficulty by requiring them to attempt an impossibility. A penny could certainly be too little as it would limit his means to less than two thirds of the usual price charged in this country.[CA16,CA17,CA18]

The squadron of the King's Dragoon Guards at Niagara was faced at once with one of the perennial problems which beset all British troops in Canada at that date. The Regimental Record relates how, 'the detachment at Niagara obtained great credit immediately after its arrival at that station from the exemplary conduct of some of the men in detecting and bringing to justice persons who attempted to tamper with them, and induce them to desert, which called forth a highly complimentary District Order from Major-General Sir George Arthur'.[28]

The 15th Foot, one of the longest serving regiments in Lower Canada, between June 1837 and a year later had suffered fourteen desertions, eight deaths and eleven men sentenced to transportation, and the 24th Foot in Upper Canada had had forty-seven men desert over the same period. The 85th Foot reported its strength weakened by constant desertion; those caught attempting desertion were awarded savage punishments, transportation for life and sentences of fourteen years' imprisonment being quite usual for such an offence. In spite of the penalties many soldiers were still undeterred. The 71st Foot, who were back in Canada for a second time after only a brief spell in Britain, were subjected to attempts by Americans to persuade men to come over to the American side of the frontier. The 71st countered this by sending parties of senior NCOs across the border in civilian clothes to contact the deserters. As many of these men had been tricked into working in the lead mines under conditions of near-slavery, they were only too glad to return to duty.[10,18,24,32]

Much of the equipment with which the troops had been sent out from England was completely unsuited to a Canadian winter. Cathcart was most concerned to ensure that his men should be adequately equipped to face the rigours of the climate. He wrote to the Horse Guards in London to secure the issue of warm overcoats which would be of sufficient length for mounted men, and approval for fur caps to be made locally which would also incorporate ear flaps for extra warmth. He also invented and had made locally 'pockets for the copper caps [needed for the newly issued percussion carbines]. They are of buff leather and worn on the belt to the right of the [regimental waist] plate. They are made as like a waistcoat pocket as possible for convenience, and look well.'[CA15]

Lord FitzRoy Somerset replied from the Horse Guards:

I am gratified to hear that you are pleased with your new command. I am sure that I consider it fortunate that Lord Hill was enabled to place the King's Dragoon Guards in the hands of an officer of your zeal, energy and experience, and I feel quite confident that you will bring the Regiment to the highest possible state of efficiency. MacDonald has arranged your pea-jacket in a most satisfactory manner and assures me that the skirts will reach the knee. He is also prepared to approve of your carbine drill and your cape case. Please let me know how your American horses come on, as they make progress in training, and keep me informed of anything that may occur of any interesting nature within your observation.[CA19]

The King's Dragoon Guards were now to be equipped for winter wear with a double breasted pea-jacket in regimental style, and over that a full-length overcoat with regimental brass shoulderscales held in by a white belt with percussion cap pouch, white pouch belt across the shoulder, knee boots, fur gauntlets, fur cap with ear flaps, and cloak folded across the saddle in a cape case. The infantry were making similar arrangements. Pictures of the Grenadier Guards, drawn at the time, show a fur cover with a flap to cover neck and ears to go over the bell-shaped shako, and fur leggings tied around the leg from below the knee so far as to cover the moccasins.

Lord Durham, the new High Commissioner, was faced with a difficult dilemma upon his arrival over how to deal with the prisoners who thronged the gaols awaiting trial. He could not try them by court martial; if they were tried by the civil courts it was certain that French juries would acquit them and English juries would condemn them irrespective of any evidence. So, on 28 June, he issued an ordinance granting a complete amnesty to all arrested for their part in the rebellion, with the exception of eight ringleaders. These eight men, Dr Wolfred Nelson, R. Bouchette, S. Marchessault, B. Viger, Dr L. Masson, H. Gauvin, T. Goddu and R. Desrivières, had pleaded guilty to high treason 'thereby to avoid the necessity of a trial and thus to give tranquillity to the Country'. They were sentenced to exile in Bermuda, and were taken in chains to the steamboat *Canada* under an escort of the 71st Foot. About a dozen others, who had fled to the United States, including Papineau, Robert Nelson, Duvernay, Cartier, Storrow Brown, Coté, O'Callaghan and Canon Chartier, were found guilty of high treason and were sentenced to death should they ever try to return to Canada. Both French- and English-speaking Canadians welcomed Durham's act as one of clemency. Unfortunately it was not the end of the story, for Lord Melbourne in London announced that the Queen had refused to endorse this action, declaring it illegal and arbitrary. When this news reached Canada it was to induce Lord Durham to resign, and brought back to Canada in October the eight exiled prisoners.[2,4,6,20,23,25,26,27]

Meanwhile, on 7 July, Lord Durham left Quebec for a tour of Upper Canada and was joined on the 13th at Queenston by Sir John Colborne, and at Niagara Falls by the Governor of Upper Canada, Sir George Arthur. After visiting Buffalo, Lord Durham and Sir John Colborne returned to Niagara where they held an inspection of the troops stationed there in order to demonstrate to their neighbours in the United States the strength of the British forces.[21]

On parade were the squadron of the King's Dragoon Guards under Captain Martin, the whole of the 43rd Foot, two companies of the 24th Foot, a battery of Artillery and the Niagara Lancers, a volunteer cavalry unit that had proved itself to be very efficient.

Old Niagara probably never did, and never will again, see such a gathering of cocked hats and radiant uniforms as on this occasion, when His Excellency was met by Sir John Colborne and Sir George Arthur with their respective staffs. The Governor General adopted the soothing system and was most liberal in his hospitalities. Willing, perhaps, first to astonish, and afterwards to mollify the Yankees, he issued public notices of a review on 17th July, and cards for two hundred persons to dinner in the evening. An immense concourse, chiefly Americans, attended; the ground was kept by two companies of the 24th Regiment and a troop of Her Majesty's Niagara Lancers.

The 43rd Foot and the squadron of the KDG then held a field day with plentiful use of blank cartridge, and in the evening there was a banquet.[21,22]

In spite of an outward appearance of tranquillity, the troops were constantly called upon to assist the civil power. On 11 July the Coldstream Guards in Quebec published an order praising the excellent conduct of a number of guardsmen who had helped a superintendent of police: 'But for them, two prisoners would have escaped, and he would have received a beating from the crowd.'

In August, on a ruling from London, Sir John Colborne was ordered to give up his command. George Cathcart visited Sir John on 22 August, and wrote:

The Colonial Office has made such a hash between the civil and military commands and responsibilities, and has established such a jumble between Sir George Arthur's civil governorship and the Major Generalship of a District, who is the junior of all, yet superior in the one capacity, and inferior in the other to the Commander of the Forces, but with Lord Durham claiming superiority over the whole. The result is that Sir John, a man of experience in this country and acknowledged to be one of the best officers of his standing in the Army, must give up his command to please the Colonial Office, and thus throw the military matters of these colonies into utter helplessness and confusion.[CA21]

Events were to overtake this predicament, when Lord Durham's decision to resign made it imperative that Sir John Colborne remain and be put in charge of both Government and the military forces.[4]

The activities of the Frères Chasseurs were now becoming more obvious, loyalists were again being threatened and started to move into the towns. Sir John Colborne began to move his forces so that they would be placed to the best advantage in case of trouble. On 30 October two companies of the Grenadier Guards were moved from Quebec to Trois Rivières. In August the 24th Foot had been moved back from Upper Canada to Montreal. In early October the 11th Foot and 65th Foot, who were newly arrived in New Brunswick, were ordered to move to Quebec, arriving there in late November and early December. Also in early October the King's Dragoon Guards were ordered to prepare to move from Trois Rivières to Chambly on the Richelieu river. Before the regiment left it received from 'the clergy, magistrates and inhabitants generally of the town of Trois Rivières' on the occasion of 'the departure of Her Majesty's Regiment the First or King's Dragoon Guards', a testimonial 'to make their sincere and grateful acknowledgements of their exemplary good conduct and excellent discipline during their sojourn in this garrison. The best wishes of the citizens for their future welfare will ever attend them.'CA22

To this Cathcart replied:

Gentlemen, I am expressing the sentiments of all the officers of the King's Dragoon Guards, as well as my own, in assuring you that we consider ourselves very fortunate in having been quartered this summer at Trois Rivières in your society. We leave you with regret, and with our best wishes for your welfare and prosperity. I will not fail to communicate to the Regiment the honour you have done to us by this address, and it will be very gratifying to them, as it is to myself, to learn that we have merited your esteem.CA24

On 16 October the two squadrons and headquarters of the King's Dragoon Guards left Trois Rivières at daybreak, embarking on a steamer which had two vessels in tow. The trip down river to Sorel was a short one, and the regiment had landed by 3 pm. At Sorel they marched past Sir John Colborne in marching order, complete with forage nets, and then covered the twelve miles to St Ours, where they halted for the night and bivouacked. On the 17th they set out for St Charles at daybreak and on arrival bivouacked for a second night. Early on the 18th, by 8 am, they had crossed to the other bank of the Richelieu river with all their horses and baggage by means of five ferry boats. Cathcart had arranged for the heavy baggage to come to Chambly all the way in *bateaux*, and the marching column had only one light cart for each of the four troops in order to carry the essential camp kettles, picket ropes and other equipment needed for the bivouac. It was Cathcart's idea for the regiment to march to Chambly, rather than be transported by river from Trois Rivières, 'as it will make a salutary sensation in the French districts which were the scene of last year's insurrection'. He was also concerned about supplies: 'The Quarter Master's department here is not so good as it should be, but we shall get on very well for this march, as I have carte blanche to arrange matters with a commissary for all our "besoins".' They arrived at the new Chambly barracks, which had been built for them, by 1 pm. There they relieved the one squadron of the 7th Hussars, which had been stationed at Chambly until then, and settled down with the infantry garrison which comprised the 15th Foot.[28,CA23]

George Cathcart had managed to bring out to Canada his wife and three small girls.

I have secured a very nice house [at Chambly] close to the barracks, in case of any alarms and excursions this winter, which are not impossible, Georgiana and the children can be securely sheltered there till the storm blows over . . .

My regiment is now, I believe, in good service order. I have well practised them to all essential points, for marches and field duties both mounted and dismounted, and I shall be proud to show them to an old and good practical soldier like Sir John. I am well mounted now. I have a clever little black horse, which I bought when I first came out, and another large black charger, which I was allowed to select out of the Regiment at troop horse price, and two bays – good to ride – but chiefly for Georgiana's carriage which will go with one or a pair.[CA23]

The King's Dragoon Guards arrived at Chambly on 18 October, and at 1 am the next morning a fire broke out in the middle of the officers' quarters of the 15th Foot. These quarters consisted of a very old single-storied range of long wooden buildings. The wood was as dry as tinder and the whole range was burnt to the ground within thirty minutes. The fire started in the porch of the quarters of two senior ensigns of the 15th Foot, Walter Carey and William Roe. Carey managed to get clear, but then dashed back into the blaze to rescue some of his belongings and became engulfed in the flames. Roe was rescued, apparently with few burns, and walked half a mile to the hospital without any help, but he died in hospital the following day.

The new barracks built for the King's Dragoon Guards was adjacent to that of the 15th Foot. Luckily the wind was in a direction which carried the flames away from their buildings; with the regiment's horses stabled there, the loss could have been severe. The men of the KDG promptly turned out and helped to rescue several of the 15th from the blaze, and then managed to save some of their property.[18,28]

Major-General Clitheroe reported the disaster to Sir John Colborne on 19 October:

Lieutenant Hammersley KDG has just brought me the report from Lieutenant Colonel Cathcart. I cannot express to Your Excellency my deep regret at the misfortune which has occurred. The fire, I am informed, was accidental. It broke out in the very middle of the officers' barracks, the cause not yet ascertained. Lieutenant Hammersley, however, distinctly states that he has no reason to suppose it was the act of an incendiary, nor has any suspicious person been seen about the barracks. The range of officers barracks is entirely destroyed. Ensign Carey was brought out, but returned to search for something, saying he would rather lose his life than have it burnt. All their effects and baggage is also destroyed. I have ordered Captain Foster to proceed to Chambly and shall go there myself, if possible today, in order to make the best arrangements for the officers.

The only suspicious circumstances is that the fire was known at Longueuil before Lieutenant Hammersley arrived there, which he did on horseback with all possible speed. They said a man had told them who had come from Chambly. However the fire must have been seen at a considerable distance.[C22]

Lord Durham had decided to leave Canada and was preparing to sail at the end of October. Sir John Colborne, instead of being superseded, now found himself being asked to take over both the government of the two provinces and command of the forces. As George Cathcart commented: 'Lord Durham's return makes a considerable sensation here, but it is an ill wind that blows no good, and Sir John being both Governor and Commander in Chief gives great strength and vigour to our military circumstances.'[CA23]

Intelligence about the Frères Chasseurs and the preparations of the Patriote leaders in the United States for a second rebellion was confusing and difficult to interpret, but it was becoming obvious that something was afoot, and that more trouble could be expected at any time. What was not clear was exactly where or when the Patriotes would strike. The oaths of secrecy which bound the members of the Chasseur lodges maintained the security of the rebel plans. Such information as did come to hand was contradictory, rumours were rife, and the countryside grew more and more unsettled. Intelligence from the United States indicated that the Patriote preparations were almost complete. A note to Sir John Colborne in Quebec dated 18 October warned him that

the information we have recently received from all parts of the United States render the possibility of hostilities during the ensuing winter so great that it has become a serious question for the Lord Durham, whether he can with honour to himself, follow out his declared intention of leaving the province immediately.[C23]

The regimental diary of the King's Dragoon Guards commented:

So secret were the plans of the rebels, so contradictory the information, and the unsettled state of things occasioned by the sudden determination of the Earl of Durham to abandon the Government at this juncture, no measures had been taken to prevent the projects of the disaffected.[28]

Feelings among the loyalist population were running high at what they considered to be the weakness of the Government in

London, and at the way in which Lord Durham had been dealt with over the issue of the prisoners. His initial leniency combined with London's rejection and reversal of his actions served to upset the loyalists and to raise the hopes and expectations of the disaffected. The loyalists' move out of the countryside into the towns increased.[2,4,26,27]

The officers of the Grenadier and Coldstream Guards in Quebec had received much personal kindness from Lord Durham, and on 25 October they entertained him to dinner prior to his departure. At this dinner Sir James Macdonell, commanding the Brigade of Guards and a member of the Special Council, made a speech praising Lord Durham and supporting his policies. This raised some criticism on the grounds that it was interpreted by some to be political interference by a soldier, and that it criticised the actions of the London authorities, and indirectly the Queen, in that he suggested that the welfare of Canada was being sacrificed on the altar of English party politics.[26,27]

On 1 November 1838, Lord Durham sailed from Quebec for England. On 3 November the Patriotes struck.

6

Rebellion Again

At the beginning of November 1838, the British regular garrison in Lower Canada consisted of the Grenadier and Coldstream Guards in Quebec. The 66th Regiment was at Sorel, with the garrison of Chambly made up of headquarters and two squadrons of the King's Dragoon Guards, together with the 15th Foot. Stationed in Montreal were the 7th Hussars, 1st Foot, 24th Foot, 71st Foot (who had one company of the 93rd attached to them), and the 73rd Foot. The 11th and 65th Foot were stationed at Fredericton in New Brunswick, and 23rd Foot remained as the garrison of Nova Scotia.

In Upper Canada the 43rd Foot, together with one squadron of the King's Dragoon Guards, were at Niagara. The 32nd and 34th Foot were at Amherstburg, the 83rd at Kingston, the 93rd, less one company at Montreal with the 71st, were in Toronto, and the 85th were in the Upper Province. The military dispositions in both provinces covered the danger points with regular troops, many of whom were soldiers who knew the country and were now familiar with winter campaigning in Canada.

In addition there were the Canadian Militia and Volunteer forces ready to support the regulars. These were of varied quality. In Lower Canada the French Canadian Militia could not be relied upon. In both Upper and Lower Canada the Volunteer units depended largely upon the quality of their officers. The Volunteer Cavalry were of a high standard, especially the Royal Montreal Cavalry, the Queen's Light Dragoons, and the Niagara Lancers.

There was one body of loyal support which was to play a decisive role in the troubles that were developing. The 1st Glengarry Fencible Regiment of Highlanders had served in

Ireland during the Rebellion of 1798. They had been employed there because they were Roman Catholics, and their chaplain, Alexander Macdonnell, claimed that they 'contributed in no small degree to repress the rapacity and cruelty of the [British] soldiers and to bring back the deluded [Irish] people to a sense of their duty to the laws'. After this, in 1804, many of the Glengarries emigrated with their chaplain to Upper Canada and settled in the eastern area of Upper Canada adjacent to the French-speaking areas of western Lower Canada. Because of their proven moderation, their loyalty to the Crown and their Roman Catholic faith, Sir John Colborne wanted to use them in 1837, but not without first gaining the consent of Sir Francis Head, at that time Lieutenant Governor. This did not material-ise, in spite of Colborne's pleas and an offer to serve from each of the colonels of the four Glengarry Volunteer regiments. However, immediately following the 1837 rebellion Sir John Colborne raised two battalions of Glengarries, who helped to garrison Lower Canada from February to July 1838, when the arrival of the regular reinforcements from Britain no longer made their presence so necessary. Sir James Macdonell, who commanded the Brigade of Guards in Quebec, was the brother of the chief of Clan Glengarry, and on arrival in Canada he visited his fellow clansmen in the Upper Province, reviewing the Glengarry Highlanders and speaking to them in their native Gaelic. Here was a reinforcement whose natural loyalty to the Crown was reinforced by the bonds of kinship and Scottish clan loyalties. Their services were soon to be called upon.[23,33]

Lieutenant-Colonel Taylor, the officer 'on particular duty' at St John's, learnt that a rising by the Patriotes was imminent in the Lower Province, and on 2 November wrote to Sir John Colborne:

A person named Potter has deposed that a man named La Berge told him that the inhabitants of St Charles and the neighbourhood are collecting arms and concealing them, with the object of attacking Chambly. Coté and Gagnon have quitted Champlain [in the USA], and a company of artillery of the USA is to be stationed there.[C25]

On 2 November George Cathcart at Chambly also received

similar intelligence of preparations for an attack on his command, and of a general uprising on the following day. He considered the situation so serious that he handed over temporary command to Lieutenant-Colonel Lord Charles Wellesley, the younger son of the Duke of Wellington, who commanded the 15th Foot, also at Chambly. He then rode the twelve miles to Montreal to make a personal report to Major-General Clitheroe and to urge him to reinforce Colonel Taylor at St John's, as the only bridge over the Richelieu river in the seventy-five miles between the frontier and the St Lawrence was at St John's.[28] Major-General Clitheroe took immediate action and despatched the 73rd Foot from Montreal, ordering them to cross the St Lawrence River on the 3rd and to march to St John's at once.

In the meantime Lieutenant-Colonel Taylor, urged by the magistrates at St John's, decided to arrest the leaders of the Patriotes before they could take action. He rode to Chambly to get backing from Lieutenant-Colonel Cathcart, who was the senior officer in the area, and to secure detachments from the King's Dragoon Guards and 15th Foot in order to effect the arrests on the requisition of the magistrates. Wellesley gave him twelve men of the King's Dragoon Guards, commanded by Captain G. D. Scott. They rode to the inn at St John's, where the Patriote leaders were thought to be meeting, but on arrival were told by the magistrates to await some infantry from the barracks at St John's itself. By the time the force was ready, the Patriote leaders had fled. The KDG detachment then rode on six miles to Pointe-à-la-Meule to raid the home of Gagnon, but found only his family and arrested his twelve-year-old son. As the KDG Regimental Diary records, 'This was the first measure taken in the second insurrection.'[28,C26]

Taylor's action was the cause of some friction between him and George Cathcart. On his return to Chambly Cathcart sent a report to Major-General Clitheroe written at 11 pm on 3 November:

I found on my arrival here that Colonel Taylor had made a requisition for an officer's party to go to St John's last night to make

109

some arrests. Lord Charles [Wellesley] sent Captain Scott and 12 men. They arrived at St John's by 10 pm, and after an hour's rest went to execute the arrests with a magistrate, but on arriving at the place were ordered to wait until the arrival of the infantry. They were kept twelve hours altogether on horseback. Gagnon had escaped, but Captain Scott succeeded in intimidating his son to produce three muskets and some ammunition. Although the KDG are ready and able to do good service, they are not able to do this hack or orderly duty without great expense to the public, and the entire destruction of the regiment, which is probably intended for other services.[CA25]

Cathcart was determined to preserve his regiment for concentrated action and not have small detachments misused by officers with no experience of handling mounted troops, nor to have his strength frittered away by constant demands for the services of odd men. He continued: 'We have one volunteer orderly here, by whom I send this [letter]. Lieutenant-Colonel Williams has been pleased to require his removal. If this is granted, and that the KDG are to be their letter party, we must prepare ourselves for that day.'[CA25]

Efficient precautions had been taken to ensure the defence of Chambly, and the area around. Cathcart wrote to his father:

The rebellion broke out here on 3rd November. I am in command at Chambly with my two Squadrons and the 15th Foot. I have also charge of the Richelieu downwards with 66th Foot. We were to have been attacked at 4 am on the morning of the 4th. We were all ready. I had arranged with Lord Charles Wellesley, who commands the 15th, to occupy with picquets [the outlying ground around the camp] to observe the canal, and a slight picquet at the Church, keeping four companies in reserve at the infantry barracks. Of my two Squadrons, one was saddled and ready to turn out mounted, in order to form an ambush behind the fort. The common was to be purposely neglected and left the weak point for it was known that the rebels, who had three guns and expected to muster upwards of 1,000 men, would attack on that side in hope of surprising the fort (an old French building) to hoist the flag of liberty upon it. Had they attempted this, my Squadron would have sallied out at a gallop along the riverside by threes right, wheeled up and scoured the common on ground most favourable to us.

They [the Patriotes] assembled on the night of the 3rd at a cluster of farm houses about 6 miles off; but it appears only they mustered about five or six hundred. I heard of this from the priest at 11.30 am on 4th.[CA26]

The priest also told him that five parishes in all had been affected, and that the gathering had taken place in the parish of Chambly at the houses of two farmers, called Berseleaux.[28] There was also information that 'there is an intended attack upon Sorel from St Charles to burn it, and then we are to be attacked here'.[CA26] A plan to set fire to St John's, with the attack on Chambly, was to be the signal for the insurrection. Robert Nelson was known to be at Napierville with a large force of Patriotes, with the hope of opening up the roads to the American frontier and receiving supplies and volunteers from the USA.

Martial law had not yet been proclaimed, so Cathcart 'got a warrant and started with one Squadron [of the KDG] supported by Lord Charles with two companies [of the 15th Foot], but I trotted on, and by one o'clock had completely surrounded the premises where the meeting was held with 80 loaded carbines, sprung and ready. The meeting had adjourned before we got there and we only got some arms and a few prisoners.'[CA26] The two companies of the 15th Foot were to make their best speed and to act either as a reserve, or in case the rebels were in a position where cavalry could not reach them.[28]

Cathcart reported that 'the terror of our brass helmets was great, and the district never recovered from it, although they fortified a camp in a woody mountain about 3 miles further back' at Boucherville.[CA26] Cathcart's official report stated:

About 11 o'clock on 4th November I received information that I could not doubt that, on the preceding night, a large body of rebels of this and adjacent parishes with arms had assembled and marched as far as a bridge on the road towards La Prairie. At that bridge they were disappointed of being met by Nelson, who was to come from St John's, so they returned to the house of one Francois Berselaux.[CA27]

It later transpired that Major-General Clitheroe's prompt action in sending the 73rd Foot to St John's had foiled Robert

Nelson's plan to attack and set fire to that town. The Patriotes at Chambly had been informed of the change of plan by a courier who reached them at 4 am on the 4th. Dr Allard of Beloeil was indeed tired of waiting for Nelson and went off to find out what was happening. He returned to tell the Patriotes: 'Gentlemen, we have all been taken in by Dr Nelson. He has betrayed us, so let us go home until further notice.'[4] So they either dispersed to their homes or made off with their arms into the Boucherville mountains.[28]

Cathcart's report continues:

I obtained, on my own deposition so as not to compromise my informant, a warrant against the said Francois Berselaux. I started with one Squadron of the KDG, and as the rebels were reported to be numerous and armed, moved two companies of the 15th as far as Booth's Bridge to support me. On arrival and surrounding the premises we caught one 'habitant' who attempted to escape and found arms and ammunition.[C27]

The arms and ammunition only amounted to a fowling piece, a rifle, a pistol and a sword, with 95 rounds of ball cartridge and 160 flints.[C28] But it was felt that 'the sensation caused by the search will have a good effect, but the duty as a frequent practice would be harrassing and lose its effect without adequate advantage. I do not intend to repeat it without urgent cause.'[C27]

These prompt measures had had the effect of discouraging the Patriotes. Cathcart commented, 'Their plans seem already to have got into confusion, and I cannot find that they have any formidable leaders or men of note.'[C28]

Martial law was proclaimed on Sunday 4 November by Sir John Colborne as soon as he got back to Montreal from Quebec, where 'he had just been sworn in on the occasion of our deliverance from Lord Durham, who had sailed'.[CA26] Martial law gave all field officers the powers of a justice of the peace for the district of Montreal. Armed with these powers Cathcart 'made frequent expeditions with my brass helmets, and with the 15th to arrest, and to seize arms, and to keep up the pressure. I had no orders for all this for Sir John [Colborne] gives me great discretionary latitude and approves and supports me always.'[CA26] Detachments scoured the countryside searching for the haunts of the ringleaders, making arrests and committing the prisoners to Montreal Gaol on charges of high treason.[15] A party of Patriotes gathered to attack La Prairie under Lefebvre, a shopkeeper. On the way they attacked the houses of two English-speakers, took some prisoners and killed one person. But they were warned that La Prairie was garrisoned by a strong patrol and armed with a cannon. This was a detachment of twenty troopers of the 7th Hussars, commanded by Lieutenant James, who chased the Patriotes and had two inconclusive brushes with parties of rebels, both sides firing at each other without effect.[C31] Another party led by Narbonne met a patrol of the King's Dragoon Guards and fled. Those Patriotes who did not go home drifted towards Napierville.[4]

As soon as the second insurrection broke out, Sir Colin Campbell in New Brunswick took steps to support Sir John Colborne. In a letter dated 7 November 1838, Sir Colin writes: 'My letter informs you of the directions which I have given to reinforce you. Sir John Harvey is preparing the two regiments, the 11th and the 65th, and he will put them in motion when all necessary arrangements are made and the weather permits.'[C29] The British Government in London was equally supportive. Lord Glenelg wrote: 'I have received your Despatches about the breaking out of the insurrection in the country bordering on the Richelieu, the proclamation of Martial Law in the district of Montreal and the entire dispersion of the insurgents. I fully approve of the measures you have taken.'[C21,C30]

The lodges of the Frères Chasseurs were not confined to St Charles and the Chambly area. Mailhot, now a general, reached St Hyacinthe on 2 November, where he was to take command of the Chasseurs from there and the neighbouring parishes, and then to seize Sorel – where however the 66th Foot were ready and waiting. The Patriotes' organisation was sadly lacking, some arms were available for distribution, others were figments of the Patriotes' hopes and imagination, there was little order and less coordination; some habitants drifted away. Eventually Mailhot led his troops to Boucherville and established a camp with the Chambly men on Mont Montarville.

The main gathering point, which was to become Patriote headquarters, was at Napierville. Dr Coté and Gagnon, who had eluded Cathcart's search, arrived there on 2 or 3 November. On 4 November Robert Nelson arrived with some 250 muskets supplied to him by American sympathisers and in company with two French officers, Hindenlang and Touvrey, who had both arrived from France. Nelson proclaimed himself the President of the Provisional Government of the Republic of Lower Canada, in front of a crowd of about 1,000 Chasseurs in the town square. By the 7th an additional 1,500 armed men had arrived and Hindenlang began to organise them into units. The total force grew within a few days to some 4,000 men, with Touvrey placed in command of such cavalry as there were. But less than a quarter of the Patriotes had firearms, the rest being equipped with pitchforks and sticks.[4,6,8]

The shortage of weapons was critical to the Patriote hopes. On 5 November Touvrey and Dr Coté went with a party to collect arms deposited across the American border, where a schooner was anchored off Rouse's Point with 200 muskets, a cannon and ammunition. They managed to force their way through loyalist Volunteers at Lacolle but on their return they were intercepted at Vitman's Quay near Lacolle by the same loyalist Volunteers who had in the meantime been reinforced by others from Hemmingford. This time the Volunteers killed eleven Patriotes and managed to capture their weapons, many of which were American Army muskets. In addition President Van Buren of the United States had issued a proclamation of neutrality which sealed the frontier and made the supply of further weapons from that source hard to obtain. So Robert Nelson now found himself at Napierville, cut off from any means of arming his supporters, and with less than a quarter of them properly equipped. With this force he was opposed by seasoned regular troops comprising cavalry, infantry and artillery.[4,6,8,25]

Sir John Colborne in Montreal was now marshalling his forces in order to march on Napierville. Robert Nelson, Gagnon and Coté had realised that they stood no chance of withstanding the regular forces being assembled against them. On 8 November they decided to retreat towards the American border, and Coté told a prisoner that they were going 'to clear the way to enable an armed body of Americans, that is to say citizens of the United States, to enter this province for the purpose of co-operating'. The Frères Chasseurs themselves may have been for the most part peasants and farmers, but some of them soon suspected that their leaders were about to desert them again for the safety of sanctuary in the United States. There were plans to seize Nelson and Coté and hand them over to the British authorities, and a group actually held Nelson and Gagnon for a time, but were forced to release them by other Patriotes who still believed that American help was on the way. Nelson, with about 1,000 men, started out for the United States frontier on 9 November. When they reached Odelltown on the frontier they found their way barred by two companies of the Lacolle Volunteers who had taken up a position in and around the Methodist church. This small force was commanded by the officer on 'particular duty' in that area, Lieutenant-Colonel Charles Taylor, who had some 200 Volunteers in all under him, plus the cannon which had been captured earlier when Touvrey and Coté had been intercepted at the Lacolle encounter. They were short of ammunition, but had the services of Sergeant Beattie of the 1st Foot and a Volunteer who had been in the artillery.

As the Patriotes advanced, the Volunteers' cannon opened fire, forcing the Patriotes to deploy on either side of the road. The Volunteers in and around the Methodist church also opened fire. The Patriotes tried to advance and outflank the Volunteers' position but reinforcements could be seen coming from Lacolle on one flank – about 150 men under Lieutenant-Colonel Odell – and a little later more help materialised from the other flank in the form of some 300 Hemmingford Volunteers.[35]

By now Nelson was no longer being heeded. As the Patriote

forces began to dwindle and disappear, he quietly left the field of battle and made his own way to safety in the United States. Hindenlang, the Grand Eagle, organised the retreat of some hundreds of Patriotes back to Napierville, but was captured. The Volunteers had accounted for at least fifty Patriotes killed for a loss of five Volunteers dead.[C32]

George Cathcart at Chambly had noted:

The rebels had assembled at a place called Napierville, here they mustered at one time nearly 3,000 men. On 8th November Sir John Colborne having previously communicated to me confidentially his intention to attack the rebels sent orders for me to bring all I could spare from Chambly to St John's. I raised a Corps of 60 Volunteers, left 100 of the 15th Foot and one weak squadron of the KDG. [This was to guard against the Patriotes gathered at Boucherville.] I marched with the rest. By 5 pm the KDG arrived and by 6.30 pm Lord Charles Wellesley with the 15th Foot arrived. Sir John was there and communicated all his plans. Sir James Macdonell with the Grenadier Guards [brought down from Quebec] and 71st Foot and 7th Hussars was to attack from the direction of La Prairie. Major-General Clitheroe with four companies of the 15th Foot, and with 24th Regiment and two guns was to attack from St John's through l'Acadie. The third column, commanded by Colonel Love with his 73rd and one company of the 15th, and supported by me with the King's Dragoon Guards, was to go up the river Richelieu as far as Isle au Noix – the infantry and guns by steamboat, and my Dragoons and gunhorses by land along the left bank. This latter move was to attack a strong post occupied by about 1,000 rebels at a crossroads half way between Napierville and Lacolle, and then cut off all retreat to the south. Sir John intended this to take place at daybreak on the 9th, but, owing to the steamers not getting up and to a railroad being broken up, it was not possible. On the 9th, however, I moved down the River Richelieu and got to St Valentines opposite Isle au Noix in time to cover the landing of the 73rd. The few rebels then disappeared and all was deserted. As the 73rd landed, I strengthened my post, but before all could land and the guns, it was dark. The moon rose at 4 am and we marched, expecting to meet our enemy at dawn. We found him gone. We then marched to Napierville and all the three columns arrived at the same moment. The King's Dragoon Guards and the 7th Hussars met in the middle of the town. We took many prisoners, but all made themselves scarce that could, and unfortunately a gap was left open by Douglas-corner. The KDG and 7th Hussars immediately persued but too late. Sir John returned with the KDG to Napierville, the 7th Hussars halted at Douglas-corner. We had been on horseback since 4 am.[CA26]

The centre column under Sir James Macdonell, with the Grenadier Guards, the 71st Foot and 7th Hussars, had assembled at L'Acadie, arriving there independently. The Grenadier Guards had crossed the St Lawrence to La Prairie on 8 November, and three companies and three guns proceeded by rail to a point four miles from L'Acadie, but were ordered to return to pick up three more companies. On the return journey the train was derailed, possibly by sabotage, and so the troops marched to L'Acadie. On arrival the village was found to be deserted. There was no staff and no supplies, and as a result 'hunger naturally caused some slight attempts at plunder', but Colonel Ellison appointed a provost marshal at once to keep order. Before the men had fed, Sir John Colborne arrived and ordered an immediate advance.

With the 7th Hussars leading, followed by the Grenadier Guards and 71st Foot and three guns, the column advanced through deserted villages to within four miles of Napierville, where it halted for the night. By dawn the next day, the whole column was in position outside Napierville. On the right the 71st Foot advanced in skirmishing order, supported by two companies of the Grenadiers. In the centre the other companies of the Grenadiers were ordered to take a series of buildings. When the attack went in only some 200 Patriotes were left to oppose them and these were soon taken prisoner.[26]

The third column, comprising the 15th and 24th Regiments, advanced from St John's through the deserted countryside to L'Acadie and on to Napierville. By fast marching they managed to overtake and disperse several Patriote bands, but when they arrived at Napierville the Patriotes had gone. As the Regimental History of the South Wales Borderers, 24th Foot, commented, 'It had been hard and trying work, mostly performed in bad weather, involving many marches over bad roads, without any real fighting to compensate the troops for their hardships.'[10,18]

The Regimental Diary of the King's Dragoon Guards comments:

Soon after the daybreak the several columns met at Napierville. The rebels dispersed on their approach, many of them saving themselves by the woods, and two or three hundred surrendering, among whom was the French officer by the name of Hindenlang, who styled himself 'Grand Eagle', who was afterwards tried and executed. No resistance was offered beyond a few straggling shots on the first approach of the troops.[28]

Cathcart continued,

Sir John determined to go immediately to Odelltown to encourage the Volunteers and start them to cut off any runaways. He asked me to escort him with the KDG. I looked them over, and the hard frozen roads had broken and pulled off some shoes. I selected 50 good men and horses and two subalterns, and halted the remainder under Captain Tyssen. By the time Sir John was ready, after not quite an hour's halt, we set off at a good trot for the sun had softened the road, passed through Lacolle and Odelltown, where the battle had been the day before, and halted within a mile of the border. There were Volunteers there, but no regulars yet, but for my 50.

I put my horses in barns quite close to his quarters, took possession of a house quite close to it also and put all my men in it. I posted three sentries and made the whole as a guard to relieve every half hour. This I find the most vigilant as well as the easiest and least fatiguing mode of keeping a good watch in cold nights with small bodies – for it only comes to one half hour's turn to each man.

My horses had been mounted from 4 am to 5 pm with only one hour's halt. Twelve hours in complete marching order and some of their work done at a good trot on excrable [sic] roads. Not a horse down. Not a sore back. And fresh and fit for service at the end. Our American horses, strange to say, beat our English ones at this work.[CA26]

At Napierville on the evening of 10 November the troops billeted themselves in the houses. On Sunday 11 November Sir John Colborne ordered all houses, except those of the loyalists, to be burnt as a punishment. The troops first engaged in a certain amount of looting and destruction, and then the town was burnt.[18,26]

On 12 November the King's Dragoon Guards returned to L'Acadie, a distance of twenty-two miles, and on the 13th crossed the Richelieu river by the bridge at St John's and reached Henryville, getting back to Chambly on the 14th.[28] George Cathcart reported:

We have not a single sore back, and only a few sprains and broken feet owing to cast shoes. I have 144 horses of the two Squadrons fresh and fit for duty, and only 34 (mostly slight cases that I should leave in even for a field day). We got plenty of sheafs of oats, unthrashed, on the march in lieu of hay, and they are as fat as when they started.[CA26]

The Grenadier Guards and the 7th Hussars returned to La Prairie on 14 November, having marched via St Remi and St George, and the 71st Foot moved to St John's. This column encountered some poor going, 'the road was so deep in mud that the artillery horses could not drag the guns through'. A company of the Guards was, therefore, diverted into a wood, which flanked each side of the road, and the men with their regulation axes commenced cutting down small trees, so as to make a corduroy road. But the edge of every axe and billhook turned in a few minutes and became utterly useless. The artillery, consequently, was left to bivouac at an adjacent farm house, two companies of Guards being left in support.[26]

Whilst the action around Napierville was taking place, Captain Manning KDG, in command of the rear party at Chambly, reported that at

about 4 o'clock on 9th November the Magistrates waited upon me, stating that a large assembly of persons was to take place. The Volunteers were ordered on duty and occupied the Fort Barracks with a Picquet of the 15th. I ordered our mounted patrols out at dusk, relieving every hour as usual, who found all quiet during the night. About 12 o'clock the sentry in rear of the 15th saw a gun flash in the pan, which was also seen by the Sergeant of our Guard, and he immediately fired in that direction. I then ordered the bush to be searched by a dismounted picquet, who discovered that some people were lurking about, whom they could distinctly hear, but could not come up to. The Magistrates have requested me to inform you they consider it would be unsafe to take any more troops from this place. The Volunteers remain on duty.[CA27]

To the north west of Montreal around St Eustache, St Benoit and Ste Scholastique, and to the north east in the neighbour-hood of St Charles and St Denis, which had been the scenes of the previous winter's rebellion, all was quiet. The memories of burnt houses, looting and imprisonment which had followed the previous year's troubles were a sufficient deterrent to immediate action in support of the new Patriote uprising. Whilst the sympathies of many French-Canadians in these areas were still with the Patriotes, the combination of inept leadership, lack of arms, and the severe consequences of rebellion made even the most enthusiastic more cautious.

The area around the Châteauguay river had remained quiet in 1837. In 1838 the Frères Chasseurs were strong and ready for action at Châteauguay and Beauharnois. Some 200 Patriotes assembled at Châteauguay on the evening of 3 November and decided to go to Caughnawaga to obtain the arms of the Mohawk Indians living there. The Patriotes hoped that they could persuade the Indians to hand over their weapons peacefully; if not, they would take them by force. Some seventy-five Patriotes left Châteauguay at midnight under the leadership of Joseph Cardinal and Joseph Duquette. These arms were needed by the Patriotes, but they also felt that by disarming the Mohawks they could safeguard their families from the savagery of an Indian attack should the Mohawks decide to support the Government while the Patriote men were in the field. They did not know that Sir John Colborne had attached Captain Campbell of the 7th Hussars to the Indians, partly to give advice and partly to prevent the Indians from scalping. As the Patriotes approached Caughnawaga, early on the morning of Sunday 4 November, they were seen by an Indian woman who had gone in search of a stray cow. She ran to the church where the Indians were gathering for Mass and told the chief. They next met Georges de Lorimier, an Indian and a relative of the Chevalier de Lorimier, who described himself as 'a Patriote, but not a rebel Patriote'. Cardinal boasted that he had twice as many men with him as the actual number, and said that they wanted the Indians' arms. De Lorimier warned the Mohawks and they ran to their houses and armed themselves. Whilst some gathered around their chief at the flagpole in the centre of the village, others ran out to take up positions on either side of the road along which the Patriotes were advancing.

As the leading Indians approached a chapel some distance to the south of the village they captured a Patriote and disarmed him, only in turn to be surrounded by more Patriotes. It was agreed that they should go to the village. Here Cardinal explained to the chief, standing at the flagpole and surrounded by his warriors, their need for arms. When the chief asked Cardinal for his authority, Cardinal tried to produce a pistol. At once the Mohawks, who had by now surrounded the Patriote party, started to disarm them and make them prisoner. The Patriotes were too frightened to offer resistance, and although eleven managed to escape, sixty-four were taken prisoner. At once they were taken by canoe from Caughnawaga across the St Lawrence to Lachine where they were handed over to the Lachine Volunteer Cavalry.

The Volunteers, who had no idea that a second rebellion was in train, changed their plans for going to church, and twenty troopers, assisted by thirty infantry of the Lachine Volunteers, were hurriedly enrolled to escort the prisoners to Montreal. It was pouring with rain and by the time they reached the city the prisoners, roped together in twos and made to trudge through the mud, presented a sorry spectacle. The news of their arrival soon spread; a crowd of onlookers had gathered as they made their way to the gaol and were handed over to the prison authorities.[4,23,25,29]

At Beauharnois, the Patriotes were better organised. Some 400 Chasseurs had gathered at Ste Martine on the evening of 3 November. They intended to capture the arms and ammunition stored in the seigneury house at Beauharnois for the use of the Beauharnois Loyal Volunteers under the command of Lieutenant-Colonel Lawrence Brown. Brown had sensed the atmosphere of rebellion, and warned the loyal inhabitants, including Edward Ellice, one of Sir John Colborne's secretaries, and his wife, Jane, to take shelter in the seigneury, which was to become a strong point which the Volunteers would defend.

Brown had only time to collect and post about a dozen Volunteers around the house, when the Patriotes attacked. The Patriote fire wounded Brown and a female servant who was inside the house, and so he withdrew his twelve men inside the building. The Patriotes soon surrounded the seigneury and kept up a brisk fire. As bullets started to smash through the windows, Brown decided to surrender and went with Ellice out of the front door, holding a lantern and calling for the Patriote leader. Dr Jean-Baptiste-Henri Brien ordered the Patriotes to cease fire.

When the Patriotes discovered that the seigneury did not contain the number of arms which they had hoped to seize, some of them became aggressive, one knocking Brown's sword from his grasp, another removing his sword belt and scabbard. Brien tried to restrain his men, only to be turned upon by them, so he led them into the house to search again for the needed arms. However, the Patriotes only found a total of twelve muskets, two sporting guns, some cartridges and a dagger. Brown and Ellice, together with sixteen other prisoners, were pushed into Ellice's carriage and sent off to Châteauguay, where they were imprisoned in the house of the curé.[4,23,25,29,33] Mrs Ellice and the other women and children spent the night in an upstairs room amidst the Patriotes, who had found a well-stocked cellar. At one point a huge, bearded and drunk Patriote confronted them with a pistol in one hand and, taking off his cap, he bowed, swaying from side to side, and said, 'N'ayez pas peur, Madame, nous ne voulons pas vous faire de mal, ne craignez rien.' Later, a more sober rebel whispered to them, 'Save yourselves if you can. I won't answer for anything tonight – everybody's drunk.'[23,25]

On the next morning, 4 November, the steamboat *Henry Brougham*, which carried the regular passenger and mail service from Upper Canada to Lachine, arrived as usual at the Beauharnois pier. Concealed behind crates and piles of timber were about 150 Patriotes under François-Xavier Prieur. They stormed on board as soon as the ship docked. The crew and about twenty passengers, including two British officers, were taken completely by surprise and were made prisoner. They were taken to the house of the Beauharnois curé, Michel Quintal.

Meanwhile, at the seigneury, Jane Ellice and the other women and children were being terrorised by drunken Patriotes. They managed to send a message to the curé. Michel Quintal came that afternoon and persuaded the Patriotes to move their prisoners to his house. The presbytery was now becoming overcrowded with the captive passengers from the *Henry Brougham* and many other refugee loyalists, both French and English.[4,23,25]

Excited and encouraged by their success, the Patriotes now split their forces. Joseph Dumouchelle took some 250 to form an armed camp at Baker's Farm on the Châteauguay river, about nine miles south east of Beauharnois, leaving Prieur and De Lorimier in command at Beauharnois. Patriote morale in the area was high; the only reverse had been suffered at Caughnawaga when the Châteauguay men had been captured by the Mohawks. They had seized the seigneury, capturing the local Volunteers, even if they had not found all the weapons they had hoped would be stored there; and they had captured the *Henry Brougham*. There were rumours that American volunteers were on the march to assist them and had already crossed the border. A message from Nelson at Napierville told them to be ready to march. They were still poorly armed and equipped, but they had six homemade 'cannon', consisting of wooden tubes bound with iron bands, which fired homemade slugs to serve as grapeshot, and more than half their number were armed with muskets or sporting guns.[4,23,25]

Sir John Colborne had taken immediate steps to deal with the situation. 'As soon as I received information of the revolt at Beauharnois, I despatched Major Philpotts with orders to Major Louis Carmichael to pass to the south bank of the St Lawrence with two battalions of the Glengarry Militia under Colonels Macdonell and Fraser and to march on

Beauharnois.'[C33] Another order to Colonel Macdonell told him, 'to assemble as many battalions of the Glengarries as you can and disperse the rebels assembled at Beauharnois'.[C34]

Captain Campbell, of the 7th Hussars, had gathered fifty of the Lachine Loyal Volunteers and 200 Caughnawaga Indians to attack Châteauguay. By the time they reached the village most of the Patriotes had left for Napierville, taking with them the loyalist prisoners captured at Beauharnois. A few shots were fired, but the village was soon taken and occupied by the Mohawks. The Patriotes on their way to Napierville soon met others fleeing from there, and in the confusion the prisoners managed to escape and make their way to La Prairie where they were welcomed by the 7th Hussars.[23]

As the Glengarries assembled, an urgent plea reached them from Major John Campbell, the officer 'on particular duty' at Huntingdon who had been ordered to move on Baker's Farm with his Huntingdon Loyal Volunteers. Colonel Donald Macdonell and 250 Glengarries from Stormount volunteered to join this force. They crossed the St Lawrence, landing at Dundee, where they were joined by Captain Solomon Chesley and fifty St Regis Indians.[33]

The main body of Glengarries, nearly 900 strong, together with the Cornwall Volunteer Cavalry troop, the Brockville Volunteer artillery company, two companies of the 71st Foot and twenty-one regular sappers, embarked at Coteau du Lac on 10 November and crossed the St Lawrence in the steamer *Neptune*. The regulars of the 71st thought the Highlanders 'a rum set of ragamuffins', but kept their feelings to themselves as every Glengarry considered himself to be a 'shentleman', and his Highland pride was easily provoked into requiring 'satisfaction'.[32,33]

The force under Carmichael and Philpotts was on the march by noon. At St Timothée they set fire to the home of François-Xavier Prieur, commanding the Patriote force at Beauharnois, and then continued the seventeen-mile march by night, arriving at Beauharnois at dawn on 11 November. With the regulars of the 71st in the lead, they ran into an ambush as they approached Beauharnois. About a hundred Patriotes were in hiding on either side of the road, and they fired on the vanguard. One of the 71st shouted, 'Oh! Somebody carry me to the rear; I'm shot through the heid!' The rest of the 71st soon dealt with the Patriotes, who fled to a nearby village where they were unfortunate enough to fall into the hands of the Indians. The column then advanced on Beauharnois. The main body of Patriotes, confronted by 1,200 troops, started to disperse, but as the 71st entered the village, a number of rebels posted behind the church opened fire, killing a soldier of the 71st and wounding two others. This last pocket of resistance was speedily dealt with, and then 'There was none but Highland bonnets, and the language that morning was altogether Gaelic.' Next day the corpses of four Frères Chasseurs were found.[23,25,32,33,C35]

Meanwhile, Mrs Ellice and the other prisoners in the curé's house had heard rumours that the troops were on their way. This seemed to be confirmed by the change of manner among the Patriotes, whose mood of confidence had evaporated, and who now either became sullen and harsh or made excuses for their involvement in the rebellion. During the fighting bullets hit the presbytery from all sides, but the prisoners were soon released by a British officer. As night came, fires started to break out, and Beauharnois suffered as badly as had St Eustache and St Benoit the year before. No one seemed to know who was responsible. The 71st thought that the Indians set fire to all the French-Canadian houses. Major Philpotts insisted that 'these fires did not originate with the troops or volunteers'. He believed that it was the 'inhabitants of the village who had been injured by the rebels and who were induced to revenge themselves in this way, because they imagined that from the lenity shown the rebels last year, they would probably meet with no other punishment'. This view was supported by the Colonel of the Glengarries, Fraser, who said, 'The fires were not the work of the Glengarries, they were started by the loyal inhabitants of the place, in revenge for what they had suffered.' But Colonel Charles Grey, commanding the 71st, admitted, 'I am told that that company of mine had not been very regular and that it aided efficiently in burning houses. I can easily believe it for I know what those with myself would do with the example that is set for them on all hands, if they were not kept very tight.' But the Glengarries had followed Highland custom and had gone off to loot what they could find. If it was the loyalists who started the fires, their action soon caught up on them: the fires spread, burning the houses of loyalists as well as those who had supported the Patriote cause.[4,23,25,32,33]

The Huntingdon Loyal Volunteers under Major John Campbell had set out to deal with the Patriotes at Baker's Farm before the Stormount Glengarries had arrived to reinforce their numbers. They got to within a mile of the Patriote camp on 7 November. Campbell saw that the Patriotes mustered more than twice his 300 men, so he remained waiting for two days for the Stormount Glengarries to reach him. But on 9 November, in view of the lack of Patriote activity, Campbell pushed forward a patrol of twenty-five Huntingdon Loyal Volunteers to reconnoitre. As they approached the Patriote camp, the Frères Chausseurs took up position and opened fire, mortally wounding one Volunteer. Campbell then withdrew his men to the houses which they had previously occupied, and posted sentries. The next morning, 10 November, the Volunteers heard in the distance the sounds of the Glengarries' pipes mingled with Mohawk war cries. They were also audible to the Chasseurs, who were justifiably afraid that the Scots and Indians boded no good for them. At the same time news came from Nelson of the Patriote defeats at Odelltown and Lacolle, with an urgent request for reinforcements. These two events proved too much for Patriote morale and they dispersed, so that when Campbell, with his reinforcements, advanced, they found the position deserted. Under Campbell's orders Baker's Farm and other Patriote houses in the vicinity were burnt and the force set out for Napierville.[4,23,25,33]

Back at Beauharnois Carmichael received reports that the Patriotes might attempt to recapture the village. The 71st and the two Glengarry Regiments countered such a possible move by marching on Napierville. Colonel Grey of the 71st commented that the Glengarries arrived leaving a trail, to use their own expression, of six miles wide as they came along, burning and pillaging. Colonel Fraser, who commands them, says they are looked upon as savages, to which I could not help answering that I thought by his own account they deserved it. His justification was that this was the second time they had been brought from home in this manner, and that the third time would be worse.

Carmichael also sent a detachment along the Châteauguay river to meet the Stormount Glengarries and Huntingdon Volunteers under Major Campbell. The two parties met at Ste Martine, joined forces, and continued towards Napierville, but at St Remi they met Colborne's regulars with the news of an invasion of Upper Canada from the United States. The Highlanders were ordered back at once, and returned to the Upper Province, but few of them were empty-handed. Even their own kinsman, John Fraser of Lachine, commented that, 'several hundreds of the Glengarries returned home as cavalrymen, mounted on strong French ponies, which they said they found loose and untied by the wayside'. And most of them carried some loot tied up in a bundle.[23,33]

The last area of Patriote rebellion centred around Mont Montarville near Boucherville. Here the grand eagle Mailhot had withdrawn after his failure to attack Sorel, and it was to here that those Patriotes who had planned to attack Chambly had withdrawn. On 10 November Mailhot fortified the seigneury and mill at Montarville, using the cellar of the seigneury to hold some loyalist prisoners. He had about 150 men with him and three home-made cannon. Mailhot posted sentries, not only to keep watch but also to prevent desertion. The Frères Chasseurs heard on 13 November that regular troops were moving against them. Many of them took to flight, dashing down the mountain firing their muskets into the air. The sound of this musketry so upset those who had remained that they took flight thinking they were being attacked, and Mont Montarville was left deserted.[4,23]

Back at Chambly George Cathcart noted that

on my return [from Napierville] I immediately communicated with my friend the Curé, who told me that the rebels whom I went after on the 4th, and who had formed a camp in the Boucherville Mountain with three guns and much ammunition and arms, and had been threatening Chambly, had broken up and that he had sent a young ecclesiastic to advise them to bring their warlike stores to him – to be voluntarily surrendered to me. As they did not arrive, I patrolled next morning with 20 dragoons to the mountain about three miles off. I had communicated with Major Johnson of the 66th at Beloil, and met him a mile and a half from the mill. We took possession of three guns, lots of artillery and other cartridges, twelve sacks of powder and about forty muskets and several hundred pikes.

I reported this to headquarters and my report arrived at 1 pm. At 12 o'clock of that day an express had been started to tell me that the rebels were in position on the mountain with three guns, and to make arrangements for the attack as soon as possible with the 66th, KDG and two guns. So my report of the capture must have arrived one hour after the messenger started to tell me to make arrangements for making it.[CA26]

Cathcart wrote to his wife in Montreal:

I had a long ride this morning into the Boucherville mountains and in the abandoned camp of the rebels. I wish I could go to Montreal, but I feel I can do a great deal just now in this moment of terror by riding about with my brass helmets and searching houses.[CA29]

On 15 November he wrote his official report:

I heard that the camp in the Boucherville mountain had broken up, and that Mailhot had crossed over at the ferry to Pointe Olivier. I also heard of some threatened disturbances at St Mary's on the opposite side of the river. I also learnt from the Curé of this place (who had been most praiseworthy in his exertions to restrain his flock from participating in the rebellion and in bringing to justice the agitators and those who coerced those peaceably disposed) that he had heard that a considerable quantity of arms and ammunition were in the mill near the centre of the Boucherville mountain.[CA28]

The local clergy were helpful, as was shown at Beloeil on 21 November when Cathcart marched from Chambly to that place with three subalterns and a troop of the KDG, together with some of the 15th Foot, to search for arms. Cathcart comments that he was to show the people the inconvenience of free quarters and a state of war. I could not afford to relax my own discipline, and never let my Dragoons loose to help themselves since we first began, and now I reap the advantage for never were men better conducted than mine are now, and have been throughout. I fear the discipline of those who were let loose will not for a long time be rectified, but the lesson to the country has been severe and salutary.

When at Beloil I began there by arresting Dr Allard, a skulker, but one who with much trouble I have proved to be a leader of the most dangerous and influential class and deeply implicated. Having by means of some perambulations with my dragoons and the free quartering of the 15th made a great sensation, and caused sufficient alarm, I made known that all I then required to induce me to leave them quiet was a voluntary surrender of all arms, and particularly the new Yankee muskets introduced this year. If they were brought to the Curate to be surrendered by him to me as a peace offering, I would move.

The priest started on an apostolic tour through his parish at daybreak next day in his sleigh, with a man on horseback preceding him (although it was broad daylight) with a lantern in his bridle hand and a bell in his right hand to preach my doctrine and enjoin obedience. By night the arms came in in sleigh loads, and we got about 30 or 40 stands.

I received orders to proceed to Ste Hyacinthe with the KDG troop I had at Beloil, and to be joined there by another ordered to march from Chambly. The river was in that state at Beloil that it could not be crossed either on the ice or in boats, although it turned out from the intensity of the frost that guns were able to cross it within forty-eight hours afterwards. This being the case, I sent my troop home and started myself round by Chambly, where I got a fresh horse and six Dragoons (one ferry boat load) and crossed the river at the rapids – not then frozen – and overtook my other troop which had already passed at the same place. When I arrived at Ste Hyacinthe, I immediately set to work to find out from people I could trust what had been doing there. Accordingly I found that not only all the principal people had been sworn to the rebellious oath, but that Mailhot, the chief agent, had arrived there on 2nd, and had held a secret meeting, where about seven of the leading 'messieurs' of that place had been present, and where he had detailed the plan of campaign.

Next day Sir James Macdonell with a battalion of Guards and

some artillery marched in. I worked hard maturing my evidence and taking depositions. I am now a sufficiently good Canadian Frenchman to take depositions and examine people in their own lingo. Next morning owing to some alarms in the Upper Province an order came to withdraw the Guards. I immediately went to Sir James and told him the state of my information and my determination to arrest seven gentlemen, who had been present at Mailhot's meeting, and that, in order to prevent escape, I required four officers of the Guards and my three subalterns to enter the seven dwellings at 4 pm simultaneously. This was done and the persons and papers secured.

I marched the column of sleighs escorted by my troop of the KDG to St Charles and on into Montreal gaol. The prisoners included Papineau's brother.

It was at St Hyacinthe that George Cathcart had served on 'particular duty', and received an address of thanks on his departure a few months previously.[CA30]

The Regimental Diary of the King's Dragoon Guards has an entry dated 25 November:

The Troop at Beloil returned to Headquarters. It having been discovered that the principal inhabitants at St Hyacinthe, persons of some rank and station in the country, had been deeply implicated in the revolt, and that a rebellious council of war had been held there, the Lieutenant Colonel took it upon himself to arrest 8 of these individuals and despatched them escorted by Captain Manning and his troop to Montreal. Various similar services were performed by the King's Dragoon Guards which proves the utility of cavalry arising from the rapidity of their movements in the suppression of internal commotions, and although it became the duty of the Regiment to resort to active and vigorous measures, their good discipline and exemplary conduct secured for them the respect and esteem even of those against whom they were called upon to act. This was evinced by the numerous signatures to an address expressive of the above sentiments afterwards presented by the Curé of Chambly and which was subscribed by men of all parties and of French and English origin.[28]

Lady Colborne, writing to a friend on 17 November,

was surprised to find that in different affairs at least 10,000 men at arms have already been conquered and dispersed. Lacolle,

Beauharnois, Napierville, Odelltown, Boucherville, and all the country round quieted, but actually that number in arms.

Sir John, with all the force he could take with safety to Montreal, was absent from Thursday 8th to Tuesday 13th, and the fatigue all went through from the horrible state of the roads, the weather etc, was very great. But the troops have borne it famously, and Sir John they all say seems to stand it better than almost anyone. He was however very glad to lie down when he came home.

We have lost, I am sorry to say, 45 killed and wounded; the loss much greater on the other side. It is very dreadful to rejoice at such things as we are obliged to now, and I am constantly obliged to recollect what horrors they intended for us, when I hear of the misery occasioned by the march of the troops through the rebels land, and to confine my pity to the poor women and children who fly to the woods, and return only to find all destroyed, for it is impossible to prevent it, or to keep proper discipline, except with the regular troops. Ordered expressly by Sir John Colborne not to be burnt, they say it is to be seen written in white chalk in all directions, but it is useless. The volunteers will revenge themselves in a degree. But not more, Sir John says, than must be expected, and with nothing of the cruelty that was openly intended had they been victors. Prisoners are coming in from arrests and skirmishes every day. We have now between 600 and 700, and the jail [sic] cannot hold them: The Court Martials must begin directly. My husband decidedly thinks that the worst is past.[C37]

7
Alarums and Excursions

In Upper Canada the American incursions continued. A considerable force of some 800 Americans, under the leadership of a man called Burge, who had been prominent in the destruction of the steamer *Sir Robert Peel* the previous May, assembled at Oswego on the American side of the St Lawrence River. They were well equipped with muskets and cannon, together with a plentiful supply of ammunition and provisions. They managed to gain the cooperation of the owners of a large steamboat, *The United States*, and with two schooners they embarked their whole force in daylight on 11 November without any interference from the local American authorities.[C19]

On the same day at Kingston, on the Canadian side, Lieutenant Johnston and forty-four men of the 83rd Regiment, together with a party of Royal Marines, embarked on HMS *Experiment*, which was accompanied by another gunboat, the naval force being under the command of Captain Sandom RN. The Americans landed half their force at Windmill Point, about a mile below Prescott, in the Johnstown District, where they took up positions around a stone windmill and some houses, which they proceeded to fortify. The British naval force managed to head off the rest of the Americans, who put back into Ogdensburg, on the American side of the river, and there a force of US regulars from Sackets Harbor, under Colonel Worth of the US Army, prevented them from joining their comrades at Prescott.

On the morning of 13 November, Lieutenant Johnston gathered his small party of the 83rd and Royal Marines, who were commanded by Lieutenant Parker, together with the Glengarry Highlanders who had arrived back in the Upper Province after their services around Beauharnois to reinforce the regular troops. This force attacked the Americans. In spite of a heavy fire, the Americans were driven from positions behind outlying stone walls, and were forced back into the windmill and surrounding houses. Lieutenant Johnston led an attack on one of these houses, but was killed in the assault and had four men of the 83rd wounded. The Glengarry Highlanders and the Royal Marines suffered more severely, losing forty killed and wounded, including four officers. The survivors were withdrawn to await the arrival of reinforcements with artillery. Twenty-eight Americans had been taken prisoner, and forty-eight killed.[14,25,C19]

An eye-witness account of this attack survives in a report written by Colonel G. Macdonell, who commanded the Lancaster Glengarry Highlanders.

I was with my Corps and a small detachment of the Royal Marines, commanded by Lieutenant Parker attached to the column of militia commanded by Colonel Richard Duncan Fraser. The enemy composed of riflemen and infantry under Von Shoutz, a Polish officer of some distinction, were advantageously posted in a windmill, adjoining stone houses, and in a field behind stone walls in great strength. Upon whom my men and the marines advanced in front of the militia column in extended order, when a smart and severe engagement ensued, and half my men including marines were either killed or wounded, among the latter Lieutenant Parker and my brother, one of the subalterns. During the firing, Edward Landus, a blacksmith, broke away singly from the line, and was observed to throw off his bayonet, and with the butt end of his musket, throwing himself upon the enemy, was observed to knock down numbers of them in a manner which is almost incredible. He was at last surrounded by the enemy and received stabs and blows from bayonets, bowie knives, and butts of rifles, and thus mangled, was left for dead by the enemy.

We received orders to charge, which we did, and put an end to the engagement, killing numbers, taking prisoners, and forcing the residue of the enemy to retreat into the windmill. During the charge we passed over Landus' body in the field, and fancying him dead did not on our return pick him up, but left him in a pool of blood. He appears to have come to in the course of the night, which was cold, rainy, and freezing. He managed to crawl, and appears to have got into the loft of a building to which there was a ladder, and which was occupied by the enemy. He laid there the whole of the next day and second night, enduring sufferings from his state seldom equalled. Towards morning and while dark, he managed to crawl back unobserved, and make his way, dragging himself along to our sentries, and was picked up by us, and sent to Prescott, where he lay in his bed for months, and recovered to the astonishment of us all.[36]

On 16 November Colonel Dundas, with four companies of the 83rd and two 18-pounder guns, landed and took up position some 400 yards from the windmill. At the same time Captain Sandom RN, with two gunboats, stationed himself opposite the American position, which was subjected to a bombardment from land and from the river for some hours, but with apparently little effect. However, some of the Americans were seen to be leaving their positions and Colonel Dundas ordered the troops to advance. Very little resistance was offered from the windmill, although a smart fire was maintained from the adjoining stone buildings, even after the Americans in the windmill had put out a white flag. Those still resisting were summoned to surrender, and a total of 114 emerged and gave themselves up, and a further sixteen wounded and thirty dead Americans were found. Twenty-six kegs of powder, six cannon and numerous muskets were captured. Some Americans managed to escape into the surrounding bush, where they were hunted down on succeeding days by the militia. In the second attack the British casualties were one man of the 83rd Regiment killed.[C38]

Lady Colborne wrote on 18 November:

I must give you the good news just arrived from Prescott. As soon as the heavy artillery, 18 pounders, could be procured from Kingston, the 83rd, commanded by Colonel Dundas, and the armed steamboat by Captain Sandom, recommenced the attack, suspended on the Americans, who had taken up a very strong position in a windmill and adjacent houses. They bore the second battering for more than an hour, but then surrendered. About 100 prisoners, 16 wounded, 6 pieces of cannon, quantity of powder, etc. Two or three hundred contrived to escape, and amongst them was their leader, a Pole, but fortunately he has been taken. I trust this example will make the Yankees more careful how they pay us another visit.[C39]

The American prisoners, who – by the time those who had been rounded up in hiding had been added – numbered nearly 200, were brought under escort to Kingston, and were lodged in the fort. The Americans are described in contemporary accounts as 'brigands' and there is no doubt that they represented some of the toughest and most unruly men amongst the pioneering elements. The body of Lieutenant Johnston of the 83rd, who had been killed in the first attack at Prescott, was found mutilated, and had been hung up, as the official report put it, 'as an object of scorn and derision'. The young officer had only arrived in Canada a few months earlier, travelling on the *Prince George* with Colonel Cathcart's wife and daughters. A negro who had escaped to Canada from slavery was murdered when he refused to join the brigands.[C19]

The prisoners were tried by court martial at Kingston, and ten of the leading brigands were executed, including Von Schoutz, the Pole. Others received sentences of transportation and the rest were eventually freed.[2]

On 4 December 1838, yet another American incursion took place, when some 400 embarked in the steamboat *Champlain* and sailed from Detroit across Lake Ontario to Windsor, where they landed, set fire to the barracks, and took up positions. They were attacked within hours by a force of militia and Volunteers from Sandwich, under the command of Colonel John Prince. Lieutenant-Colonel Richard Airey, commanding the 34th Foot, wrote from Amherstburg to the Adjutant General on 6 December:

These people dispersed, some recrossing the river and some taking to the woods on the first fire. Twenty-one of the brigands were killed in running away and four were shot when taken, by order of Colonel Prince. Twenty-five are now prisoners under my military charge here, in consequence of Sandwich not being considered a safe place for them. I lament to report the death of Staff Assistant Surgeon Hume, barbarously murdered. One militia man was killed and two militia men burnt (to death) in their houses.[20,C40]

Sir George Arthur, the Lieutenant Governor of Upper Canada, was incensed by the news of the shooting of four prisoners, because he feared that it would make martyrs of them, and he was sure that they were better dealt with by the due processes of the law. There is no doubt that Colonel Prince and his militia had been infuriated by the murder of Hume and the other militia men. Hume's corpse, like that of Lieutenant Johnston at Prescott, had been subjected to exposure and ridicule. However undisciplined and unjustified the summary shooting of four prisoners was, it had the effect of discouraging further American inroads. An even larger force was preparing to leave Detroit but was stopped by the firm action of General Brady, commanding the US troops in that area. It seems the American authorities were now doing their best to prevent any more incursions by their citizens.[C19]

On 14 December Sheriff McLeod of Niagara reported that

on the afternoon of the 12th, ten waggons loaded with strangers arrived at Youngstown (on the American side of the frontier), and in the evening after sunset, ten more loaded [waggons arrived]. It was soon found out they were Patriotes, entire strangers. They had about fifty rifles, six or eight muskets and bayonets, some pistols and bowie knives. They amounted to about 100 or 110 at most, principally young men from Ohio. They stated that they came in quest of a cannon and arms that had been taken from them some time ago, that they had reason to believe was in the Fort. Some of them asserted they were going into Canada on a hunting expedition, and in search of land. They expected to be joined by 1500 more hunters at that place.

Yesterday morning, I saw a party of about twenty or thirty of them walking towards the Fort. On their arrival at the gate the guard turned out and charged them with the bayonet. They seemed to parley with the guard for about ten minutes, and then walked to their companions that were waiting. The sentries (at the Fort) were immediately doubled. From what I hear from the other side, I think we may expect an attack somewhere on the frontier; not by the people residing opposite, but by strangers from other parts. They may kill a few, but there can be no doubt as to the result. The country will turn out in mass to oppose them.[C41]

At the end of December Sir John Colborne, in answer to

136

representations from the Lieutenant Governor of the Upper Province, Sir George Arthur, sent the 73rd Regiment there as reinforcements.[C49]

In Lower Canada, 1838 ended with the dashing of Lieutenant-Colonel George Cathcart's arrangements for the comfort of his men. A letter of 5 December from Lord FitzRoy Somerset in London informed him that 'Your pea-jackets have gone to the bottom. They were shipped on board the "Colborne" which has been wrecked in the St Lawrence. This is a great misfortune.'[CA31] However, later in the month he heard from Montreal that

At Bonaventure are a quantity of red coats (damaged), trousers, boots and belts (say five hundred of each), three cocked hats, three Epaulets, and a few swords and belts. All of which articles it has been advisable by us not to sell at present. It is therefore desirable that the pleasure of His Excellency thereon be known, in order that the affair of the bark 'Colborne' may be closed.[CA32]

On 2 January 1839, George Cathcart wrote to his father:

I have had a very anxious and uncomfortable time, for when I went to Chambly we were led to expect the outbreak, and soon I was in a state of siege, and the secret oath was to exterminate all loyal subjects. My Regiment is in good order, very well conducted, and really very happy.

All is quiet here now, but the Canadians of Lower Canada know that they are in the natural course of things in progress of being supplanted by our increasing British population and the only way to keep them from openly resisting this now that they have once declared themselves, is by coercion and surveillance. Those who are taken with arms must be punished by Court Martial under Military Law.

The sympathisers in the State of Vermont made an inroad on the 29th December on sleighs from Swanton, and they burned three houses and six farms in the township, and ran away again. All our frontier of Lower Canada for a belt of five or six miles in depth is fortunately occupied by English or American settlers who are interested in the preservation of their valuable property, and well able to defend themselves, since they are armed and well organised. This forms a splendid cordon of volunteers who are at daggers drawn with the sympathisers, and of course form a salutary barrier between that party and the French Canadian districts. But that state of affairs will never last unless we hold a higher tone of discussion with the general Government of the United States, and tell them that if they admit their inability to control the separate state governments, we must deal with each of those separate states and not through the medium of the general Government. We must treat those states along our frontier who harbour pirates as hostile, and deal with them accordingly. We would only blockade or otherwise molest those states who were hostile to us. This would immediately separate the north and the south of the Union, since the Southern cotton growers would desire peace and free trade, and nothing would give them more satisfaction than to see the northern parts blockaded. But with Lord Palmerston and Co, we must submit to being spat upon and insulted by the villainous Yankees without redress.[CA33]

However, on the following day, 3 January, all proved to be not so quiet. It was learnt that a large body of Americans were gathering at Swanton, Highgate, Plattsburg and Burlington around Lake Champlain. The Regimental Diary of the King's Dragoon Guards records:

A threatened invasion of refugees and sympathisers, and symptoms of a revived internal insurrection rendered a movement into Henryville necessary, and a Squadron of the King's Dragoon Guards accompanied a column commanded by Major General James Macdonell to the frontier, where they remained as an advance post until the necessity for it ceased.[28]

On 13 January George Cathcart explained the operation to his father:

We had strong reason to expect an attempt to burn Phillipsburg, or Missisquoi Bay, by the sympathisers. To prevent it and to encourage the Volunteers, Sir John determined to send a force there. I was ordered to go and take command with one troop of the KDG, the 66th Regiment and two guns, and all the Volunteer cavalry and infantry on the border. Nothing occurred, but the reports of an attack in force gained ground, and Sir James Macdonell moved down with a wing of the Guards and the 15th Regiment, and came to Henryville himself.

I patrolled and reconnoitred the border, and our visit had the good effect of encouraging the Volunteers, but we all marched back again without a chance of doing anything more.[CA30]

The 15th Regiment received the order to march on Henryville at 11 am on 5 January:

The division, in complete marching order, arrived at its destination before sunset; although the distance was only seven miles, the march had to be performed through uncleared woods, and over roads in many places breast-deep in snow, where the men were obliged to file in single rank.[18]

Another alarm on 3 January drew a troop of the 7th Hussars under Captain Campbell to Ferrebonne where a body of the Patriotes was thought to be assembling, but on arrival all was quiet and the troop returned to Montreal on 5 January.[29]

Sir John Colborne's policy of pacification was described by the Grenadier Guards:

The general conduct and discipline of the Battalion during the whole period connected with this expedition [to Henryville] was excellent, and as the professed object of it was to punish the disloyal inhabitants by living upon them, and treating them as a conquered race, it is much to the credit of the Battalion that with the exception of occasional offences, which were summarily dealt with, there was no ill-treatment of the population, no serious instance of insubordination, and no General Court-Martial. This was to be attributed both to the esprit de corps of the men as well as to the firmness and ability of the Commanding Officer who under no circumstances allowed the slightest relaxation of discipline, and even in the most difficult circumstances was particular about cleanliness. The marching of the battalion was excellent, and received commendation at the time. Throughout the winter, though it was held by some that the cold would produce rheumatism, the men marched with their greatcoats rolled for, during the march, they did not require them, and after it was over they felt the benefit of the extra covering. During the winter months the soldiers had no beds, but slept on straw, with their blankets as a covering.[26]

One of the guardsmen wrote home:

We seized some arms, took some prisoners, frightened the people, and had some devilish cold marches. Our last was to Henryville and lasted six days. We were sent there on account of a report of the Yankees threatening an invasion in that quarter, but they thought better of it, so we returned. Our Battalion has behaved itself throughout beautifully. The men marching like Rough and Readys as they are, and when in quarters exceedingly orderly. The weather is very severe now, the thermometer often 20 degrees of Fahrenheit below Zero.[37]

The Coldstream Guards had remained in Quebec on garrison duty. A sentry of the Coldstream saw a goose being chased by a fox. The goose took refuge behind the sentry, and from then on attached itself to the post and was given the name of Jacob. Some weeks later the same man who had saved Jacob was on guard again during the night. A party of Patriotes planned to kill the sentry on duty. They stealthily crept up undetected under cover of darkness, drew their knives, and as they charged forward they were met by the goose with flapping wings and loud squawks. This gave the Coldstream sentry time to fire his musket at them, and rouse the guard.

Jacob, the goose, was from then on adopted by the battalion, and continued to stand guard with the duty sentry. He wore an officer's gorget suspended on a blue ribbon around his neck. He returned to England with the battalion, but in 1846 was run over by a van in the narrow gateway of the old London Portman Street Barracks. Jacob's head was preserved, and to this day is kept at Coldstream Regimental Headquarters in London with the gorget around his neck.

Even though the Patriotes in Lower Canada commanded a large measure of support and sympathy from the French-Canadian population, the same was not true of the Upper Province, where after the tragi-comic rebellion of 1837, nearly all the later trouble had come from American intruders. And in the Lower Province, the number who had actually been prepared to take up arms probably did not number more than 8,000 out of a population of 650,000. But those who had persisted through 1838 in open rebellion now had to face the result of their actions. Open rebellion for the second year running could not be treated with the leniency which followed the 1837 uprising.

The prisoners taken in Lower Canada were mainly confined in the gaol at Montreal, where conditions were as good as the keeping of 850 Patriote prisoners allowed. Those taken prisoner in Upper Canada were moved to the Lower Province, mainly to Quebec, for reasons of greater security. The Upper Canadian prisoners were surprised by the superior conditions they found in the gaols of the Lower Province. 'My eyes! How these Frenchmen live! How old Kidd, the jailor of Toronto, would stare, could he but see such a table.'

The courts martial on the prisoners started on 17 November 1838, with Major-General Clitheroe presiding, and were to continue until May 1839. The court consisted of twelve officers to assist the President of the Court, with the Deputy Judge Advocate prosecuting, aided by two barristers, and two barristers appearing for the defence. One hundred and eleven prisoners were charged with high treason, and ninety-nine of these received the death sentence, although it was only carried out in twelve cases. Fifty-eight prisoners were sentenced to transportation, two were banished, and twenty-seven released under bond for good behaviour.[2,4,6,23,25]

On 15 January 1839, Colonel Day wrote to the Civil Secretary giving the names of eleven prisoners charged with high treason for their part in the Napierville action. They included Narbonne, who had been involved in the previous year's rebellion and who had threatened 'to slit the throats and bellies of all the Tories', and Hindenlang, the French officer captured during the retreat from Odelltown. On 7 February Lord Glenelg wrote to Sir John Colborne, sending him 'a letter from Count Molé, interceding for a Frenchman named Charles Hindenlang, who is stated to have been taken prisoner at Odelltown. I have to request that you will give such consideration to Count Molé's intercession, as the facts of the case, and the circumstance of Lower Canada appear to you to justify.'[4,C50] Count Molé appealed to the generosity of the British Government on Hindenlang's behalf on the grounds that he had been misled in New York, and that he was the only

French citizen to have joined the insurgents.[C43] Both Narbonne and Hindenlang were among the twelve on whom the death sentence was carried out.

On 18 January Lord Glenelg wrote to Colborne, giving

instructions for the disposal of such of the prisoners in Lower Canada as may be tried for rebellion and sentenced to transportation, or whose sentences may be recommended to be commuted. I have to acquaint you that measures will be adopted for removing such prisoners as early as possible direct from Canada to the penal colonies. As it will be impossible to effect their removal until the opening of the navigation, no immediate steps can be taken for this purpose, but you will of course not send to this country [Britain] any prisoners under sentence of transportation, but retain them in the Province until you receive further instructions with respect to them.[C44]

On 27 March, the Marquess of Normanby, who had succeeded Lord Glenelg wrote:

With respect to the prisoners who are under sentence of transportation in Upper and Lower Canada, the necessary orders have been issued to the Lords Commissioners of the Admiralty to send to the St Lawrence as early as possible a vessel capable of conveying not less than 200 convicts from Canada to Australia.

This was followed on 16 April with the news that

HMS Buffalo is under orders for Quebec with detachments for the troops serving in Canada, and that after landing these detachments she will take on board persons who may be under sentence of transportation to Australia, and will proceed with them directly to their destination.[C45,C46]

The attitude of the British Government was made clear to Sir John Colborne by the Marquess of Normanby:

I have also to express the highest satisfaction with which my colleagues and myself have learned that in your opinion it will not be necessary for the public safety to carry into effect any further sentences of death in cases of high treason. It is, I am convinced, no less gratifying for yourself than to Her Majesty's Government to be able to dispense with a mode of punishment which can never be resorted to without reluctance, and I feel confident that the leniency shown towards the great mass of prisoners arrested for participation in the rebellion will have a beneficial effect in attaching the lower classes of the French Canadians to the government of the country, and in disabusing their minds of the false opinions which had been incalcated by designing and ill-effective persons.[C45]

At this time a boundary dispute with the State of Maine looked as though it might develop into hostilities. Some of the New Brunswick militia were embodied, and Nova Scotia also prepared to come to their assistance. This threat worried Sir John Colborne.

The movements of the militia in the State of Maine towards the frontier will create much embarrassment and give the Patriotes and brigands some hopes of an improvement in their prospects. I have no doubt that any hostile action with our troops on the disputed territory should attract to that quarter many of the refugees of Canada. I however think we had no alternative to adopt than to make arrangements for driving the intruders from our territory should they persist in their intention of occupying it.[C47]

A few months later the situation had quietened for the time being. The Marquess of Normanby commented that he 'had learned with much satisfaction that the arrangements entered into between the British authorities and the State of Maine are such as to allow the return to Quebec of the four companies of the 11th Regiment, the detachments of Royal Artillery which had been sent to the Madawaska settlement'.[C48]

An entry in the Regimental Diary of the King's Dragoon Guards, dated 6 February 1839, noted that 'Major-General Sir James Macdonell having returned to the command of the Quebec District, the Commander of the Forces was pleased to place Lieutenant-Colonel the Hon George Cathcart in command of that portion of the Montreal District on the right bank of the River St Lawrence, and he was stationed at St Johns, being the most central situation of the district'.[28] This command included 2,500 regular and 1,500 Volunteer forces and covered five counties down to the frontier. The regular units were:

The King's Dragoon Guards with two squadrons
The 7th Hussars with one squadron
Two companies of the Grenadier Guards
The 15th Regiment
The 65th Regiment
The 66th Regiment
The 71st Regiment
Two batteries of the Royal Artillery.

The Volunteers were put under the command of three officers on 'particular service'; Lieutenant-Colonel C. Taylor at Odelltown and Hemmingford, who had commanded the Volunteers at the Battle of Odelltown, Lieutenant-Colonel Williams at Missisquoi Bay and Major Head at Shefford and Polton.

On 6 February the Grenadier Guards, less the two companies under command of Colonel Cathcart, were moved back from La Prairie to Montreal and there they were quartered in a large store-house near the St Lawrence River, called the Point-au-Callière barracks.[26]

The same day George Cathcart wrote to his father:

I shall lose no time in visiting every part of this extensive command, and getting acquainted with my troops, because retaliation and a little border warfare may still be in store for us. When the navigation opens and the seed time comes round again, they will be quiet, as they will have things to do, but until the middle of March we must look out.[CA34]

Cathcart was as good as his word, for on 11 February he was reporting to Montreal that, having established himself at St John's on 9 February, he contacted Colonel Taylor at Odelltown and Napierville and inspected the frontier, returning to St John's via Bedford, where he saw Colonel Williams and visited Ile aux Noix, Clarenceville and Philipsburg. He reported:

They all remark an increase in the number of Canadians in and about Champlain, and a stir and excitement among them. I find that a company of United States regular troops came from Plattsburg and searched two houses, which are said to belong to persons well affected to the British interests; it is also said that this American company took back to Plattsburg some arms which had been previously deposited in some less secure place. But the general impression on the Odelltown frontier is that nothing beyond some attempt of incendiaries and assassins are to be apprehended there. Against those they are well prepared.

I find the picquets well posted, and the men to have become admirably adapted in their own rough way for real outpost duty. On the several outpost duties there are about 120 men on duty every night, so not above 200 men could be got together to cover Lacolle in case of a surprise without several hours previous notice. I cannot think that any serious attempt could be made by a large body of Brigands without 24 hours' previous notice having been obtained. The two companies of the 15th at Napierville would at once be moved up to Lacolle by Lt Col Taylor to hold that post with the collected volunteers. I should in that case be disposed to move the whole of the 71st to Odelltown. I have caused the Commissary to secure sleighs at l'Acadie to be ready, if required, to move 200 men. I would wish to move the 71st to some place half way between l'Acadie and Odelltown, and to bring the Squadron of the 7th Hussars to Douglas Corner with a view to cutting off the invaders. A Squadron of the King's Dragoon Guards might well be posted at Gagnon's house.

The ice is no longer safe to cross [the Richelieu river] anywhere between Ile aux Noix and Rouse's Point, so that if the 65th were to be called to the left bank they might be disappointed by the enemy crossing at Rouse's Point for an attack on Caldwell's Manor, and the false movement of the 65th could not be retrieved. I have desired Lt Col Senior therefore to consider himself as the support of the troops in Caldwell's Manor. At Clarenceville where I met Lt Col Senior and Captain Grattan, I found the troops well posted and very alert.[CA35]

Four days later Cathcart wrote to his father:

Here we are in the state of an army in the field with our outposts along 40 or 50 miles of frontier, on the alert, and subject to nightly petty attacks by brigands, who are harboured in the neighbouring states, and who take advantage of any unguarded points to come in – burn – and run away. I have been round my outposts and have made arrangements which will render these inroads more difficult. I have established a system of inlying picquets at certain points about 5 miles back from the frontier, at which we hold two sledges, each capable of carrying eight men and the driver. These are kept at the alert from 9 pm till 6 am each night, and I require the officer of the picquet to inspect that the horses are harnessed and the sledges ready at the door so that in less than 20 minutes a reinforcement of 16 men can be at any point on the frontier where shots are heard or a fire seen.

All this outflank duty is admirably performed by Volunteers regularly clothed, and paid, and who from practice are as clever at that duty as Cossacks or Hungarians could be.

I have stationed my regular force in support at:

L'Acadie	71st Regiment
Ile aux Noix	65th Regiment
Napierville	Two companies of 15th Regiment
St John's	15th Regiment (less two companies)
	Troop K.D.G.
	Battery of Artillery
La Prairie	66th Regiment
	Two companies Grenadier Guards
	Squadron 7th Hussars
Chambly	King's Dragoon Guards (less one troop)
	Two companies 11th Regiment
	Battery of Artillery.

I have some very good Volunteer cavalry down on the frontier with some of my own NCOs to help them. One Squadron KDG is ready to advance if necessary to a place 8 miles on the road to Ile aux Noix where they can easily cross on the ice and act on either side. We have a good and constant flow of information so I do not think the brigands can collect in sufficient force to make big inroads with less than 24 hours' notice, which suits me as I should be too quick for them, and they would not easily get back.

But the sad state of affairs cannot be put right until our Government make it clear to the States that we are not afraid of war with them.[CA36]

On 21 February there was an attack on a post commanded by Captain Hoyle. George Cathcart commented, 'Some men approached the post at night and not answering the challenge, he let fly at them but without effect.'[CA46] 'The fuss made about the last [attack] has, I think, induced them to try to scare the Volunteers. They may have got more than they bargained for.'[CA37] Deserters from the US Army also posed intriguing problems. Cathcart refused to authorise the sale of arms of a deserter from the US Army to Volunteer Wheeler, who had purchased the same. Arms are never the property of soldiers, militia or volunteers, and therefore the purchase was illegal. Nevertheless, as the case is a novel one, the Lieutenant Colonel sanctions the arms being kept by the Volunteer, provided they are not claimed in 8 clear days from the capture by a competent authority.

On 22 February there was an attempt

to burn the barns occupied by our Squadron of the KDG by night. Our sentries were on the alert and the picquet pursued them, but the rascals took to the ice, and two of our picquet who were on the point of cutting them off, got in and were in some jeopardy, on which the rascals cheered. This accident prevented their getting a shot at them. I hope they may come again tonight.[CA46]

George Cathcart was an active commander and on another visit to Odelltown on 26 February he rode across the frontier and paid a visit to Champlain village in the United States. On his return to Odelltown he commented to Colonel Gore at Montreal that he

saw Captain Sweeney's Troop [of the Royal Montreal Cavalry] and was really surprised to see how well they can move and how perfectly manageable they are. The Infantry Volunteers are also a fine body of men and well appointed. Every one of them had their arms in good order and well flinted, which is a sure sign they think about having them ready for use. Whilst I was at Odelltown a detachment of the Montreal Volunteer Artillery arrived. The gun taken by the Volunteers [at the Battle of Odelltown] is of course valued with a sort of religious veneration by the people there; it is in good order itself and has a good enough carriage, but of the limber they only have the axle tree and wheels. It would be a very gratifying attention to these fellows, who certainly earned their gun, if you could cause the limber to be completed for them and supply them with an ammunition cart. Without it, it is of no use to them, and to have one of the Montreal Volunteer guns down would not please them half so much.

As to the reports and alarms from the frontier, I think they are much exaggerated, and that there is no longer the slightest chance of an inroad of 100 men in any one place this season, so long as the frontier is guarded by Volunteers.[CA39]

On 16 March, Cathcart was writing to Lieutenant-Colonel Williams at Phillipsburg to be sure to give prompt support to his outposts and to station a cavalry picquet of an NCO and six men from Captain Moore's Troop of the KDG at Moore's Corner on the frontier.[CA40] This precaution was justified by a report on 3 April from Philipsburg where a meeting with the United States authorities had been arranged in order to hand over some Canadians who had taken refuge after burning farms.

The good intentions were all a Yankeee flourish and nothing is to be expected from them as to giving up the 4 Canadians whom they have ascertained to have been the perpetrators of the burning at Millers.

There are, I believe [Cathcart continued] no regular States Troops on that side, but a large Militia force (I mean several companies) had been assembled. General Mason is there to command them. The intention is to prevent an attack, but I query whether some of the militiamen would not be disposed to join in it rather than prevent it. If I have anything to warrant it, I would wish to move the 15th to Bedford, and a Troop or Squadron of the KDG to Henryville, and the Guns might go to Bedford. Clarenceville is strong enough and the 65th can support it or control the south river if necessary.[CA41]

The frontier was now quietening down and by the end of March the two companies of the Grenadier Guards at La Prairie rejoined the rest of the regiment in Montreal, and George Cathcart could write to his father,

I think the border situation is now pretty well subdued and Maine seems to be tired of her warlike preparations. We still have frequent burnings by rascals who cross the line for a few hundred yards in the night and then run back. A few nights ago one party came in armed and with a lantern. They were seen by one of our Volunteer sentries and challenged three times without answering, whereupon the picquet was turned out and pursued them into their lines, wounding two of them.[CA44]

The incursions from the United States and burnings of Canadian farms and buildings eventually drove the Canadian farmers on the frontier to retaliate.

Two days later there was an alarm when Cathcart

ABOVE *The bivouac of the 1st and 66th Regiments at St Hilaire.* BELOW *The attack on St Charles by 1st and 66th Foot. Lithographs after paintings by Lord Charles Beauclerk, Captain, Royal Artillery, by A. Flint, 1840. By kind permission of the National Army Museum.*

ABOVE *The attack on St Eustache by 1st, 32nd and 83rd Foot.* BELOW *The bombardment of St Eustache by the Royal Artillery with soldiers of the 1st Foot waiting to attack. Lithographs after paintings by Lord Charles Beauclerk, Captain, Royal Artillery, by A. Flint, 1840. By kind permission of the National Army Museum.*

Lieutenant-Colonel George Cathcart, KDG. Lithograph by J. Richardson Jackson after a painting by T. Y. Gooderson, 1857. By kind permission of Major-General the Earl Cathcart.

LEFT *St Stephen's Garrison Church, Chambly.* RIGHT *The church at Odelltown, with the cannon captured by the Volunteers at Odelltown. Author's photographs.*

The old French fort at Chambly. Author's photograph.

LEFT *Trooper of the 7th Hussars in winter dress. Watercolour by Christopher Fulton. By kind permission of the artist.* RIGHT *Soldier of the 66th Regiment in winter dress. From a watercolour by Sir James Archibald Hope. By kind permission of the David M. Stewart Museum, St Helen's Island, Montreal. Photographed by Giles Rivest.*

'The 43rd Light Infantry as they turn out in their sleighs at the Falls of Niagara, 1839.'
Watercolour by Sir Richard A. Levinge, Bt.

Sergeants of the King's Dragoon Guards and 15th Foot in winter costume. Watercolour by Sir James Archibald Hope. By kind permission of the David M. Stewart Museum, St Helen's Island, Montreal. Photographed by Giles Rivest.

The 71st Regiment escorting Patriote prisoners. Lithograph by J. H. Lynch after a painting by M. A. Hayes. By kind permission of the National Army Museum.

LEFT *A Grenadier Guardsman in the march on Napierville. Watercolour by Sir James Archibald Hope. By kind permission of the David M. Stewart Museum, St Helen's Island, Montreal. Photographed by Giles Rivest.* RIGHT *Jacob the Goose. By kind permission of the Regimental Colonel of the Coldstream Guards.*

An officer of the King's Dragoon Guards. Unknown artist. By kind permission of the Parker Gallery.

LEFT *Privates of the 71st Highland Light Infantry in winter dress, marching order, Canada. Watercolour by Colonel T. Unett, 19th Regiment. By kind permission of the National Army Museum.* RIGHT *Officer of the 7th Hussars in Canada, 1842. Watercolour by R. I. McDonald. By kind permission of Christopher Fulton.*

'An Officer's Trophy Room': *print of a painting by Cornelius Krieghoff, showing an officer of the King's Dragoon Guards. Sigmund Samuel Canadiana Gallery of the Royal Ontario Museum.*

found the Missisquoi frontier in a very warlike attitude. Brigadier General Mason of the Vermont Militia having called out his Brigade and posted strong picquets immediately opposite ours. The intention, I believe, is a real wish to prevent force on their side. The outrage committed in burning Millers Farm no doubt alarmed them as to the consequences to be expected, and the two burnings on their side, however wrong and to be regretted if done by our own people, has had the good effect of awakening them to a sense of their own interests.[CA42]

On 9 April he reported that 'measures are to be taken by the Americans on their own account to seek for the incendiaries of Alberg, and there is not the slightest suspicion of any of our people having been concerned'.

But there were other alarms, for 'Colonel Taylor warns me that Chambly Barracks are to be burned forthwith. My people are on the alert at all times, and we have an admirable specimen of a fine regiment in the detachment of the 11th now with us.'[CA43]

The overall position was such that Cathcart was able to write requesting permission to leave St John's and resume command of the King's Dragoon Guards at Chambly. On 15 April the Adjutant General wrote that he was 'much obliged to you for your exertions since you have been at St John's, and as things look a little more peaceable, there is no objection, whatever to your re-establishing yourself at Chambly'.[CA45] The KDG Regimental Diary has an entry for 18 April that George Cathcart 'resumed his regimental duties being at the same time still in command of the right bank of the St Lawrence'.[28]

George Cathcart, although confident about the operational situation, was not so happy about his personal circumstances, which had attracted no additional allowances or promotion. 'The Government have pitched about twenty battalions into Canada and made no provision for command or staff, and therefore there is no organisation at all except in temporary expedients such as my appointment.'[CA44]

By June the situation had quietened down, so that George Cathcart was writing to his father:

149

The troops have been drawn into Montreal, and the greater part of the Volunteer Force reduced. I am allowed to live quietly at Chambly. My officers have cleared a part of a very pretty common to make a cricket ground. We are told that we are to have some disturbances again, but it will be our own fault if we are not prepared to prevent them – at least as regards the interior – as to the border warfare – the only way to prevent that will be a show of firmness on the part of our home government towards the States. They have shown that they can prevent the mischief if they wish it. But it was not until after the speech of Sir Robert Peel, which reminded them of their own policy under similar circumstances in Florida, when General Jackson took possession of Pensacola, and the reflection that we might do the same to Plattsburg and Buffalo, together with some little show of retaliation on the part of our volunteers, that they set to work in earnest, and then with complete success.[CA47]

Captain Martin, commanding the detachment of the King's Dragoon Guards at Niagara, reported an incident at the end of May

of the burning of a barn and shed, and the plundering of the house of a Mr Taylor, near that of the late Captain Ussher who was murdered near Chippewa a few days previous. The barn and shed of a Mr Miller were destroyed by incendiaries who came across from the Yankee shore. The 43rd barracks, the Hotel at Drummondville and Sherriff Hamilton's house were set on fire, and I am perfectly convinced that nothing but the utmost vigilance on the part of our sentries prevented it.[CA48]

Colonel Mickle wrote from Stanstead to George Cathcart:

You have been very kind in permitting a Sergeant of your Regiment to drill the Shefford troop of cavalry. I would take it as very kind indeed by your permitting him to instruct the Stanstead troop to give them an idea of the carbine exercise on horseback.[CA49]

A District General Order issued at Toronto on 16 December stated that

Captain Martin, Commanding the Squadron of King's Dragoon Guards at Fort George [Niagara] having handsomely proposed to give instruction in the Cavalry exercise and movements to the Militia Dragoons as may be ordered to attend him for that purpose, His

Excellency the Lieutenant Governor directs that a Sergeant, Corporal and Private from each troop of Cavalry and Volunteer Dragoons at Toronto, Hamilton and Niagara District with their horses be immediately sent to Fort George for a fortnight or even three weeks, should Captain Martin think it necessary.

One such detachment sent to Fort George came from Captain Denison's 1st West York Troop of Cavalry from Toronto, which was in later years to become the present Governor-General's Horse Guards and the affiliated Canadian Regiment to 1st The Queen's Dragoon Guards, themselves the successors of the King's Dragoon Guards in Niagara in 1838. This must be one of the earliest recorded instances of a close link between affiliated Canadian and British regiments.[53]

American Independence Day on 4 July led to information that there might be renewed disturbances. George Cathcart visited Odelltown on 3 July and reported:

There is not the slightest symptoms of any hostile movement and nothing more than the usual preparations for the celebration of the 4th July. I learnt however that notices had been stuck up at Rouse's Point, inviting all Canadians to Swanton for a public meeting. It was believed that the notorious Bill Johnson was to be there.[CA50]

I have decided to move one Squadron KDG, one demi-battery, and one Company of the 11th Regiment to St John's, and intend to send the dragoons and guns to Bedford, and the Company of the 11th to take the duties of St John's, and the fresh Company of the 71st to proceed to Bedford as an additional escort and security for the guns.[CA51]

The meeting at Swanton took place and attracted about 500 people, but plans to attack Philipsburg were abandoned when news of the troop movements was heard.

As the situation quietened more attention had to be given by commanding officers to the routine administration of their units. George Cathcart and Lieutenant-Colonel Whyte received an instruction that 'Materials in the Regular Cavalry are provided by the Quarter Master on the Colonel's account, who is expected to make his Saddlery last 12 years, and for the

Colonel's interest, Oil and other things required to keep the leather in proper order are freely supplied by the Quarter Master'.[CA52] The accounts of the King's Dragoon Guards for 1 January to 31 March 1839 show that expenditure on the Colonel's account amounted to £67.4s.1½d., which included the cost of running the Regimental Headquarters, and the armourers', saddlers' and farriers' expenses.[CA53] The officers' mess accounts showed the wine fund in credit by £16, the mess fund in debt to the tune of £91, and the band fund £144 in debt.[CA54] But Cathcart thought that 'We have a very good brass band. Last autumn we completed our instruments by an importation of £250 worth, and as we have a very good master who can arrange for it, it makes very pretty music indoors or outdoors.'[CA44]

On 1 April 1839 the strength (all ranks) and dispositions of the regular troops south of Montreal were:

St John's	Royal Artillery	39
	15th Regiment	392
Chambly	Royal Artillery	81
	King's Dragoon Guards	223
	11th Regiment	203
La Prairie	7th Hussars	73
	66th Regiment	485
Napierville	15th Regiment	164
	65th Regiment	337
	71st Regiment	527

There were therefore about 2,700 regular troops stationed between the frontier and Montreal.[CA55]

As the troops moved around they were often billeted upon local people, and this gave some cause for friction, especially over payment for the billeting of the horses of the Royal Artillery and cavalry. There was confusion over the date from which such payments could be claimed, and a typical argument arose between Captain Fylden of the Royal Artillery and the proprietor of the Cross Keys Inn at St John's which had to be referred to Montreal for decision.[CA56,CA57]

There was also some friction between officers at Clarenceville. Lieutenant Colonel Williams and Captain Grattan had both written privately to George Cathcart, each complaining about the conduct of the other. Cathcart had replied urging them to settle their differences, but six weeks later Gratton had to be replaced by Captain McCumming of the 15th Regiment.[CA58,CA59]

George Cathcart was ever mindful of the comfort of his men:

I find in this sloppy muddy weather it is impossible to live without Jackboots, and I accordingly live in them. I wore nothing else all winter. The boots made large enough to wear a long stocking over my sock, inside of the boot, and pulled over the knee. This was regimental for the officers. The men had long stockings, but as they gave us 8/6d per man in consequence of the great wear and tear of last autumn, I have been able to give every man a pair of Jackboots to wear during the muddy and sloppy seasons of spring and autumn, which are dreadful here. They are all paid for, and the men very happy in them. Of course this is only for stable duties, watering order and drill order – or actually in the field. But if a General comes to see us, we must put on our Wellingtons, and make up our minds to wet feet. Our Jackboots are quite waterproof. They have the art of making them so here by putting the smooth side of cowhide leather outside, and then making a particular sort of composition of wax and boiled oil.[CA44]

Replacement of horses after the hard conditions of a Canadian winter led George Cathcart to write, 'I have been to Burlington [in the United States] to buy horses, and passed a very pleasant day there. The people were civil, and I got very good horses.'[CA47]

On 24 May the KDG Regimental Journal records, 'The King's Dragoon Guards and as many of Her Majesty's troops as could be spared from the outposts assembled at Montreal for a General Review for Her Majesty's Birthday.'[39] Cathcart wrote:

We had a very grand review at Montreal. Sir John [Colborne] commanded in person. He had six regiments of Infantry and two of Cavalry. The review was a manoeuvre and very well managed on a difficult and cramped piece of ground, chiefly in one line or echelons of brigades. Sir John gave me the Cavalry Brigade with orders to play my own game and make movements and charges as opportunity offered. The Infantry were in three brigades. Col Ellison of the Guards had the Grenadier Guards and 66th. Col Wetherall the Royals and 15th. Col Grey the 71st and 24th. I got one capital charge when the line was retiring covered by its skirmishers. I formed both regiments on the extreme right in two lines, and sent Whyte with the Hussars to charge the whole length of the front of the line, and then retire from the right of squadrons, and pass to the rear through my regiment which was advancing at a trot to support. As soon as the 7th were through, we galloped, and on coming to some broken ground where the 7th charge had halted, we broke into files from the right of threes, and did the second division of the sword exercises at a gallop – then halted. These American horses have such good mouths that they never break away, and we can do these things at a gallop as closely and regularly as at a walk. We had not a single horse or man down that day, although the ground was in a very bad state, and many large ditches were in our way.[CA47]

More inspections and field days followed. Major-General Clitheroe had inspected the King's Dragoon Guards at Chambly just before the Queen's Birthday Parade, and watched them conduct a field day. On 19 July he carried out another inspection at Chambly, and on 8 August the King's Dragoon Guards and the 7th Hussars converged on La Prairie, and encamped on the common. There, on 9 August, Sir John Colborne gave command of the parade to George Cathcart, as the senior officer, and watched the Cavalry Brigade being put through its paces. The two regiments returned to their quarters on the following day.[28]

During the summer months the 15th Foot suffered an outbreak of opthalmia, and in spite of the efforts of the regimental surgeons, the disease persisted, although no other regiment seems to have been so affected.[18]

The 24th Foot remained in Montreal, but the 85th Regiment was plagued throughout 1839 by desertions. An entry in the Regimental Diary records that on 11 November two men tried for attempted desertion received sentences of transportation for life in one case, and fourteen years' hard labour in the other. But even these draconian measures did not prevent men from trying.[10,24] The 65th Regiment spent most of its service in Canada split up, and during 1839 it had four companies at Ile aux Noix, and four in the Upper Province. The 32nd were stationed at New London in Upper Canada, with the 83rd at Kingston, the 93rd at Toronto and the 43rd at Niagara.[10,11,14,22,24]

On 10 September George Cathcart paid a visit to the detached squadron of the King's Dragoon Guards.

I have been to inspect my Squadron at Niagara and visit the falls. I found the Squadron well mounted, but I own I like our Vermont horses better than the Upper Province horses. I returned as soon as I had cast some horses, and done other regimental business, but not without a flying visit to Buffalo and Navy Island. I passed a day with Sir George Arthur at Toronto. The 'Responsible Government' men in the Upper Province give some uneasiness there, because the plausible doctrine unites a faction composed of radicals and separatists, and even the Methodists with their wide-spreading influence join in the cry in the hope of having the loaves and fishes with the established clergy. Although I do not believe they are aware of the mischief they are doing. Sir George Arthur is a very temperate and sensible man, and at the same time quite prepared to act. The regular army of which he has about 6,000 at his disposal [in Upper Canada] – the Militia – the free blacks – the lower orders of Irish (who are all loyal), the Clan Regiments, (the Glengarries, the MacNabs) and those who are loyal from principle and interest, and those who care little about loyalty, but who desire no better than a quiet life – give the Government a powerful ascendancy in the Upper Province. So that although we may have troubles there, there is no immediate danger.

As to the Lower Province, we have now the French Canadians in complete subjection. We have a regular police with stipendiary magistrates, who if they do their duty cannot fail to prevent conspiracy, or at all event to give timely warning so that I hope for a quiet winter. I am still in command of the frontier towards the Yankee sympathisers, but hope they will see the cruelty and nonsense of so vexatious a border warfare.

I am going to Burlington to buy 14 horses. I have got means to mount the band. Hammersley, who was sent out to buy horses in the first instance before the 7th [Hussars] came out is on his way home to the Depot [in York] as I have no steady men there owing to rapid promotions. I shall return incognito through some of the sympathising districts in order to judge what they are up to, and if I am found out, I shall ask if they have any horses to sell.[28,CA60]

The state of the depot of the King's Dragoon Guards and 7th Hussars in York had given George Cathcart some worry. He wrote to the Horse Guards from Chambly:

I have reason to know that the system as regards the training of young officers at the Depot of the two Cavalry regiments serving in Canada is as bad as possible and that every description of boyish and unworthy irregularity is tolerated. The consequence is that young men are in danger of being irretrievably spoiled as officers and in danger of contracting habits unbecoming gentlemen. I regret to say that both reports from home, and specimens sent out confirm me in this opinion. I have therefore to submit my earnest wish that a proper Field Officer should be placed at the Depot with particular instructions to attend strictly to the formation of young officers both as soldiers and members of society. Should it not be thought fit to appoint a Field Officer for the purpose, I know of no one better fitted than Major Biggs of the 7th Hussars.[CA63]

Sir John Colborne also judged that things were settling down. He reported to London:

Although I have received many communications from New York informing me of the determination of the Patriotes not to abandon their schemes of disturbing the tranquility of these provinces, and of even at an early period renewing their incursions, I am persuaded that they have not the means of conveying into effect their evil intentions within the Province. The police magistrates are active, and no circumstances have occurred to induce me to suspect that the habitants encourage the refugees to disturb the frontier. The United States officers are vigilant, and have promised to transmit to me any intelligence they may receive as to the projects of the brigands. McKenzie of Upper Canada has been tried at Rochester in the State of New York under the Neutrality Act, and sentenced to be imprisoned for eighteen months.[C51]

Keeping such a large regular force supplied and equipped had its difficulties, as a note from the Office of Ordnance in London made clear:

500 Cavalry carbines with pouches and slings, 500 swords with belts, and 100 pistols were ordered to be sent to Quebec. The present stores can readily furnish the carbines and swords, but the pouches, slings and belts must be procured from contractors. It is with much difficulty that the pistols can be collected together, any further number must be manufactured. A work necessary subject to many delays and must occupy considerable time.[C52]

The original intention had been to return the Grenadier Guards to Quebec, but Sir John Colborne felt that the situation was still too unsettled, and kept the battalion in Montreal. Discipline within the Guards was excellent; they were not troubled with the problem of desertion, did not have a single soldier before a garrison court martial, nor did they have any trouble with drunkenness, in a place where bad spirits were cheap and readily available. A picquet of fifty guardsmen had to clear a court in Montreal when loyalists threatened a jury which refused to convict a man accused of murder. On 26 September two companies of the Grenadiers provided an escort for the prisoners who had been sentenced to transportation for life, and were being marched to Quebec to be placed aboard ship.

At the end of August Sir John Colborne inspected the Grenadier Guards in Montreal and expressed 'his great approval of the conduct of all ranks of the Battalion while stationed in this Garrison'.[26] In October Sir John Colborne gave up his command, and handed over to Lieutenant-General Sir Richard Downes Jackson as Commander of the Forces in Canada, and to Poulett Thomson as Governor. On arrival in England Sir John was made a peer in the title of Lord Seaton in recognition of his outstanding service. George Cathcart found the new Governor to be in poor health. 'He is an ill-mannered and shy man who never seems to speak to anybody.' On the other hand he liked Sir Richard Jackson, who confirmed him in his command of the troops south of the St Lawrence River; and he visited Chambly on 1 November and inspected the troops there.[28]

In November some further troop dispositions were made. The headquarters and two companies of the 71st Foot were sent to St John's, but as the ice at Ile aux Noix was still unsafe the relief of the 65th Regiment on the other side of the Richelieu river could not take place. Two companies of the 24th Foot were at Chambly, with the 66th Regiment at La Prairie, and two companies of the 15th Foot were to relieve the 11th Foot, who were to proceed to Quebec. In all George Cathcart had nineteen companies of regular infantry, in addition to the two squadrons of cavalry.[CA61],[CA62] Cathcart made his arrangements for the winter by deploying the Volunteer cavalry as a screen along the frontier, with regular infantry contingents to back them up at Beauharnois, Ile aux Noix and St John's. He maintained his headquarters and reserve forces at Chambly.

8

Garrison Duties

The year 1840 saw the internal situation in both Lower and Upper Canada quietening down, except for continuing uneasiness on the United States frontier. For the British soldier life reverted to garrison duties with an occasional alarm, which more often than not came to nothing. Pressures upon the London Government to meet the needs of a growing and sometimes troublesome empire with an all too small regular army led to the reduction of the regular force in Canada as soon as was expedient.

The 15th Foot, who had been in Canada since 1827, were put under orders for embarkation to England in May. Before leaving Montreal 8 sergeants, 9 corporals and 261 privates volunteered to serve permanently in Canada, and were transferred to other regiments. On 29 May the remainder of the regiment, numbering 23 officers and 319 other ranks, were inspected by Major-General Clitheroe before embarking on the troopship *Atholl*, which landed the regiment at Portsmouth on 27 June, where they occupied the barracks at Haslar. The 11th Foot left Canada at the same time, and transferred a number of men to other regiments. In October the 66th Regiment, who had served in Canada for thirteen and a half years, left for England in the troopships *Atholl* and *Sapphire*, landing at Gosport on 3 December. Even with these reductions there was still left in Canada a force of two cavalry regiments, two battalions of Guards, and twelve infantry regiments.[12,18]

The need for a substantial force in Canada was evident. Not only was a show of strength essential in those areas which had been disaffected, but the frontier with the United States required a constant watch, and an argument had arisen with Maine about the interpretation of the Treaty of 1783. Both sides agreed to the arbitration of the King of the Netherlands, but when his solution offered a compromise which the British were willing to accept, the United States rejected it outright.

The new Governor General, Poulett Thomson, was created Lord Sydenham, and on 10 February he was sworn in at Kingston, the new seat of government. At the same time the legislative union of Upper and Lower Canada came into being, having been agreed upon in January by the Chambers of both provinces. Under the new constitution, Ministers were to be responsible to the legislature, and so one of the main reforms fought for by Mackenzie and Papineau was accomplished, even if not in the form they desired. The elections under the Act of Union took place in May, and the new Assembly met on 14th June.[20,36]

The situation on the frontier south of Montreal still required watching. George Cathcart wrote to Lieutenant-Colonel Taylor on 18 April:

I agree with you that some place halfway between the two Cavalry troops would have been the desirable station for Headquarters. Cavalry are, as you say, of great use for the expedition with which they can get from one place to another at any season, and when on the spot they ought to be either mounted, or, if used dismounted, as good as so many infantry men or nearly so, but they are so few and necessarily so dispersed that they can do little without the ready support of infantry. With that support placed in a central situation and to be available in an hour's time at any point, a few Cavalry may do a very great deal towards the security of that part of the frontier likely to require looking after.[CA46]

A month later he was writing to Montreal:

There may be no great risk in bringing the Napierville Company into St John's for the summer months, but I cannot say that the Napierville station could be permanently dispensed with. You are aware that the two troops of Cavalry are now only half troops, and that one company [of Volunteers] is stationed at Hemmingford so that for the whole frontier we have but very few Volunteers. The reason why the Volunteers were reduced was because there was a support of regular troops available at Napierville.

The squadron of the King's Dragoon Guards at Niagara

was due for relief, and on 20 May D Troop, dismounted, embarked at Chambly en route for Montreal and Niagara, to be followed by G Troop on 10 June. George Cathcart wrote to his father:

I am just now relieving my Squadron at Niagara, one troop at a time, with all their appointments, but leaving the horses at their respective stations. It is a long march, but the men are easily transported by steamer. This gives me only three troops at Chambly at present.[CA66]

A month later he was writing:

I have completed the change of my Squadrons from Niagara, and the one comes down after having been out two years under the command of an excellent officer, Martin, and in so good a state did it come in, that all repairs of saddlery have been completed already, and with the help of some of the 71st tailors, I have got it quite on a par with the rest. In the field too it has lost nothing but has only a few novelties and a little improvement in riding to learn to make it quite up to the mark.[28,CA67]

The Niagara troops arrived in Chambly on 4 July.

As the situation became quieter, so life for the British soldier shifted from active service to garrison duties. The new Governor General, Lord Sydenham, visited Chambly in June. Cathcart relates how

I showed him my three troops in review order, making three Squadrons rank entire in the barrack yard. They marched past with carbines carried, and trotted past after the parade and saluted. I sounded the Officers Call and presented all my officers. We then rode to St John's, where we embarked on board the steamer and left it at Ile aux Noix after looking at that fort. I had arranged with Major Denny of the 71st, who has a very well appointed barge, to have it there. The Governor went on board and with the piper in a splendid costume in the bow, and a crew of 71st men dressed like man o'war men, we had a delightful row. When we got within four miles of St John's, another barge with the band of the 71st on board put out from a creek in the river and accompanied us playing.[CA66]

I have many sons of old friends in the 71st, which is my 'Tenth Legion' of my little command. Sir Hew Dalrymple, a Captain, who is a very gentlemanlike young man and a good officer. A son of Sir

William Cummings, very like his Papa; also the eldest son of Sir John Hope of Pinkie, a sensible young man.

All is quiet and well enough here as far as can be expected in this state of suspense with the great question of Union pending. I have lost my much esteemed friend and Colonel [of the KDG], Sir Henry Fane, but have received a very civil letter from my new one.[CA66]

I have got a new Riding Master, and a most zealous and efficient one he is, and so popular that NCOs and men come to ask to be put into a class to ride with him. I have now several excellent rides, one of Sergeants and Sergeant Majors, one of Corporals with one or two of select men, who go through the whole business with lances, leaping bar etc., and with their stirrups of a right length, and hands in the right places. But this has taken some trouble for I found both seat and hand very ugly and very bad.[CA67]

George Cathcart was not only a capable and zealous officer, he was intelligent enough to see that Canadian conditions required new answers and he was not afraid to experiment. There is a long and detailed correspondence between him and the Horse Guards, starting in January 1840 and going on through that year, on a variety of subjects from the design of forge carts, shoe cases and cavalry cloaks, to the usefulness of hammer hatchets and the new practice of placing a folded blanket under the saddle. In addition Cathcart drew up his *Instructions for Cavalry in Canada* which are a model of clarity, experience and commonsense.

On the subject of hammer hatchets he reported that

the fences in this country are made of logs 10 feet long, secured between two upright poles at their junction without nails, but one peg is generally used to confine the upright posts. These fences are easily thrown down, and I have established a drill by which a Fencing Party of 1 Corporal and 3 Privates can clear the road across the country, without delay, for a column. On these occasions the hatchet is of great service in cutting through the peg which is the only security for the fence.

In his *Instructions for Cavalry in Canada*, Cathcart writes:

By looking out for a favourable part of the fence and a weak post, the drill may be done with so much ease and expedition that three men, going on at a gallop, may open the road for a Troop advancing at a trot, without occasioning a check. The hammer has proved useful for driving in staples and for securing the horses during active operations.[CA68, CA69]

Cathcart's experiment with carrying blankets caused wide interest. He reported:

The Regiment has carried the blankets received as Field Equipment on the march or in the field folded in four under the saddle, and although we have had frequent severe trials, and generally get over our marches at a six miles an hour trot, I have never known a single case of a sore back. I am convinced that a proper blanket would be a valuable addition to the Horse Appointments of a Heavy Dragoon.[CA68]

On 14 May the Horse Guards in London reported that Lieutenant-General Sir Hussey Vivian, as President of the Board of Cavalry Officers, had requested information on the manner in which the blankets were folded; and they pointed out the difference between the construction of light cavalry and heavy cavalry saddles, and the weight they were expected to support. There were fears about the additional expense, and so the idea was not well received.[CA70]

Cathcart returned to the attack pointing out that there would be no extra cost. He was suggesting that the expensive shabraque (blue cloth with a yellow binding, price 8/6d), which was already issued as a 'horse cloth' and was of no use for anything else, be replaced by a good, but cheaper, blanket, which would serve several needs. He also quoted from experience:

On 9th November 1838, one Squadron of the King's Dragoon Guards marched to St Valentine's in the evening, a distance of 10 miles and bad roads, at a trot so as to keep pace with a steamboat having troops on board, and arrive in time to cover their landing. The horses remained saddled that night. At 4 am they marched, and one Troop, after the affair at Napierville, accompanied Sir John Colborne at a rapid pace to the frontier, as an escort, where they arrived at 6 pm, and with the exception of perhaps one hour in that time (14 hours) never halted. Several long marches succeeded this day and the Squadron returned to the barracks at Chambly without a single case of a sore back. This trial was in winter, partly in frost and partly under heavy rain. On 4th July a Squadron marched from Chambly at 4 am and arrived after sunset at Phillipsburg, a distance of 41 miles, remaining saddled and in bivouac, and marched a distance of 10 miles at day break. This march was under a powerful sun, and the Squadron returned without a single case of sore back.[CA71]

At first the conservative cavalry colonels remained unconvinced. A War Office Instruction reported: 'Lieutenant-Colonel of the 1st D.G. in Canada reports they have adopted the practice of carrying the blanket under the saddle on the march and in the field. The Board of Cavalry Officers have never contemplated the use of a blanket in the Heavy Cavalry in the manner mentioned.'[38] However, after further consideration, a later letter from Sir Hussey Vivian said, 'I see no objection to the change proposed.'[CA72]

George Cathcart also managed to secure a change in the way cavalry cloaks were made for service in Canada:

I found that the 19th Light Dragoons in Canada had adopted the measure of making their cloaks into coats with sleeves, but this was for the purpose of constant wear in winter in a peculiar climate, and with the appointments worn constantly during winter over the coats. The cloak in its present form is preferable to a closer fitting coat with sleeves for a dragoon dismounted on sentry, the rain runs off freely and it is easily dried and rolled. It is a better thing for a man to sleep in on his guard bed or in bivouac, as it covers his legs and envelopes his whole body. It is a better covering for a man and horse on the march or as a mounted vidette. No active skirmishing can be performed with any cloaks on [without sleeves]. It admits of being rolled and easily carried, whereas the coat without cloak straps and with the regulation saddle could not be carried, and would be abandoned as an encumbrance.[CA73]

On 8 January he wrote: 'I have been able to obtain from the Secretary at War the grant of cloaks which are more suitable to the service in this country than open cloaks.'[CA74]

When the King's Dragoon Guards were ordered to Canada they had been issued with the new pattern cavalry swords, but there were still '107 remaining of the old pattern, many of which

164

are the old Waterloo swords. In consequence of the numerous Corps of Volunteers I was able to sell 120 cast swords to great advantage, having obtained for them 10/- each.'CA74

During 1840 George Cathcart revised the Standing Orders of the King's Dragoon Guards and these were published on 1st September at Chambly. They give an insight into some of the social attitudes in the British Army of that time.

The Commanding Officer has thought fit to revise the Standing Orders of the King's Dragoon Guards, and embody the principles and regulations, according to which all regimental duties are now to be performed to enable young Officers to learn their duty, and to secure an uniform observance of the same regimental system, under any circumstances of detachment or separation, or temporary command.

The Commanding Officer is equally responsible for the maintenance of discipline and due subordination, whether on Parade, at the Mess, or in any other situation. No discussion on any point of duty is tolerated either at Mess, on Parade, or elsewhere.

The majors and captains of the regiment were

to attend particularly to the instruction and forming of young officers, not only as to their military duties, but as to their habits when off duty, and will not fail to call them, when necessary, to that due sense of decorum worthy of officers of the King's Dragoon Guards, so essential to the maintenance of the reputation which the Regiment has so long upheld . . .

[No officer] will ever be tolerated or countenanced, as hangers on, in the King's Dragoon Guards, with the ignoble motives of wearing the uniform, and enjoying the idle comforts and society of the Mess, without the pride and spirit to desire to distinguish themselves by the perfect knowledge and soldier-like performance of their duties.

The Orders throughout strongly insist on the attention officers must pay to their men. 'He will frequently visit his men's rooms, and see that everything is neat and clean, and kept so during the day.' Captains were to see that 'their Subalterns attend to their Troop duties, and will study to instruct them, and to instil into them an interest in the concerns of the Troop'.

The Captain is bound to see that the necessaries supplied to the men are the best money's worth that can be obtained uniting cheapness with durability . . . There is nothing that requires the attention of the Captains more than the care of their recruits, who ought to be treated with every encouragement, compatible with duty, by the Non-Commissioned Officers and Men of the Troop, and should each be attached to a smart soldier of unblemished character for a comrade – one who is likely to teach him honest and soldier like habits, and not lead him into drunkenness or dissipation. It cannot fail to be a gratifying reflection to an Officer in command of a Troop, that, by duly entering into the spirit of this Order, and studying the characters and tempers of his recruits, he may be able to form many good soldiers, out of materials which, if neglected or harshly and improperly dealt with, would grow up in sullen discontent to be an incumbrance to the Regiment, leading the miserable existence of confirmed and habitual defaulters.

The Surgeon of the Regiment was to 'be careful that he be not imposed upon by malingerers. But he must not, by harsh language or hasty measures towards the men he may suspect, incur the risk of deterring others from reporting themselves ill.' The Quarter Master 'is to be constantly supplied with every article to be of the very best quality, and purchased on the most advantageous terms for the men, in order that the Soldier may be convinced he is charged at the lowest price'.

Marriage was to be discouraged. 'It cannot be too often repeated to the men that they are on no account to marry without leave, and their marrying at all must be discouraged as much as possible.' 'It is impossible to point out, in too strong terms, the inconveniences that arise, and the evils which follow a Regiment encumbered with women.' The Quarter Master was made responsible for the supervision of the regimental wives 'regarding the washing, drying of clothes, and any irregularity of conduct and slovenliness of dress, and any case of sickness or distress'.

On the excellence of its Non-Commissioned Officers the state of a Regiment very much depends . . . Although familiarity, connivance or undue indulgence cannot fail to lead to contempt of authority, and a relaxed state of discipline, firmness, strict impartiality, friendly advice, attention to the comforts of the men, and, above all, his own good example, cannot fail to insure to the Non-Commissioned Officer the respect and esteem of the Men of the Troop; and he will find his influence far greater, if thus supported, by fair means, than if asserted only by harsh language, uncalled-for severity, or a domineering manner.

The Corporal's position is a difficult one, but he will remember it is one of trial; and a man who shews himself capable of performing his duties properly as a Corporal, and preserves his character for sobriety, will be sure of promotion; and, as too many fail, those who are fit for it, and can take care of themselves, will not have long to wait for their advancement.

Since this was a cavalry regiment, great attention was paid to the care of the horses. Standing Orders told each private soldier. 'A good dragoon is known by the care he takes of his arms, accoutrements and appointments, and by his fondness for his horse, and its condition, which is his best test of his willing attention to it.' And this advice was reinforced to officers and NCOs. 'The care of the Horse, good grooming, the state of the Horse Appointments, the quantity and quality of the forage, are the subjects which require constant attention from all Cavalry Officers and Non-Commissioned Officers.'

Standing Orders laid down the daily routine of duties for a cavalry soldier in Canada:

Reveille at half-past five (in the field at daybreak).
Morning stables at six.
Breakfast at eight.
Stables at half-past eight.
Turn out for Watering Order at a quarter before nine.
Forage at a quarter before eleven.
At half-past eleven the Guard Report, and prisoners will be disposed of by the Commanding Officer in the Orderly Room.
Mid-day Stables at a quarter before twelve.
Horses fed, and Stables dismissed, at a quarter before one.
Dinner at one.
Evening Parade. Turnout at a quarter-past two.
General Parade at half past two.
Evening Stables at seven.
Bed down and feed with hay, at twenty minutes before eight.

Dismiss at eight.

First post at nine o'clock; second post at ten minutes past nine.

George Cathcart encountered difficulties with his second-in-command, Major Slade, who had been sent out from England in June 1839. Major Slade applied for leave in England on 27 March, and was turned down by Cathcart on the grounds that 'the rule of the service is for an Officer to have served two years, and most of the Officers have already established that claim, and were I to allow you, one Captain will be deprived of his turn'.[CA75] Major Slade was, however, persistent and pressed his claim on grounds of urgent private affairs. On 28 March, Cathcart had to write again:

Your brother's affairs may be settled by power of attorney without inconvenience to yourself or Her Majesty's service. If it is indeed necessary that you should go to Turin and superintend a lawsuit there, a twelve months leave would be required, but I fear in that case, considering how long you have been on half pay and how short a time you have done duty with the KDG, the Commander in Chief would hardly allow you to absent yourself for so long a period, and remain in full pay, and I certainly could not recommend it.[CA76]

Nevertheless he forwarded the application to Montreal and the Commander of the Forces granted Major Slade six months' leave. In September Major Slade obtained a medical certificate to say that he was unfit and applied for an extension of leave.

Cathcart wrote to the Horse Guards on 10 October:

The Regiment under my command came out on this service without a Major, the six service Troops being then commanded by a Captain. It was not until June 1839 that Major Slade arrived, and I was sorry to find that having been sixteen years on half pay and labouring under bodily infirmities, had not only forgotten all the details of duty both as regards the field and the orderly room, but could neither walk nor ride in a manner necessary for the efficient performance of his duty. By his zealous attention however he had rendered himself sufficiently acquainted with his duty to give me some assistance in the orderly room. After he had been scarcely nine months doing duty and often on the sick list, he applied for leave of absence on urgent private affairs. It now appears that he has never been farther than England, and that his business has been perfectly arranged without him. I submit my wish that should a further extension be applied for, a Military Medical Board be ordered to examine and report whether Major Slade is fit for the service.[CA77]

On 28 November Major Slade was writing to Lord FitzRoy Somerset at the Horse Guards for a further extension of leave, and added:

In regard to the letter from Colonel Cathcart that your Lordship was good enough to read out to me the other day, I do not think he could have really meant to express himself against me in the strong manner he has done, for it was only a short time since that I received from him a communication to the effect that if I wished to have the command of the King's Dragoon Guards, he was ready to sell. Colonel Cathcart no doubt expected to have seen me arrive at the Regiment, or at least to have heard from me before the 9th of last month, the day my leave of absence expired. His disappointment at neither seeing nor hearing from me, coupled with his own wish of returning to England this autumn (which my absence may probably have prevented) has, I fear, been the cause of his angry feelings towards me.[CA78]

Cathcart wrote to both Major Slade and Lord FitzRoy Somerset on 12 January 1841:

I should have been entirely at a loss to account for so extraordinary and apparently unwarrantable an assertion that he had received a communication FROM ME, that if he wished to have the command of the KDG, I was ready to sell, had I not by the same post received two other letters. One from the Major offering me £12,000 for my commission, and the other from a well-intentioned but mistaken friend who acquainted me with the unauthorised overtures he had made to Major Slade. I hereby declare I never contemplated any dealings of the sort with Major Slade, and that not one word, and not one letter, has ever passed between the Major and me on the subject. I have no intention to retire from a service to which I have devoted 31 years of my life, and of which I am still as fond as ever.[CA79]

Major Slade was not the only officer to give trouble, for on 14 August Cathcart wrote to the Adjutant General in Montreal about the conduct of Captain Scott KDG. Surgeon Staunton of the Royal Artillery claimed that he had given Captain Scott a heavy dose of laudanum at 6 am, which had caused the captain to oversleep, but Colonel Cathcart discovered that Scott

left the barracks at half past five am, having been playing at whist and drinking more or less all night, that would certainly have incapacitated him for his duty in the field had he not fallen into the hands of a most culpable medical friend who had dined, and I believe been in company with him all night, and who administered the 'rather too large dose' under the effects of inebriety himself. Captain Scott is now on the sick list and under medical treatment by the Surgeon of his own Regiment. As he is an Officer of very irregular habits in respect to drinking instead of supporting me in the management of young Officers, and is to them a constant bad example and companion in irregularity, I am anxious that the Major General should take the most serious notice of the case.[CA80]

George Cathcart produced during 1840 his comprehensive guide for the use of cavalry in Canada, which – apart from the instructions for fencing parties already mentioned – contained instructions for every possible contingency, including cavalry against cavalry, cavalry skirmishing, patrolling, relieving skirmishers, dismounted service and picquets and videttes. Typical of his common sense are his opening remarks on dismounted service in Canada:

Is is well known that twenty or thirty men well posted, at some broken or barricaded bridge, for instance, may stop the progress of any army for a considerable time; or the first occupation of some stone house or mill may decide the fate of a day. Infantry march only at the rate of three miles an hour at most – by the dismounted service, two thirds of the Cavalry force, transported with expedition to the place, can be dismounted, and become, if properly armed, equal, for that duty, to Infantry of equal numbers, and may maintain a post long enough for the Infantry to come up and relieve them.

On picquets and videttes he comments: 'The regulations – common sense – and the necessity of the occasion – render any amplification on this subject unnecessary.'[CA69]

An inspection in August drew the wry comment, 'I was inspected yesterday by an Infantry General, who as regards books does well enough. The weather was so bad we could not go out, but this morning, although very greasy, we will give him a field day.'[CA81]

On 28 April 1840 the Grenadier Guards were moved from Montreal back to Quebec. Lieutenant-Colonel Ellison had been succeeded in command by Lieutenant-Colonel Lyster, who was found dead in his bed two days after the battalion arrived in Quebec. He was described as 'highly appreciated in the fashionable circles in London, he seemed more fitted for society than the camp, yet when arrangements were necessary consequent upon either weather or marches, no officer could have been more active or energetic, and none discharged his duty with more ability'.[26]

Both the Grenadier and Coldstream Guards practised their men in winter warfare. They were practised in the skill of wearing snow shoes, and parties of thirty men from each battalion were sent into the wild with some Indian guides to learn how to build log cabins and live off the wilderness. The Treasury in London gave an initial grant of £1.10s per man to provide winter clothing for every soldier serving in Canada, this to be followed by a further allowance of five shillings for each subsequent winter. From this money a fund was built up to provide a winter coat and cap for every man.[26,27]

The 24th Foot moved from Montreal to Kingston in May 1840, and when the 11th and 15th returned to England in June, the 24th received a substantial draft from those electing to serve on in Canada. The 32nd Foot remained in Upper Canada, stationed at New London, and then moving to Toronto. During the winter of 1839/40 Colonel Maitland, their Commanding Officer, who had played so prominent a part in the disturbances in the Upper Province, died. The 85th Regiment in Lower Canada were inspected by Major-General Clitheroe on 21 August 1840, and apparently the inspection did not go well! An entry in the Regimental Diary records that he was 'a silly old Guardsman'.[10,11,24] A case of insubordinate conduct on the part of a private in the 65th Regiment came before George Cathcart, who commented:

Sergeant McMahon's conduct appears to have been calculated to irritate the prisoner. It is inconvenient, however, to allow such a man as Knight appears to be to gain anything like an advantage over the Sergeant. It is fortunate that Knight put himself so decidedly in the wrong by refusing to leave the Guard Room when ordered to do so.[CA82]

Although the situation along the frontier south of Montreal had improved, Cathcart wrote to his father on 22 September 1840 that

my frontier is not quite quiet and some little mischief appears to be brewing which requires precautions that have been taken to reinforce certain points. These things amount to the burning of barns by French Canadian refugees, and such petty acts, but as the object is to provoke retaliation with a view to recruiting the sympathy of the lawless Yankees of the border, it is necessary to be on our guard. I am a little anxious now for I have been obliged to prepare barracks for a company of Volunteers to be brought from Beauharnois, and the Engineers are so slow about it, and make so much fuss, that I am afraid of an attack to burn them before they can be garrisoned. However, I have a small picquet in each, and the company is on its march.[CA83]

A month later he was writing:

The Volunteer cordon on my front will suffice without more trouble to keep the troubled spirits within bounds, and if not, I have plenty of help at hand. I have now the whole line of the frontier from Lake St Francis to Frelighsburg to take care of, Beauharnois having been added to my former command.[CA84]

The dispute with the United States over the Maine frontier was still troublesome, and the British Government decided to retain a strong force in Canada, including the Brigade of Guards, until it was settled. Cathcart commented that

I would like to see the boundary question settled. The opinion of our Engineers, which is no doubt true, places the matter more remote from adjustment than ever. It establishes our undoubted right to the whole, and on that evidence, instead of the faulty evidence then produced, the King of Holland could only have awarded the whole disputed territory to Great Britain. It would be new for a State to give up what was its own by right, except by exchange or by treaty of peace after a war. I cannot see how it is now to be settled without a war. A lull would be a bad thing, for the undecided question would then be reopened the moment the army was reduced, and then it would be a question of pounds, shillings and pence whether to send back the troops or succumb. I trust nothing will prevent our going home next spring.[CA83]

A month later he wrote: 'I do not see now that we have established our undoubted right to the whole, how we can admit of a compromise.'[CA84] The dispute was eventually settled in 1842 by the complete surrender to the United States of all that they wanted by a British Government that had veered from a position of extreme aggressiveness to complete capitulation.

Meanwhile Sir Richard Jackson, Commander of the Forces, had decided to hold a field day at Chambly involving the King's Dragoon Guards, the 67th and the 71st Regiments. George Cathcart told his father:

I am to assemble the 71st Light Infantry in addition to the 67th, the KDG, and a battery [of the Royal Artillery] to give him a field day, but rainy weather has set in, and as the 71st must be encamped, we must wait in hopes of a spell of fine weather. I have two dispositions ready for him, one a sally from the garrison, a short and cramped business of necessity; the other a very pretty movement on a more extended scale. I mean to move out as the advance guard of an army, and force the passage of a river supposed to be occupied by a similar advanced guard. I mean to make a false demonstration with two Squadrons of the KDG and a demi-battery on the bank below the bridge on the main road. I shall invest the bridge with a central column of the 67th, a demi-battery and one Squadron of the KDG. I shall then pass the 71st across on pontoons about half a mile higher up to take the enemy in the flank, and then favoured by their flank movement, storm the bridge and carry on the war afterwards on the other side. It will be good fun, and do good in establishing mutual confidence between me and my troops in case we have anything to do. The 71st are perfect and we understand each other right well, but the 67th are newly arrived. I like them and think them up to anything, though not sufficiently officered.[CA83]

Later he described the event:

I had the 71st over from St John's encamped on our cricket ground, also the pontoons. We had little rain, but everything went off as well as possible and Sir Richard was very civil and appeared much pleased. I hear he has talked about it much since.[CA84]

The winter of 1840/41 'was unusually mild, but a great deal of snow has fallen, we may expect some hard weather, but the neck of the winter will at all events be broken'.[CA85] The troops in Lower Canada consisted of the King's Dragoon Guards and the 67th Regiment with a battery of the Royal Artillery at Chambly; a squadron of the 7th Hussars and the 65th Regiment (less a company at Ile aux Noix) at La Prairie; the 71st Foot at St John's with a company at Napierville, with some sappers and miners at St John's. A squadron of the 7th Hussars, together with the 1st, 23rd and 85th Foot, were in Montreal. The Brigade of Guards remained in Quebec. In Upper Canada the 32nd Foot and 93rd Foot were in Toronto, the 24th at Kingston, and the 43rd and 83rd Regiments were also in the Upper Province.[10,11,14,22,24,26,27,28,29,30,31,32,33,34,39]

During January, the 24th, 32nd and 65th Regiments were put under orders to return to the United Kingdom. The 24th Foot was at a strength of 660 NCOs and men, of whom 200 volunteered to exchange into other regiments still serving in Canada. Many of these volunteers were men who had volunteered in June 1840 to exchange into the 24th Foot from the 11th and 15th Regiments, when these regiments went home. The 24th embarked in the transport *Prince Regent* at Quebec in June and arrived in Plymouth at the end of July, having completed twelve years overseas, during much of which time they had been broken up into separate company contingents. The 65th embarked at La Prairie for Quebec on 15 June, having sent 199 volunteers to other regiments, of whom 79 went to the Royal Canadian Regiment. The remainder sailed from Quebec in the transport *Abercrombie Robinson*, nearly 400 strong, arriving in Portsmouth on 22 July. The 32nd Foot moved from Toronto to Quebec in July, embarking on the transport *Apollo* in July and landing at Portsmouth on 17 September. The *Apollo* had brought the 68th Regiment from the West Indies to Canada, and the 56th and 70th Regiments had also arrived to relieve the 24th and 65th Regiments.[10,11,34]

On 13 July the King's Dragoon Guards were inspected at Chambly by Major-General Clitheroe, who was about to move. George Cathcart wrote home:

I am now also about to have my duties and responsibilities much increased in my military command, for Major General Clitheroe is going to be removed to the Upper Province to command there. Sir James Macdonell will not quit his garrison of Guardsmen at Quebec, so that I am to have the ordering of the troops south of the St Lawrence. In short all the troubles and responsibilities of a Major General without the pay. I have now the 56th, 70th and 71st [Regiments], the KDG, and one Squadron of the 7th Hussars, one battery of field artillery, besides the Volunteers.

The Volunteers consisted of the Huntingdon Volunteers and two troops of the Royal Montreal Cavalry along the frontier, and the Queen's Light Dragoons at Philipsburg and Missisquoi.[CA87]

Some tension had been caused by 'the arrest of Mr McLeod the sub-sheriff of Niagara by the State of New York, but as yet on my frontier no mischievous agitation appears to have been commenced upon it by the outlaws and sympathisers and other evil disposed persons. I trust Lord Palmerston's success in the East will give him courage to assume a more decided tone in his negotiations with the US Government.'[CA85]

The affair of Major Slade KDG was still causing George Cathcart some concern. In January he wrote to his father, 'I trust they will soon send me an efficient Major, for in the three years I have commanded an 8 Troop Regiment, I have not had the assistance of one field officer, for I cannot reckon the inefficient services of Major Slade during the nine months he was here of any use to me.'[CA85] In June he was complaining again:

They have used me and the Regiment very ill in suffering it to remain for three years without an efficient Major. I got the Regiment in a very bad state. Colonel Teesdale, only looking for the best way of getting out of it, had been absent for two years, and both the Majors of his day left, one being a man not disposed for anything but home service, and the other being totally unfit, and therefore obliged to quit. My Quartermaster was just appointed, having been Paymaster's clerk with no practical knowledge of his department, and the former Quartermaster having gone mad, when the order came, declared himself so, and left no books or papers. I have now got things right and to my satisfaction and from the date of my responsibility I can answer for anything. But under these circumstances to have abandoned the Regiment without a Major and with only a young inexperienced Captain – and though not a bad Captain, not a fit man to command a regiment – to succeed me would not have been a safe measure. I expect my new Major (an excellent one) in the course of July.[CA88]

In June the Cathcarts learnt that their son had died in England the month before, and so Georgiana Cathcart and the daughters returned to Britain, sailing from Halifax in June. George Cathcart had applied for leave as he had served for four years in Canada. At the end of June a large draft for the King's Dragoon Guards arrived from the depot at York. 'I have now 5 Troops at Headquarters and a fine set of recruits just arrived.' In August Major Martin arrived as second-in-command and proved to be a very capable officer. On 25 August George Cathcart reported: 'My Major is arrived, and as he is a very sufficient one, I have nothing to detain me [from proceeding on leave] but owing to many officers being on leave, it is not easy to supply my place in the command of the division'.[28,CA86,CA89]

In April the Grenadier Guards also received a draft of an officer and fifty-four men, bringing the strength of the battalion to 827 rank and file. Meanwhile the Act of Union, joining the provinces of Upper and Lower Canada, had gone through. George Cathcart commented, 'The affairs in this

176

Province are going on well enough. It was some time before the new united House of Assembly began to work, but they have worked well of late and the Governor General has carried all his important measures, and latterly with increased majorities.'[26,CA89]

In September Lord Sydenham, the Governor General, died, having fallen from his horse and been dragged for some distance. George wrote home that

He conducted business to the last with the full possession of his faculties. He had intended to have been carried to his bed to a special room in which he would have assembled the two Houses, so that he might prorogue the first United Canadian Parliament, since he had personally put the Union into effect, and carried out the details in a most satisfactory manner. When this proved impossible he immediately ordered a Warrant to be prepared for Major General Clitheroe at Kingston to prorogue Parliament in his capacity as Deputy Governor. He then took the sacrament and when told there were hopes, he replied that he knew better. He was then in a dying state, but having recovered a little, he asked if Parliament had been prorogued, and on being told that it had, he said, 'Then my duty is performed and I die contented.' He died very shortly afterwards.[CA90]

On 25 September Sir James Macdonell reviewed the King's Dragoon Guards at Chambly. On 22 October George Cathcart left Chambly on leave for England, and Major Martin took over command of the regiment. The combined depot of the King's Dragoon Guards and 7th Hussars at York had been the cause of some concern. On his arrival in England George Cathcart received a letter from the Horse Guards:

You should inspect minutely the Depot Squadron of the First, or King's Dragoon Guards, and also that of the 7th Hussars, and that you transmit a report of the Officers, Non-Commissioned Officers, Men and Horses. You will also be pleased to add any observations that you may think necessary on the state of Drill and Discipline.[CA91]

There had been complaints from a tradesman concerning unpaid wine bills, involving officers of both the KDG and 7th Hussars.[CA92,CA93,CA94] A batch of horses received from the 14th Light Dragoons had produced only one sound bay mare out of a total of twenty-two horses.[CA95] Both Lieutenant-Colonel Cathcart of the KDG and Lieutenant-Colonel Whyte of the 7th Hussars had complained about the command of the depot and in November the War Office directed that the combined depot of four troops be commanded by an adjutant, and the duties of riding master be performed by another officer, both officers to be nominated from the two regiments.[CA96]

In January 1842 George Cathcart had reported to the Adjutant General: 'There has been considerable neglect and unattention at this Depot, the state of the horses proves it. I cannot too strongly recommend that at least one old Officer should be attached to the Depot of this Regiment.'[CA102]

The year 1842 proved to be quiet and uneventful in Canada. The depot of the 23rd Foot in England received drafts which enabled it to form a 2nd Battalion which then embarked during May, at Portsmouth in HMS *Resistance*, arriving in Montreal on 30 June and then moving to Kingston. The 1st Battalion, which was in Montreal, sent two companies under Captain Crutchley to suppress some election disturbances which had broken out at Belleville. The 43rd moved in July from the Upper Province in Montreal, and the 83rd marched at the same time to Toronto.[14,22,31]

The King's Dragoon Guards at Chambly were inspected during June by Major-General Sir James Hope, and in July a draft of twenty-four soldiers arrived from the depot in York. The regiment suffered yet another setback with new kit coming out from England. Major Martin wrote to George Cathcart:

The appointments sent out by the 'Great Britain' were, on the Quartermaster's seeing them, abandoned by him, in consequence of the injury they received by the vessel running ashore. They were sold by public auction at Montreal for the benefit of the underwriters. The Quartermaster on the day of the sale purchased the pouches and some of the belts. I find on inspection that 105 of the pouches are as good as when they came out of the maker's hands, not in the slightest degree scratched, but the belts were completely spoiled.

He also referred to the inspection:

The new General, Sir James Hope, saw us on our drill ground in review order. The men were in their new clothing and looked remarkably well. He was quite delighted with our movements, which was something I believe he was unaccustomed to. He visited the Hospital, some of the stables, and rooms, the Sergeants' Mess room, the regimental school, and saw our books in the Orderly Room. He saw the 56th and the Artillery also. The 56th Regiment goes home immediately and the 39th replace them here.[28,C97]

On 10 June Major Martin had to inform George Cathcart that he had 'received [Lieutenant] Powell's application to be allowed to sell out of the service as being the only means by which he can extricate himself from the pecuniary difficulties in which he is involved'. Cathcart wrote to Powell's parents:

I am sorry to say that your son has on several occasions been in difficulties, not merely of a pecuniary nature, and I have befriended him on all those to the full extent of indulgence which, as Commanding Officer, I could have been justified in doing. But under the present circumstances I should have reported him unfit for the service. It appears that he has now [resigned] of his own accord. I have not yet received any official papers respecting his resignation, but should it pass through my hands I feel compelled by a sense of duty to recommend the acceptance of the resignation with leave for him to sell his commission.

In July a Mr Blathwayt was prepared to buy Powell's commission in favour of his son, who was a cornet in the regiment, and who then succeeded Powell in his lieutenancy. CA98,CA99,CA100

On 31 August a private of the King's Dragoon Guards, Joseph Simpson, was discharged and received £13. A report relates how

he went into the bush to some women for some brandy, went to sleep, and found £10 had been stolen from him. Caroline Ash, alias Greenwood, gave up £5 next morning to James Stanley who said he was a policeman. Caroline said a man named Kenyon of the KDG had stolen the money and gave it to her. Angellie Hebert gave up $10. She admits it belongs to Simpson. She says Caroline told her she had made a good theft. The whole affair appears to have been accounted for in Caroline's possession and there does not appear to be any good understanding between Kenyon and Caroline.[CA101]

In August the Brigade of Guards in Quebec received orders to return to England. On 29 September 1842 the headquarters and six companies of the Grenadier Guards embarked on board the troopship *Resistance* at Quebec, followed by the two remaining companies on 18 October in *Pique*. The battalion was reunited at Wellington Barracks in London by 14 November. Before leaving Quebec a number of men of both the Grenadier and Coldstream were given a free discharge with a modified pension from the Army in recognition of their outstanding service, so that they could settle in Canada. During four and a half years in Canada the Grenadiers had only seven deserters. The Coldstream embarked headquarters and six companies on 5 October in HMS *Calcutta*, the remaining two companies travelling on 18 October in *Pique* with the two Grenadier companies. The Coldstream battalion landed at Spithead on 31 October and marched to barracks in Winchester, and eventually to St George's Barracks in London.[37,38] Later in the autumn the 7th Hussars were put under orders to return to England, and on 25 November a detachment of twenty men of the King's Dragoon Guards under a subaltern proceeded to Montreal in order to relieve the squadron of the 7th Hussars in the barracks there. George Cathcart had returned from leave, arriving in Chambly on 8 November 1842. The officers of the KDG had felt 'put out' that the 7th Hussars should be going home before them, but George Cathcart brought news with him that the KDG would be leaving Canada the following year.[28]

In May 1842 the 71st Regiment formed a reserve battalion in Scotland, which embarked at Portsmouth on 11 August, landing in Montreal on 23 September, and joining the 1st Battalion. The two battalions were commanded, as one regiment, by Lieutenant-Colonel Grey, with a major in command of each battalion. There was a good deal of rivalry between the two, as the veteran 1st Battalion looked down on the new 2nd, but an inspection in 1844 found the 2nd Battalion 'every bit as good as the 1st'. [32]

December 1842 was an exceptionally severe month, but it was followed by a mild January, when the snow had gone and there was little frost. The ice in the St Lawrence River showed signs of breaking up and so navigation was opened very much earlier than usual. In 1843 the situation in Canada was returning to normal and Cathcart was writing to Lord FitzRoy Somerset:

Everything is quiet here. The English party are discontented and sullen, but are not likely to be easily excited, and there do not appear to be any agitations on that side with mischievous intentions at present. The French party is in high feather, but the two races do not seem more disposed to intermix than heretofore.[CA103]

In February the KDG detachment which had replaced the 7th Hussars in Montreal was reinforced with a further ten men, but in May the situation was sufficiently quiet for the whole party to return to Chambly.[28]

The garrison in Canada was now to be substantially reduced. The Royal Scots, the 1st Foot, were under orders to go to the West Indies, and left Canada in October. The right wing of the regiment embarked in the transport *Premier*, but the ship hit a rock in the St Lawrence during the night. Although it was in danger of breaking up, a firm discipline was maintained, and at daybreak a line was got ashore and all were landed safely. The Royal Scots were greatly helped by some French Canadians and the regimental children were got ashore by being 'tied up five or six together in blankets, like dumplings, and lowered into the boats'. As a result the two wings of the Regiment did not come together again until late in 1844 in Barbados.[39]

Of the two battalions of the 23rd Foot, the 1st Battalion was also ordered to leave Canada and sailed for the West Indies in September, and the 2nd Battalion moved from Kingston to London, Ontario.[31] The veteran 1st Battalion of the 71st Foot left Canada in October bound for the West Indies in the transport *Java*. The 85th Regiment embarked for service in the

West Indies at the same time. The 83rd Foot moved to Trois Rivières in May from Toronto and from there to Quebec, where in June the regiment embarked in the *Countess* and *Jamaica*, setting sail for England on 17 June and arriving at Spithead on 10 July, where they were landed and stationed at Gosport. The 43rd Regiment remained in Canada, moving from Montreal to La Prairie in May, and to Quebec in September 1843. The 93rd Foot remained at Toronto, and did not return to Britain until 1846.

At Chambly the King's Dragoon Guards spent the first part of 1843 preparing for their return to England. In January George Cathcart was writing to Lord FitzRoy Somerset about the cost of transporting a good proportion of the regiment's horses to England.

We have 270 Troop Horses here now fit for duty, perfectly broke and trained for Cavalry purposes and equal to the weight they have to carry. But I think it would not be worthwhile to take home any horses that would be worn out within a year or two in the natural course of things. I have looked through the Regiment with this view and would recommend that 35 horses per Troop should be taken home. This would leave us 60 to sell here, and replace at home. The whole number I would thus propose to take home would be

Troop horses	210
Officers	40
	250

It should be considered what is the use of a dismounted Regiment of Dragoons or during the 18 months that must elapse before the Regiment could again be fit for mounted service, when the men must all be employed in nursing and breaking in young horses, and are not therefore available either for infantry or cavalry duty.[CA103]

On 12 May the King's Dragoon Guards were ordered home, and in June the regiment received instructions that 178 Troop horses were to be selected for transport to England, leaving 79 horses which were to be transferred to the Commissariat Department and sold by public auction in Canada. Cathcart informed Major-General Brown, the general in Montreal, that 'as the voyage is attended with some risks, I do not think it would be advisable to bring home more than enough [horses] to complete the Regiment with the 170 horses of the 7th Dragoon Guards', which were to be transferred to the KDG on arrival in England.[CA104]

Cathcart wrote to his father in May:

I am glad to think that I shall probably have an efficient regiment to show as soon as I land, with horses and men that understand their duty. We expect to sail in July and to arrive about the first week in August. I do not know what to do with my tails. I have never cut the docks, but only squared them off at 24 inches, for the flies are troublesome here. I will not meddle with them now, but I believe I must keep my Canada Squadrons separate when we get our English horses, and so have two bang tailed Squadrons and two bob tailed. The American horse looks better in profile than when seen from behind, as his quarters are not so full as the English breed, and his appearance would therefore be improved by the lop of his tail.[CA105]

The two regular cavalry regiments, the KDG and 7th Hussars, had been well mounted in Canada. John Godley wrote in 1842:

At La Prairie there are now two regiments, the 71st and the 7th Hussars. I was much struck by the excellence of cavalry horses; indeed it is universally allowed that the two cavalry regiments now in Canada were never so well mounted before. Most of the horses come from Vermont, the Yorkshire of New England, and the price which is given by the British (125 dollars) is large enough to secure the pick and choice of the whole country . . . The horses are generally large strong bays, showing a good deal of blood, and with high showy action . . . The Canadian horse (or 'punch', as he is called) is of a totally different stamp – short, plain, and cobbish, but extremely hardy and active; they generally bring from fifty to seventy-five dollars.[40]

Before the King's Dragoon Guards left Chambly, George Cathcart arranged a parade to celebrate the Queen's birthday. The whole garrison was on parade, and after a *feu de joie* each regiment marched past, and then back to their respective barracks. Cathcart had arranged a special occasion for his own regiment:

On the parade ground I had spread a tablecloth on which were placed two kettledrums with their banners. The kettledrums were filled with excellent punch. The three Squadron standards with their bearers and escort of troop sergeant majors with swords drawn took post behind and the kettledrummer with two silver soup ladles, instead of drum sticks, stood ready to bale out the precious contents. When each man had received his share in a goblet, the band played 'God Save The Queen', and then I called upon the Regiment to drink Her Majesty's health. I then sounded the dismiss, and as the men doubled off to their quarters, they raised a cheer which could be heard a mile off.[CA105]

The change from military to civil control in the formerly disaffected areas is well illustrated by a letter from the Adjutant General in Montreal to Captain Sweeney, commanding at Odelltown on the frontier. There were still occasional instances of burnings:

I regret to hear of the burning. You did quite right to report the circumstances, but we must not meddle in 'matters civil'. The magistrates must manage their own matters. Your exertions in stimulating them to act are not only laudable, but, as I well know, much required; but they must now only be used in a private capacity.[CA106]

Before the King's Dragoon Guards left Chambly, the Regiment received an address signed by sixty-one leading members of the community:

Five years, nearly, have elapsed since your arrival in the Province, and though the circumstances of your arrival afford no pleasure in the retrospect, and the interval which ensued has been often clouded, yet we contemplate with unalloyed pleasure the whole period of your presence here. In the beginning it afforded protection and allayed differences, and throughout its whole length it has been unmarked by violence, licentiousness, or disorder of any kind, and latterly it has exercised a benign influence, holding up an example of order, and social enjoyment, and social improvement, which has been, and will hereafter be, beneficial to us all.

To you, Colonel Cathcart, as the moving spirit of the body, we owe much. To you, Gentlemen, the Gallant Officers of the First Regiment of King's Dragoon Guards, we have to acknowledge the same spirit which has animated your leader. To the Non-Commissioned Officers and Privates of the Regiment, acknowledgments and thanks are due for an orderly behaviour, which, in five years, shows no instance of violence or disturbance of the public peace.

Colonel Cathcart, Gentlemen, Soldiers, we part from you with deep regret, and we can only wish you a safe return to your native land.[CA107]

On 9 July the King's Dragoon Guards began its march to Quebec for embarkation with the departure of the 1st Troop, followed on 12 and 17 July by the 2nd and 3rd Troops respectively. On the 22nd, headquarters and two troops left Chambly, and on 3 September the rear party with 6th Troop finally cleared the camp. The regiment was transported in five vessels during September, arriving at Ramsgate at the end of the month, and marching on 1 October to Canterbury Barracks, having lost only nine horses during the voyage. At Canterbury they were joined by the depot squadron and, for the first time since 1828, the King's Dragoon Guards were together as a regiment of eight troops. One hundred and ninety-nine troop horses were transferred to the Regiment, left behind by the 7th Dragoon Guards who had embarked for service overseas. On 20 October the regiment was inspected by Major-General Lygon, Inspector General of Cavalry, who found it complete and ready for immediate service with a total strength of 445 NCOs and men, and 374 troop horses.

George Cathcart, having brought the regiment back to England, made application to retire on half pay, which was approved by Her Majesty, and he handed over command on 19 January 1844 to Lieutenant-Colonel Hankey, having himself been promoted to full colonel.[28]

The troubles in Canada were spread over a period of six years, and had engaged the active service of two regular cavalry regiments, two battalions of the Guards, and seventeen regiments of Foot, apart from contingents from the Royal Artillery and Royal Engineers, and the very considerable commitment from the Royal Navy. The Canadian Volunteer and militia involvement was as considerable, and the Volunteer cavalry and artillery proved to be particularly useful and effective. The British Regular Army involvement over this period in Canada constituted a significant proportion of its total strength, at a time when other calls upon its services were equally urgent – not least after the disastrous outcome of the First Afghan War. It is all the more extraordinary that so little attention has been given to a period of service which helped to shape the future of Canada, and which for nearly a century affected attitudes towards its powerful neighbour, the United States of America.

1st King's Dragoon Guards

1838	1839	1842
	COLONEL	
Sir Henry Fane GCB	Sir Henry Fane GCB	Hon Sir William Lumley GCB
	LIEUTENANT-COLONEL	
Sir George Teesdale	Hon George Cathcart	Hon George Cathcart
	MAJOR	
James Delancey	John H. Slade	Richard Martin
Sir William Alexander Maxwell Bt		
	CAPTAIN	
John Spencer Manning	John Spencer Manning	James Smith Schonswar
Richard Martin	Richard Martin	Hastings David Sands
Charles Amherst	Charles Amherst	Alfred Scott
David Tyssen	David Tyssen	Burrell Fuller
John Thomas Evans	John Thomas Evans	Henry Martin Turnor
James Smith Schonswar	James Smith Schonswar	Fred Hammersley
William John Major Hughes	Hon William Drake Irby	Tho Ommanney Pipon
Hon Wm Drake Irby	George Denniston Scott	Edmund James Power
George Denniston Scott	Hastings David Sands	
	LIEUTENANT	
Thomas Coventry Brander	Thomas Coventry Brander	Manaton Pipon
Frederick Hammersley	Frederick Hammersley	Richard Hollis
Hastings David Sands	Alfred Scott	Thomas Richard Mills
Alfred Scott	Burrell Fuller	Bingham Newland
Burrell Fuller	Henry Martin Turnor	John Blackburn Hawkes
Henry Martin Turnor	Benjamin O'Neale	George W C Jackson
Benjamin O'Neale	Viscount Amiens	Cornelius Powell
Viscount Amiens	Stephen Percy Groves	John Borlase Maunsell
Stephen Percy Groves	Tho Ommanney Pipon	William Warner Allen
Tho Ommanney Pipon	Edmund James Power	
Edmund James Power	Manaton Pipon	
Manaton Pipon	Richard Hollis	
Richard Hollis		

1838	1839	1842
	CORNET	
William Charles Grant	Thomas Richard Mills	James Peach Cleaver
Thomas Richard Mills	Henry Keown	Richard Burke RM
Henry Keown	Bingham Newland	Geo Wm Blathwayt
James A–Seton	J–Blackburn Hawkes	Lockhart Little
Bingham Newland	J–Broughton Egerton Ward	Talbot Dillon Chester
	B–Leigh	William Tershill
		Jas Mark Phillippe Child
	PAYMASTER	
David Scott Kinnaird Maclaurin	David Scott Kinnaird Maclaurin	David Scott Kinnaird Maclaurin
	ADJUTANT	
Richard Hollis	Richard Hollis	Richard Hollis
	QUARTER-MASTER	
John Brown	Joseph Missett	Joseph Missett
	SURGEON	
William Jones MD	William Parry	Thomas Lewis
	ASST SURGEON	
Alexander Smith MD	Alexander Smith MD	Wm Ord Mackenzie MD
	VETERINARY SURGEON	
John Mellowes	John Mellowes	John Mellowes

Volunteer Corps

A General Order dated 29th December 1837 listed all Volunteer Corps, with their authorised strengths, in the Lower Province:

1st Battalion Montreal Militia (to include the New Glasgow Volunteers) of 7 Companies; to be paid
1st Volunteer Brigade (Lt-Col McCord)
Royal Montreal Cavalry: 2 troops in Montreal; 1 troop in Lachine to be paid
Artillery: 2 6-pounders and 72 men to be unpaid
Rifles: 3 Companies to be unpaid

2nd Volunteer Brigade
1st Battalion (Lt-Col N. Bethune): to be unpaid
2nd Battalion (Lt-Col John Molson): to be unpaid
3rd Battalion (Lt-Col John Maitland): to be unpaid

3rd Volunteer Brigade
Montreal Light Infantry (Lt-Col B. Holmes): to be unpaid
1 troop Light Dragoons (Capt Walter Jones): to be paid
French Canadian Loyal Volunteers (Capt Barron): 28 men to be unpaid

ISLAND OF MONTREAL

Major Penner's Command
Lachine Loyal Volunteers (Capt V. Roi Lapensee) and 41 men to be unpaid
Lower Lachine Loyal Volunteers (Capt Begly) and 60 men to be unpaid
Tannery Loyal Volunteers (Capt Charles) and 45 men to be unpaid
Cote St Paul and St Pierre Loyal Volunteers (Capt Clarke) and 61 men to be unpaid

REAR OF MONTREAL

St Eustache Loyal Volunteers (Capts Globenski and Chouquet): 2 Companies embodied but disbanded on 27 November
Two Mountains Loyal Volunteer Cavalry (Capt Maclean): 1 troop of 65 men to be paid
St Andrew's Loyal Volunteers: 2 companies of 60 men each to be paid
Rawdon Loyal Volunteers (Lt-Col Griffith): 2 companies of 100 men each to be paid

Kilkenny Loyal Volunteers (Capt Irwin): 25 men to be unpaid
New Glasgow Loyal Volunteers (Capt Stevens): 85 men to be unpaid
New Paisley Loyal Volunteers (Capt Renny): 35 men to be unpaid
Vaudreuil Loyal Volunteers (Major Matheson): 120 men to be unpaid

SOUTH SIDE OF RIVER ST LAWRENCE

Beauharnois Loyal Volunteers (Lt-Col Brown): 500 men to be unpaid
Huntingdon Loyal Volunteers (Lt-Col Davidson): 400 men to be paid, with the special responsibility of covering the Canadian/American frontier from St Regis to La Cole
Hinchinbrook Loyal Volunteers (Lt-Col Davidson): 100 men to be unpaid
Hemmingford Loyal Volunteers (Major Scriver): 100 men to be unpaid

RIGHT BANK OF THE RIVER RICHELIEU

Henryville Loyal Volunteers (Lt-Col Beardsley): 97 men to be unpaid
Clarenceville Rangers (Capt Vaughan): 60 men to be paid
Missisquoi Borderers (Capt Botham): 50 men to be paid
1st Company St Armand Loyal Volunteers (Capt Thomas): 64 men to be unpaid
2nd Company St Armand Loyal Volunteers (Capt Kemp): 78 men to be unpaid
3rd Company St Armand Loyal Volunteers (Capt Baker): 81 men to be unpaid
Frelighburgh Light Infantry (Capt Starke): 50 men to be paid
St Armand East Loyal Volunteers (Col the Hon Robert Jones): 200 men to be unpaid
St Armand West Loyal Volunteers: 250 men to be unpaid
Caldwell's Manor Loyal Volunteers (Lt-Col McAllum): 50 men to be unpaid
Missisquoi Loyal Volunteers (Capt May): 60 men to be unpaid
Sorel Loyal Volunteers (Capt Peel): 60 men to be unpaid

LEFT BANK OF THE RIVER RICHELIEU

Lacolle Loyal Volunteers (Lt-Col Odell): 275 men to be unpaid
1st Company St John's Loyal Volunteers (Capt Lay): 38 men to be paid
2nd Company St John's Loyal Volunteers (Capt Lindsay): 30 men to be paid
Chambly Loyal Volunteers (Capt Augustus Hatt): 80 men to be unpaid

ISLE AUX NOIX

Lacolle Loyal Vounteers (Capt March): 60 men to be paid
Veteran Company (Capt Knight): 60 men to be paid

Shefford Loyal Volunteers (Capt Knowlton): 400 men and 1 troop of 50
    Cavalry to be unpaid
Napierville Loyal Volunteers (Capt Loop Odell): 50 men to be unpaid
East Sherrington Loyal Volunteers (Capt Douglas): 50 men to be unpaid
St George Loyal Volunteers (Lt-Col F. Languedoc): 160 men to be unpaid
West Sherrington Loyal Volunteers (Capt MacAllister): 39 men to be unpaid
Granby Loyal Volunteers (Capt Lyman): 50 men to be unpaid
Eastern Township Loyal Volunteers (Col Heriot): 600 men to be paid
Lennoxville Queen's Mounted Rangers (Capt Austin): 1 troop to be unpaid

COTEAU DU LAC

Loyal Volunteers (Capt Cox): 50 men to be paid with the task of
    maintaining communication with Upper Canada

QUEBEC

Royal Quebec Volunteers, 7 Companies of 84 men each to be paid and come
    under command of Col Baird, CO of the 66th Foot
Royal Quebec Volunteer Artillery, 3 Companies to be paid and to come
    under command of Lt-Col Kilby RA
Veteran Company (Capt Colman, late 15th Foot) to be paid

Those Volunteer Infantry units who were to be paid were awarded 1/– per
day for each private soldier, and the Volunteer Cavalry were paid at the rate
of 4/– a day. Some units such as the Montreal Militia were to be furnished
with a great coat and a cap, and with 'trowsers or pantaloons', a pair of
moccasins and mittens.

The Royal Quebec Volunteers, having a high proportion of married men
whose families were being deprived of their labour, were given 'an extra
issue of 2 bushels of Pease or Potatoes to each company'. The Veteran
Companies were to be given 'such clothing as can be spared and a fur cap'.[c3]

191

Private Manuscript Sources

COLBORNE PAPERS

C1 Letter to Sir John Colborne dated 1 November 1837.
C2 Letter to Sir John Colborne from Lord Glenelg dated 27 February 1838.
C3 General Order dated Montreal, 29 December 1837.
C4 Journal kept by the late Amury Girod, November 1837.
C5 Letter to Viscount Palmerston 21 February 1838.
C6 Letter to Sir John Colborne from Sir Colin Campbell dated 27 December 1837.
C7 Letter to Lord Glenelg from Lord FitzRoy Somerset dated 27 February 1838.
C8 Letter to Sir John Colborne from Lord FitzRoy Somerset dated 6 January 1838.
C9 Despatch to Sir John Colborne from Lord Hill dated 9 January 1838.
C10 Extract from a letter to Sir John Colborne from Lord Hill dated 15 January 1838.
C11 Extract from a letter to Sir John Colborne from Lord Lynedoch dated 26 April 1838.
C12 Report from Toronto to Sir John Colborne dated 19 February 1838.
C13 US State Dept Memorandum dated 7 February 1838.
C14 Letter from Lord Glenelg to Sir John Colborne dated 30 January 1838.
C15 Letter from Sir John Colborne to Lord FitzRoy Somerset dated 3 March 1838.
C16 Letter from Robert Nelson to J. B. Ryan dated 25 July 1838.
C17 Letter from Sir John Colborne to Lord Glenelg dated 2 May 1838.
C18 Letter from Sir George Arthur to Maj-Gen Clitheroe dated 30 June 1838.
C19 Report from the Select Committee of the House of Assembly of Upper Canada appointed to report on the state of the province, Toronto 1839.
C20 Letter from Lord Hill to Sir John Colborne dated 9 January 1838.
C21 Letter from Lord Glenelg to Sir John Colborne dated 11 December 1838.
C22 Letter from Maj-Gen Clitheroe to Sir John Colborne dated 19 October 1838.
C23 Memorandum from Graham to Sir John Colborne dated 18 October 1838.

C24 Letter from Sir George Arthur to Maj-Gen Clitheroe dated 30 June 1838.

C25 Letter from Col Taylor to Sir John Colborne dated 2 November 1838.

C26 Letter from Col Love to Sir John Colborne dated 4 November 1838.

C27 Letter from Lt-Col G. Cathcart to Sir John Colborne dated 4 November 1838.

C28 Return of Arms and Ammunition found at home of François Berselaux dated 4 November 1838.

C29 Letter from Sir Colin Campbell to Sir John Colborne dated 7 November 1838.

C30 Letter from Lord Glenelg to Sir John Colborne dated 10 December 1838.

C31 Letter from Lt James to Major Biggs dated 4 November 1838.

C32 Letter from Lt-Col C. Taylor dated 9 November 1838.

C33 Letter from Sir John Colborne to Lord FitzRoy Somerset dated 11 November 1838.

C34 Letter from Major Hall to Col Macdonell dated 5 November 1838.

C35 Letter from Col Carmichael to the Military Secretary, 10 November 1838.

C36 Letter from Major Philpotts to Sir John Colborne dated 17 November 1838.

C37 Letter from Lady Colborne dated 17 November 1838.

C38 Report from Lt-Col Dundas, 83rd Regiment at Prescott dated 16 November 1838.

C39 Letter from Lady Colborne dated 18 November 1838.

C40 Letter from Lt-Col Airey to Adjutant General dated 6 December 1838.

C41 Letter from A. McLeod, Niagara, to Sir John Colborne dated 14 December 1838.

C42 Letter from Col Day to the Civil Secretary dated 15 January 1839.

C43 Letter from Count Molé to the Foreign Office, London, dated 20 January 1839.

C44 Letter from Lord Glenelg to Sir John Colborne dated 18 January 1839.

C45 Letter from the Marquess of Normanby to Sir John Colborne dated 27 March 1839.

C46 Letter from the Marquess of Normanby to Sir John Colborne dated 16 April 1839.

C47 Letter from Sir John Colborne to Sir John Harvey dated 18 February 1839.

C48 Letter from the Marquess of Normanby to Sir John Colborne dated 6 May 1839.

C49 Letter from Lord Glenelg to Sir John Colborne dated 3 January 1839.

C50 Letter from Lord Glenelg to Sir John Colborne dated 7 February 1839.

CATHCART PAPERS

CA51 Letter from Lt-Col G. Cathcart to DQMG Montreal dated 4 July 1839.

CA52 Instruction from Horse Guards dated 1839.

CA53 Lt-Col commanding KDG Accounts 1 January–31 March 1839.

CA54 KDG Mess Fund Accounts, 1 April 1839.

CA55 Return of Strengths of Units, 1 April 1839.

CA56 Letter from Lt-Col G. Cathcart to DQMG dated 28 February 1839.

CA57 Letter from Lt-Col G. Cathcart to DQMG dated 11 April 1839.

CA58 Letter from Lt-Col G. Cathcart to Lt-Col Williams dated 27 February 1839.

CA59 Letter from Lt-Col G. Cathcart to DAG dated 8 April 1839.

CA60 Letter from Lt-Col G. Cathcart to Lord Cathcart dated 13 October 1839.

CA61 Letter from Montreal to Lt-Col G. Cathcart dated 6 November 1839.

CA62 Letter from Lt-Col G. Cathcart to DQMG dated November 1839.

CA63 Letter from Lt-Col G. Cathcart to Horse Guards dated 10 December 1839.

CA64 Letter from Lt-Col G. Cathcart to Lt-Col C. Taylor dated 18 April 1840.

CA65 Letter from Lt-Col G. Cathcart to Col Gore dated 30 May 1840.

CA66 Letter from Lt-Col G. Cathcart to Lord Cathcart dated 26 June 1840.

CA67 Letter from Lt-Col G. Cathcart to Lord Cathcart dated 26 July 1840.

CA68 Letter from Lt-Col G. Cathcart to Adjutant General Montreal dated 4 January 1840.

CA69 Instructions for Cavalry in Canada dated 1840.

CA70 Letter from Adjutant General Horse Guards to Lt-Col G. Cathcart dated 14 May 1840.

CA71 Letter from Lt-Col G. Cathcart to Adjutant General Montreal dated 8 August 1840.

CA72 Letter from Sir Hussey Vivian to Adjutant General Undated.

CA73 Letter from Lt-Col G. Cathcart Undated.

CA74 Letter from Lt-Col G. Cathcart to Deputy Adjutant General Montreal dated 8 January 1840.

CA75 Letter from Lt-Col G. Cathcart to Major Slade KDG dated 27 March 1840.

CA76 Letter from Lt-Col G. Cathcart to Major Slade KDG dated 28 March 1840.

CA77 Letter from Lt-Col G. Cathcart to Commander-in-Chief Horse Guards dated 14 October 1840.

CA78 Letter from Major Slade to Lord FitzRoy Somerset dated 28 November 1840.

CA79 Letter from Lt-Col G. Cathcart to Lord FitzRoy Somerset dated 12 January 1841.

CA80 Letter from Lt-Col G. Cathcart to Adjutant General Montreal dated 14 August 1840.

CA81 Letter from Lt-Col G. Cathcart to Lord Cathcart dated 12 August 1840.

CA82 Letter from Lt-Col G. Cathcart to Major French, 65th Regt. dated 5 July 1840.

CA83 Letter from Lt-Col G. Cathcart to Lord Cathcart dated 22 September 1840.

CA84 Letter from Lt-Col G. Cathcart to Lord Cathcart dated 11 October 1840.

CA85 Letter from Lt-Col G. Cathcart to Lord Cathcart dated 25 January 1841.

CA86 Letter from Lt-Col G. Cathcart to Lord Cathcart dated 26 July 1841.

CA87 Return of Effective Strengths dated 23 August 1841.

CA88 Letter from Lt-Col G. Cathcart to Lord Cathcart dated 25 June 1841.

CA89 Letter from Lt-Col G. Cathcart to Lord Cathcart dated 25 August 1841.

CA90 Letter from Lt-Col G. Cathcart to Lord Cathcart dated 24 September 1841.

CA91 Letter from J. Macdonald Adjutant General to Lt-Col G. Cathcart dated 29 November 1841.

CA92 Letter from Capt Martin KDG to Lt-Col G. Cathcart dated 30 April 1841.

CA93 Letter from Lt-Col G. Cathcart dated 19 July 1841.

CA94 Letter from Capt Pipon to Lt-Col G. Cathcart dated 16 August 1841.

CA95 Return of Horses, Depot 1st KDG.

CA96 Letter from War Office to Lt-Col G. Cathcart dated 6 November 1841.

CA97 Letter from Major Martin to Lt-Col G. Cathcart dated 24 June 1842.

CA98 Letter from Major Martin to Lt-Col G. Cathcart dated 10 June 1842.

CA99 Letter from Lt-Col G. Cathcart to Mr Powell dated July 1842.

CA100 Letter from Lt-Col G. Cathcart to Mr Blathwayt dated 10 July 1842.

CA101 Report on a Theft. KDG record dated 31 August 1842.

CA102 Memorandum to Lord Hill from Lt-Gen Sleigh dated 13 January 1842.

CA103 Letter from Lt-Col G. Cathcart to Lord FitzRoy Somerset dated 24 Jaunuary 1843.

CA104 Letter from Lt-Col G. Cathcart to Maj-Gen Brown GOC Montreal, dated 22 March 1843.

CA105 Letter from Lt-Col G. Cathcart to Lord Cathcart dated May 1843.

CA106 Letter from A. G. to Capt Sweeney KDG dated 24 June 1843.

CA107 Testimonial signed by 61 prominent people of Chambly.

Bibliography

1 Hatch, Robert M., *Thrust into Canada*, Houghton Mifflin, 1979
2 Craig, Gerald M., *Upper Canada: The Formative Years*, McClelland and Stewart, 1963
3 Katcher, Philip R. N., *The American War of 1812*, Osprey, 1974
4 Ouellet, Fernand, *Lower Canada 1791–1840*, McClelland and Stewart, 1963
5 Papineau, L. J. A., *Journal d'un Fils de la Liberté*, La Maison Réédition, 1972
6 Ryerson, Stanley B., *Unequal Union*, Progress Books, 1983
7 Kilbourn, William, *The Firebrand*, Clarke, Irwin, 1956
8 Stanley, George F. G., *Canada's Soldiers*, Macmillan (Canada), 1954
9 Bell, Sir George, *Soldier's Glory*, G. Bell, 1956
10 Atkinson, C. T., *The South Wales Borderers, 24th Foot, 1689–1937*, CUP, 1938
11 Swiney, Col G. C., *Historical Records of the 32nd (Cornwall) Light Infantry*, Simpkin, Marshall, Hamilton, 1893
12 Groves, J. Percy, *The 66th Berkshire Regiment*, Hamilton, Adams, 1887
13 Beauclerk, Lord Charles, *Lithographic Views of Military Operations in Canada under His Excellency Sir John Colborne, during the Late Insurrection, accompanied by notes, historical and descriptive*, London, 1840
14 Anon, *Memoirs and Services of the 83rd Regiment*, Hugh Rees, 1908
15 *Journal of the Army Historical Research Society*, vol. 16
16 Traill, Catharine Parr, *The Backwoods of Canada*, London, 1836
17 Davis, Robert, *The Canadian Farmer's Travels in the USA*, Canada, 1940
18 Jones, Robert J., *A History of the 15th (East Yorkshire) Regiment*, published by the Regiment, 1958
19 *Journal of the Army Historical Research Society*, vol. 16, 1937
20 Fortescue, Hon J. W., *History of the British Army*, vol. 11, 1910
21 Moore Smith, G. C., *Life of John Colborne, Field Marshal Lord Seaton*, John Murray, 1903
22 Levinge, Sir Richard, *Historical Records of the 43rd Regiment*, W. Clowes, 1868
23 Senior, Elinor Kyte, *Redcoats and Patriotes*, Canada's Wings, 1985
24 *The History of the Corps of the King's Shropshire Light Infantry*, vol. 2, published by the Regiment, 1970
25 Schull, Joseph, *Rebellion: The Rising in French Canada, 1837*, Macmillan (Canada), 1971
26 Hamilton, Lt-Gen Sir F. W., *History of the Grenadier Guards*, vol. 3, John Murray, 1874

27 Ross of Bladensburg, Lt-Col, *History of the Coldstream Guards*, A. D. Inis, 1896
28 'Records of the King's Dragoon Guards', MS in Museum of 1st The Queen's Dragoon Guards
29 Barrett, C. R., *The 7th (Queen's Own) Hussars*, R.U.S.I., 1914
30 Brereton, J. M., *The 7th Queen's Own Hussars*, Leo Cooper, 1975
31 Broughton-Mainwaring, Major Roland, *Historical Record of the Royal Welch Fusiliers*, Hatchards, 1889
32 Oatts, Col L. B., *Proud Heritage: The Story of the Highland Light Infantry*, Nelson, 1959
33 Macveigh, James, *Historical Records of the 93rd Sutherland Highlanders*, James Maxwell, 1890
34 Wylly, Col H. C., *The York and Lancaster Regiment*, published by the Regiment, 1930
35 Stanley, George F. G., *The War of 1812*, Macmillan (Canada), 1983
36 *'C' Series Public Archives of Canada*, vol. 26, pp. 104–7
37 Letters of M. Leicester, Grenadier Guards, 1839–40, MS, National Library of Ireland
38 'Uniform and Equipment of the Royal Scots Greys', *Journal of the Army Historical Research Society*, vol. 16, 1937
39 Brander, A. M., *The Royal Scots*, Leo Cooper, 1976
40 Godley, John Robert, *Letters from America*, London, 1844
    Guitard, Michelle, *Le Camp Militaire de Chambly (1812–1869)*, Parks Department, Canada, 1980
    Kelly, Greg, *William L. Mackenzie: 1837, Revolution in the Canadas*, Toronto, 1974
    Lossing, Benson, *The War of 1812*, Harper and Bros., 1868
    Lindsey, C., *The Life and Times of William Lyon Mackenzie*, 1862
    Mackenzie, W. L., *Narrative of the Rebellion*, 1837
    Manning, H. T., *The Revolt of French Canada*, Canada, 1969
    Papineau, L. J., *Histoire de l'Insurrection du Canada*, 1840
    Senior, Elinor Kyte, 'The Glengarry Highlanders and the Suppression of the Rebellions in Lower Canada 1837–8', *Journal of the Army Historical Research Society*, vol. 56, no. 227
    Senior, Elinor Kyte, *British Regulars in Montreal*, McGill-Queen's University Press, 1981
    Stacey, C. P., *Quebec 1759*, Macmillan (Canada), 1959
    Standing Orders of the First, or King's Dragoon Guards, Montreal, 1840
    Order Book, Military General Orders, 1838–39, L 22, Denison Family Papers, Metro Toronto Public Library

Index